Gluten-Free
Baking Classics

The Heirloom Collection

90 New Recipes and Conversion Know-How

ANNALISE G. ROBERTS

Full Court Press
Englewood Cliffs, New Jersey

Published in the United States of America by Full Court Press *(fullcourtpressnj.com)*

ISBN 978-1-938812-39-2
Library of Congress Catalog No. 2014953989

Editing and book design by Barry Sheinkopf for Bookshapers (bookshapers.com)
Cover design by Annalise G. Roberts, with Donald Strum and Dounia Loeper, and Barry Sheinkopf
Food photography by Gary Franco, GF Studio, New Jersey
Food styling by Kathleen Cwirko, GF Studio, New Jersey
Baked goods for photographs made by Annalise G. Roberts

Recipes for Traditional Pie Crust and Tart Crust first appeared in *Gluten-Free Baking Classics*, 2006, and *Gluten-Free Baking Classics*, second edition, 2008, by Annalise G. Roberts

Library of Congress Cataloging-in-Publication Data

Roberts, Annalise G.
Gluten-free baking classics the heirloom collection: 90 new recipes and conversion know-how/Annalise Roberts

p. cm.
Summary: "Discussion and primer on gluten-free baking, and recipes for gluten-free flour mixes, pastries, breads, and other baked goods" —Provided by publisher.

Pictured on the front cover: Banana Pecan Crunch Cake
Pictured on the back cover: Alsatian Apple Tart

TO MY FATHER

Whose love of farms and planting seeds and farmers markets and specialty grocery stores and cooking and baking bread and gathering friends and family around a table to enjoy a meal knew no bounds. His passions helped shape my world. I only wish I could have shown him this book before he left us in June of this year. I miss him beyond words.

Acknowledgements

My deepest gratitude and thanks:

To Barry Sheinkopf for your keen dedication in crafting a beautiful book, and for helping me to navigate the path to getting it published.

To Gary Franco for employing your incredible talent and artistic mind to produce great photographs for this book. Your ability to work with light and to know just how to frame the shot was awe-inspiring.

To Kathleen Cwinko, whose patience and skill helped to make my baked goods look delicious. Your sense of humor and enthusiasm made the long hours fly by.

To Shelly and David—again—if not for you, this book might never have happened.

To all my taste testers, for you approached your task with a never-ending zeal: Conrad, Alex, and Bradford; Susan and Fritz Zeigler; Mary and Greg Frazier; Betsy and Paul Rosengren; Madhuri Shukla; Brandon, Justin, Donna, and Eugene Chrinian; Peter and Milana Reckseit. And to all the others I fed and questioned, sometimes over and over, until I got it right.

To my incredible field testers who offered up your time and kitchens to test recipes for this book: Jola Maczynski, Susan Goodstadt-Levin, Pat Priesing, Shawn McBride, Doris Schapira, Jason Dietel, Pam Philips, Jeanne Cobetto, Amy Luczak, Monica DiBisceglie, Janine Tuttle, Mary Buckely, Martine Giddings, Diana Gitig, Katie DeYoung, Jillian Kosminoff, Jennifer Granich, Rita Yohalem, Phil Baer, Gayle Gorga, Maria Roglieri, Bonnie Nelson, Upsorn Hutchens, Sue Lampropoulos, Mary Beth Galvin, Erin Pencek, Laura Reynolds, Michelle Bylaw, Jayne Butler, Betty Barfield, Shelly Carpenter, Kathy Bohn, Lanie Cohen, Sherry Alexander-Duder, Kathleen D'Auria, Alison Beck, Carla Krueger, and Maureen Huggins.

To Cynthia Kupper at Gluten Intolerance Group, for answering my many questions about Bette Hagman and early gluten-free baking in this country.

And last, but not least, to the many people in the gluten-free community who've supported me in my work and encouraged me to keep writing books.

Table of Contents

INTRODUCTION

ACROSS THE INTERMINGLING CULTURES IN THIS COUNTRY, WE TEND TO CELEBRATE HAPPY moments, holidays, birthdays, weddings, and even religious rites with baked goods. We grow up eating foods that connect us to our families and our heritage. That's why it's important for many of us on a gluten-free diet to be able to hold onto the culinary details that act as a touchstone in our lives. And it's why being able to successfully convert a wheat based recipe into a gluten-free version is so critical to those in our community. When I wrote my first cookbook, *Gluten-Free Baking Classics*, I wanted it to contain a broad assortment of the kind of basic, must-have recipes that most people long for when they first begin a gluten-free diet. I included recipes for pizza, sandwich bread, chocolate chip cookies, pie crust, French bread, corn muffins, layer cakes, brownies, biscuits, and over a hundred more. Sometimes however, you can get hungry for something other than the basics. And that's what happened to me. I started developing recipes for some of the baked goods I grew up with and I had just about given up on (*kifli* and apple turnovers), or was curious about (whoopie pies and *churros*), or convinced myself I could do without (lemon buttermilk Bundt cake, and lady fingers). Along the way, I added recipes that my readers decided they wanted to have back in their lives (Pineapple Upside Down Cake and Brioche).

The result is this cookbook of timeless and culturally diverse heirloom favorites. While these might not be the recipes you typically look for when you first go on a gluten-free diet, they're the ones that eventually make their way onto many of our wish lists. And they're all designed to work each and every time you make them.

But there is more. When I was considering what to include in this book, something intriguing struck me. I noticed that as I went about trying to create baked goods I had never made before, like whoopie pies, not only did all the experience I acquired converting my own wheat based recipes in the past come in handy (in terms of knowing how much flour, fat, liquid or xanthan gum to use), but I was also using another important skill: I was spending a lot of time evaluating which recipe or recipes to base my new gluten-free versions on. I had seamlessly incorporated it into my process, however, now I suddenly realized how important it had become to the end result. I was making ample use of this skill in order to make sure that I didn't waste my time and ingredients converting a recipe that wasn't any good to begin with.

When you know what the taste, texture and appearance of a baked good is supposed to be like, all you have to do is work towards that goal. But what if you're not sure? What if you've never tasted something before, or if you're not really confident of what the best version of it should be like and you still want to make it?

I started to focus on how I develop new recipes — the ones I knew well, and those I didn't — and decided to try to explain it in this book. I decided to teach gluten-free baking in a more deliberate way so that you can learn what you need to do to successfully convert a recipe by yourself, avoid missteps, and trouble shoot mistakes. My hope is that this book will show you what is possible and how to do it.

1

THE WILD WEST DAYS OF CELIAC

FIRST THERE WERE ONLY THE PIONEERS, THE ONES WHO BRAVELY TRAVELED INTO THE NEW uncharted territory of the "wild" West. The pioneers had made the decision to move on and change their world in order to improve their lives. There were few road maps, almost no one to help them on their journey, and very little communication along the way with others who had gone before. In the celiac world, these were the (unlucky) few diagnosed before 2002.

Then very slowly, settlers started down the lightly traveled paths of the pioneers. There were no established towns or cities for them to come to, because the pioneer folk who were living in the new uncharted territories lived pretty much by themselves in very small communities. In the celiac world, I was a settler at the time of my diagnosis. No one I knew had ever heard of celiac disease. Doctors, except for a select few, could never be counted on to diagnose their patients correctly or give accurate advice about how to deal with it; nutritionists and dieticians often provided outdated and incorrect food advice (for example, I was incorrectly told not to eat anything made with distilled vinegar); and the leaders of the two largest national support group organizations couldn't agree on diet protocols. The relatively small number of celiac settlers who existed at this time had to find their own way by searching for the few accurate resources that were available.[1]

Then more people came and started to settle down. There were more day-to-day basics, but few conveniences and no luxuries. The growing—but still small—communities tried to develop a sense of order, ward off unscrupulous gunslingers, and help

---

[1]*In fact, there was an incredible amount of misinformation circulating around the medical community at the time. For example, I was (incorrectly) told to stop eating wheat immediately, before my endoscopy, and many of the people I met had been told by their doctors that they could start eating wheat again when their symptoms went away, or had been told that their children would out grow it.*

the newcomers. But there was still no one in charge, no spokesman, and few rules or standards. There was also an overall jostling for position among the folks who were there as people started to stake out their claims for leadership, land, and commerce. In the celiac world, there was still no main clearing house for guidance and advice in the way the American Heart Association, the American Cancer Society, the National Breast Cancer Foundation, or the Lupus Foundation of America are often the first place people go to supplement the information they get from their doctors. In place of gunfights, there were petty rivalries between the national support group organizations, newly formed independent support groups, and hospital research centers as they competed for the attention and money of people who had been diagnosed. Moreover, the growing number of celiac websites often provided conflicting information from both self-proclaimed experts and the participants in community chat rooms, as patients, who had been left with few authoritative resources to turn to, tried to help themselves.

Here Comes Everybody

Then that famous golden nugget was discovered, and the Gold Rush began as people answered the call to "Go West, Young Man." Individuals, families, and entrepreneurs poured in, coming from all directions. In many ways, that is the same explosion of awareness, excitement, opportunity, and involvement that we are witnessing now in the celiac world. As more people have been diagnosed with celiac, and medical researchers finally came to admit that gluten intolerance does in fact exist outside of celiac disease (even though the patient community had been saying this since at least 2004), the market has exploded for all things gluten-free: Restaurants, large corporations, small and mid-sized food companies, grocery stores, farm markets, and cooking schools all jumped into the pot. To flame the fire, this rush to embrace "gluten-free" coincided with the catapultic rise of blogging and social media. These forces have resulted in a huge throng of people shouting for attention and aggressively trying to fill the void left painfully empty by culinary professionals and the medical community.

The Consequences

The explosion has led to a better understanding of the spectrum of gluten sensitivity and to more people being correctly diagnosed with celiac and non-celiac gluten intolerance. This is a good thing. All of a sudden, everyone seems to know someone who has celiac or is gluten-sensitive. There is also a lot more talk about the hundreds of symptoms, most of which are not related to the digestive tract, and the fact that you don't have to actually have celiac in order to have symptoms. Moreover, the lines of delineation between those with celiac (one percent of the population with zero tolerance for gluten consumption) and those with non-celiac gluten intolerance have become more clearly defined, and as a result, it is easier for people to understand what they need to do to get and stay healthy.

The explosion has also helped, directly and tangentially, to educate doctors and other medical practitioners not to ignore the symptoms. Incredibly, I still meet people every week who complain that it took them seven to ten years to be correctly diagnosed. But now I am beginning to have hope that people will have the knowledge and confidence to switch to more informed doctors when their own doctor ignores their pleas.

Secondly, the explosion has led to more and better gluten-free prepared food, baking flour, and baking mixes in grocery and specialty stores. We've also seen more food choices in restaurants, and more cookbooks. This is particularly good for those who are newly diagnosed because it makes it easier for them to embrace their diagnosis. But in reality, it is good for anyone who wants to eat gluten-free food.

There are, however, things that concern me. The explosion has done nothing to deflate the number of competing national support groups and websites all clamoring for attention, support, and limited dollars. Instead of one coherent message going out to the media, to food companies, to restaurants, doctors, medical personnel, insurance companies, and Congress, the groups are each sending out their own messages and often diluting the overall impact. There also appears to be a low level of acrimony between many of those working at the national level, and there are turf wars over the work to be done. It has led to a duplication of effort and a squandering of resources. How much better it would be if the groups divided up the work and then specialized in an area for which they are best suited.

And my final concern: As the number of cookbooks and food magazines dealing with gluten sensitivity increases, there are a seemingly endless number of flour mixes. There is, in fact, a general lawlessness among food writers and those who develop recipes. There are no rules or standards, not for home cooks or for those in business. Although there is no real gluten-free cup-for-cup replacement for wheat flour, not having a universally accepted gluten-free equivalent of an all-purpose-flour isn't necessarily a good thing. It makes it harder for newcomers to develop their technique, become competent, and move up the learning curve. It means that everyone who starts down the path basically has to start from scratch in evaluating which road map to use. It also means the gluten-intolerant are more apt to bite into something dry or dense or grainy or gummy or rubbery or weird tasting or flavorless—or several of the above all at the same time.

So Where Do We Go From Here?

When it comes to baking, it's probably safe to say that most people who give up gluten simply want to be able to recreate the baked goods they've always enjoyed (hopefully in moderation): the pizza, cookies, cake, and crusty, chewy breads they left behind. So I'm not convinced it's worth creating a whole new category of baked goods using gluten-free flours, although some other enterprising baker could possibly do just that. I'm also not convinced about the wisdom of what I call free-style baking, as in just use these guidelines for flour exchange, or these ratios, and throw in any flour you want or any flour you have in your cabinet; this leads to inconsistent, and often compromised results. And while the surprise aspect of never having the same thing twice might please some, the huge disparity in the quality of gluten-free fresh bakery products, shelf-stable bakery products, baking mixes, and recipes really means that there is much work to be done in just being able to dependably reproduce the basics.

The result? One of my goals in this book is to try to tame a bit of the Wild West aspect of the gluten-free baking community. I want to create a starting place for gluten-free bakers, help them build a solid foundation for tackling recipes, help them to move up the gluten-free baking learning curve so that they can successfully innovate and be creative, and finally, help them to develop consistency. Consistency is a mark of being great in anything, from throwing a curveball, to dancing the tango, to writing good, clean software code. The difference between a great baker and everyone else is having the skill set to produce top quality baked goods over and over on purpose. And while I can't promise to make you a great baker, I can promise to give you the tool kit to start you on your way.

Finally, my primary goal in this book is to provide you with a collection of dependable gluten-free recipes for baked goods that mimic high-quality wheat versions. I want this to be the book you turn to when your baked goods have to be good, when you don't want to take a chance. I want it to be a cookbook whose recipes and advice you'll come to know and trust and return to time again.

2

GLUTEN-FREE BAKING FUNDAMENTALS: THE FLOURS

Finding a Starting Place for Gluten-Free Baking

Baking with gluten-free flours means rethinking how you use recipes, buy ingredients, mix dough and batters, and use baking pans and your oven. Most of us simply want to be able to make gluten–free versions of the baked goods we've always enjoyed. But I'm not a big believer in "good enough" baking: they should be *really* good, not just "good enough." They should look, feel, and taste as good as or better than their wheat-containing counterparts. Even with that goal in mind, I also believe you should be able to make gluten-free baked goods without it being a painful, time-consuming experience.

Many of the recipes for baked goods in this country have historical roots in Europe, where bakers fine-tuned the art of making pastry with dairy and eggs, and made breads with increasingly refined wheat flour. As seeds, grain protein formulations, farming techniques, and milling became increasingly industrialized, the all-purpose wheat flour and bread flour produced for baking became more standardized. Over time, the consistency and relative quality of the ratios and base recipes that bakers used for wheat baking rose because they had access to this relatively consistent flour; and today, most wheat recipes are calibrated to use it (except those that focus on using heritage wheat). The dependable ratios and base recipes also make it easier for bakers to evaluate recipes, and they provide a solid foundation for creative recipe development and for adjusting to nuances in flour protein content, moisture, weather, and altitude.

But there hasn't been an equivalent all-purpose gluten-free flour or gluten-free bread flour that *everyone* in the gluten-free community turns to. Many early bakers used rice flour, potato starch, tapioca starch, and sometimes cornstarch, alone or in some combination. These were the most frequently used flours for gluten-free baking up until about 2006, when sorghum, millet, and other whole-grain flours started to become accepted and popular. Moreover, certified gluten-free bean flours went on the market in the mid-1990s, and while their strong flavor was not appreciated by everyone, their higher protein content and ability to create relatively lighter baked goods helped to win them fans. As a result, bakers also started to include bean flours in many recipes.

Although there were several gluten-free cookbooks in the United States before 1990 (including *Good Food, Gluten Free*, by Hilda Cherry Hills, first published in England in 1976), the idea of using a blended flour mix for home baking in this country was popularized by gluten-free pioneer Bette Hagman in her *The Gluten-Free Gourmet* cookbooks, the first of which was published in 1990. The original formula, which she fine-tuned with the help of home economists at the University of Washington, became well known and popular because it was better than any one flour alone, and it provided a good, solid starting place for recipe development. However, after Hagman's first three books came out, many of the newer gluten-free writers tweaked her blend to develop a proprietary flour mix for their own cookbooks. Ultimately, as the number of cookbooks grew, so did the number of blended flour mixes (although some of the newer writers, in order to further differentiate themselves, used a unique combination of flours for every recipe). As a result, a gluten-free baker who uses recipes from five different cookbook writers might ultimately need five different blended flour mixes, or more, in their pantry.

Some may herald the benefits of all this flour diversity to accommodate taste differences and nutritional needs, but I'm not convinced the advantages outweigh the inconveniences. There is no parallel in wheat baking for this kind of foundational free-for-all, and I think the downside is that it has contributed to a lack of consistently good-quality gluten-free baked goods across the country. For every good gluten-free cookie, there are dozens of mediocre and bad ones, proportionately more, I think, than you would find in the wheat world.

The flour free-for all also makes it incredibly difficult to evaluate a new recipe, even for experienced gluten-free bakers. An experienced wheat baker can look at the list of ingredients (and directions) for a wheat recipe, estimate the end result, and then figure out what, if anything, he/she might want to do to tweak it. It is an important skill that saves time and money, and helps protect the baker from disappointing results. But there is no equivalent in gluten-free baking. The lack of a common pedagogical discipline means there is no common starting place. If, every time you bake, you end up using a different variety of flours, even while maintaining a fixed ratio and weight, you will get a different end result. And while this might be just fine with creatively minded bakers who never want to make the same thing twice, it is not consistent with learning a skill. In reality, there is something much more important that needs to be understood and embraced by those who really want to be successful.

I believe the key to great gluten-free baking is *dependability and sustainability*. You need a dependable flour mix, you need to know how it works, and you need to understand its nature so that you can predict how it will work in different situations. You need dependable recipes, recipes you can turn to and be confident you will get good results, recipes that are good enough to be a base for creative enhancement. And then, it all needs to be simple enough physically, mentally, and emotionally so that it is sustainable.

In this country, the blended flour mix that has been used more than any other for the past two decades, and the one that has provided the most inspiration for variation and tweaking, is the original formula Bette Hagman first used: 2 cups rice flour, ⅔ cups potato starch, and ⅓ cup tapioca starch. It remains an excellent starting place on which to build (although she specified white rice flour because that was the only one available at the time).

Building a Foundation

When I start any discussion about gluten-free baking, I typically explain it in terms of art and science: The science part is which flours you choose to use together, how and where you purchase and store them, how you mix and measure them, and how you replace the gluten in wheat; the art part is understanding the essential nature of the gluten-free flour blends you use, so you can maneuver your way around recipes and be creative.

When I baked with wheat, I used one all-purpose flour for my cakes, pie crusts, cookies, and muffins, and a second, a bread flour, when I made bread (which I often used in some combination with all purpose or whole wheat flour). I had a container for each of the two flours in my pantry, and another small one, for the whole wheat, in my refrigerator. But given the essential nature of the many gluten-free flours available to us, it really is necessary to use a blend of flours in order to get good results (although there are a few gluten-free bakers who will tell you otherwise). I have never made a single-flour-only gluten-free baked good, or tasted one made by someone else, that was really delicious (by this I mean a baked good that uses only bean flour, or just tapioca flour or rice flour). Easy to make, yes. But a taste, texture, and appearance that mimics or comes remarkably close to wheat? Not so much.

I wanted my gluten-free baking to mimic my wheat baking: I wanted two containers of flour to reach for, consistency of product, and an ability to build on my understanding. I started with Bette Hagman's rice flour mix, and I quickly realized that white rice flour combined with potato starch and tapioca flour leads to a flavorless flour blend, which in turn leads to empty- tasting baked goods. Hagman also didn't differentiate between brands of rice flour in her books, so unless you buy several and test them, you'd never understand the difference. The first time I ever baked a gluten-free recipe, I made muffins with a white rice flour that had a huge grind—except I didn't know it was a huge grind at the time. The muffins didn't resemble any muffin I'd ever made with wheat: They were gritty, heavy, and dense. My then eleven-year-old son took one bite, put it down and said to me, "Mom, you could take down a buffalo with this muffin." He was right.

I tried Hagman's bean flour mix next. It made a lighter, less gritty baked good but tasted so weird, and had such a lingering aftertaste, that I could never even bring myself to use up the bag I'd bought. Fortunately, though, I had bought the bean flour from Authentic Foods, which was the only company making it in the United States at the time (it was a proprietary blend developed by its founder, Steve Rice). I noticed that his product line included extra-finely ground white and brown rice flours, and that he touted the benefits of the fine grind. I bought them both and started baking. It was a revelation. The finely ground flour made all the difference in the texture and appearance, and at the same time, the brown rice version added back in the taste I was missing.

I searched for affirmation from the authors of the very few other gluten-free cookbooks that were available at the time. There was no mention anywhere of the differences in rice flour grinds. On the other hand, Rebecca Reilly knowingly wrote about the taste and nutrition benefits of brown rice flour over white in her book *Gluten-Free Baking* (2002). Her words helped give me the confidence to move forward using the extra-finely ground brown rice flour as the major component of my all-purpose blend. Ultimately, I found that I was able to recreate a wide array of baked goods using my new brown rice flour mix, and I started converting my favorite recipes using it in place of all-purpose wheat flour.

But gluten-free breads made with white or brown rice flour (and combined with potato, tapioca, and/or corn starch) came up short. They lacked all the most important characteristics of good wheat bread: a rich, nutty, grain taste; a tender, crisp crust; and chewy texture laced with air pockets. Moreover, rice-based artisan breads didn't look or taste anything like the good wheat artisan breads I was used to; they tended to be glossy, gummy, and dense looking. I searched the market place and discovered certified gluten-free flours made from millet and sorghum flours, two ancient whole grains indigenous to the African continent and cultivated all over Asia. During 2004, I started testing simple bread recipes using the new flours mixed with starch. Ultimately, I was able to make gluten-free breads with a texture and appearance that came as close to wheat as any I had seen. Protein-rich millet adds a beautiful golden glow, a rich grain taste, and helps to give breads a more "wheat-like" structure and appearance; sorghum has a somewhat milder grain taste and is a little more nutty in character; it also provides protein for nutrition and structure. Finally, I had two flour blends on which to build and develop a repertoire of recipes.

BROWN RICE FLOUR MIX

Brown rice flour (extra finely ground)	2 cups
Potato starch (*not potato flour*)	⅔ cup
Tapioca flour (also called *tapioca starch*)	⅓ cup

WEIGHT EQUIVALENTS

Authentic Foods Brown rice flour	1 cup = 4 ounces (113 grams)
Potato starch	1 cup = 6 ounces (170 grams)
Tapioca flour	1 cup = 4 ounces (113 grams)

1 CUP BROWN RICE FLOUR MIX MADE WITH AUTHENTIC FOODS BROWN RICE FLOUR = 4.4 OUNCES (125 GRAMS).

Authentic Foods makes a flour blend called *GF Classic Blend* that is calibrated to be exactly like my Brown Rice Flour mix. It's a nice convenience. You don't have to measure and mix the individual flours detailed above; you just cut open the bag and pour the contents into a storage container.

What to look for when you buy brown rice flour

Ideally, look for stabilized, finely ground brown rice flour. A large grind can make your baked goods gritty, heavy, and/or crumbly. In addition, stabilized rice flour has a longer shelf life and doesn't break down as quickly when baked, so your baked goods stay fresher longer. Finally, white rice is not a whole grain and is not as nutritious. In fact, it is mostly a starch, with very little protein left after processing. The more complex proteins left in the brown rice not only provide better nutrition, they add flavor and help keep your baked goods fresher for a longer time. White rice has almost no flavor, and when combined with potato and tapioca starch, which are also almost flavorless, it leaves an empty taste.

Authentic Foods, in California, sells *powdery-like-wheat* brown rice flour that is stabilized to increase shelf life and sealed in a high-quality bag that is light and air resistant (stabilizing helps keep the protein and oil-rich bran in the flour from going rancid quickly, although it adds to the cost). It is certified gluten-free. For me, it has proven to be the "hands-down" winner in repeated blind taste tests. It may look pricey, but not when compared to the price of buying ready-made gluten-free cakes, muffins, and cookies that are often of a lesser quality than those you could make at home. I strongly believe that the high-quality rice and very fine grind of Authentic Foods will make a big difference in your finished product. Other brands have a larger grind that you can actually feel between your fingers; they aren't as powdery, and it really does make a difference. In my classes, I actually pass around little cups containing several brands of flour (one in each cup) so people can feel the grind variation for themselves.

Authentic Food's (e-mail and phone below) flour can be ordered online or purchased at select grocery and natural food stores. Bob's Red Mill and King Arthur Flour Company make brown rice flours that tie for second place in terms of grind size, although King Arthur's is also stabilized. They are both more readily available in grocery stores across the country. Arrowhead Mills brown rice flour has a big grind, is extremely gritty, and is not stabilized (although I use their millet flour to make gluten-free bread). Finely ground brown rice flour can also be found at Asian grocery stores around the country, but contamination could possibly be an issue, so check for certified GF labeling or make an inquiry before you buy. The most important thing is: If you want, or need, to use other brands of brown rice flour, try to find one with the finest grind you can afford.

But if you can't buy finely ground flour for reasons of cost or logistics, see *"Can I grind my own flour?"* (page 18 below) for information about how to make grittier rice flour less gritty.

Take note: 4.4 ounces of the Brown Rice Flour mix made with Bob's Red Mill or King Arthur brown rice flour will not behave exactly like 4.4 ounces of the Brown Rice Flour mix made with the Authentic Foods product in a recipe. But it will be close enough to give you a nice baked good. The flours are processed and packaged differently (Authentic Foods is less dry), and the larger grind absorbs liquid differently.

BREAD FLOUR MIX

Millet flour	2 cups
Sorghum flour	1 cup
Potato starch (*not potato flour*)	1 cup
Tapioca flour (also called *tapioca starch*)	1 cup
Corn starch	1 cup

WEIGHT EQUIVALENTS

Millet Flour	1 cup = 4.75 ounces (135 grams)
Sorghum Flour	1 cup = 4.5 ounces (128 grams)
Potato starch	1 cup = 6 ounces (170 grams)
Tapioca Flour	1 cup = 4 ounces (113 grams)
Corn Starch	1 cup = 4.75 ounces (135 grams)

1 CUP BREAD FLOUR MIX IS BETWEEN 4.25 OUNCES (121 GRAMS) AND 4.5 OUNCES (128 GRAMS).

The difference between the two numbers amounts to about one tablespoon of the flour mix, and is dependent upon which brand of millet and sorghum you use. Also, if you add up the total of each flour to make 6 cups of the mix and divide by 6, you will get 4.8 ounces (136 grams) per cup. The difference between this number and my designation of 4.25 and 4.5 as total weight per cup of the mix (for use in recipes) is due to aeration of the flour mix before measuring for use in a recipe (see the *How to Measure and Mix Gluten-Free Flours* section below). The bread flour mix is half whole grain and half starch, and so it takes in more air during aeration than the Brown Rice Flour mix (above), which is two-thirds whole grain.

A large grind works as well as, if not better than, a fine grind for my bread recipes. Arrowhead Mills makes an excellent millet flour that, in my experience, has proven to be more consistently fresh than Bob's Red Mill (but they will both work well). However, Bob's makes an excellent sweet white sorghum flour that I really like. If you want to buy other brands of these flours, I suggest you compare them to Bob's Red Mill and/or Arrowhead Mills in order to best evaluate whether they'd be a good replacement in terms of taste and freshness.

Sweet Rice Flour

Some of the recipes in this book use a small amount of sweet rice flour, which helps give certain baked goods a better texture in the form of tenderness. It adds a kind of softness that is sometimes interpreted as "chew". Only a small amount is ever used at a time because too much results in a denser, tighter, gummy product. I recommend that you use a finely ground sweet rice flour, such as Authentic Foods, or your baked goods will be gritty.

To illustrate exactly what sweet rice flour can do in a gluten-free baked good: Years ago I created a recipe for a simple cream-filled chocolate cookie. Several months later, during the summer, I decided to try to make gluten-free ice-cream sandwiches for my newly gluten-intolerant son (who had watched with sadness as his younger wheat-eating brother enjoyed a regular ice-cream sandwich at a friend's barbecue). I used the chocolate cookie recipe (mentioned above), made a thick roll of dough, pressed it into a rectangular shape, chilled it, sliced it, and then pricked each slice with a fork before baking (I wanted my gluten-free version to look and feel like the store-bought ice-cream sandwiches he missed). The cookie was delicious, but a bit too hard once it was frozen. I took out some of the brown rice flour mix and added back in an equal amount of sweet rice flour. The sweet rice flour worked its magic: The ice-cream sandwiches were more tender, and they bent a little when frozen (both recipes are in *Gluten-Free Baking Classics*, Surrey, 2008).

Other Whole Grain Flours

There are gluten-free bakers across the country who use a variety of whole grain flours in addition to, or instead of, brown rice flour in their cakes, cookies, muffins, and pie crusts (including millet, sorghum, teff, amaranth, garbanzo bean, and quinoa). I do not. I have the most success recreating classic baked goods when I use my brown rice flour mix. However, I do like to add ground nuts along with my flour mix when a recipe lends itself to it (like the Banana Pecan Crunch Cake and Cherry Almond

Muffins recipes in this book).

On the other hand, when it comes to baking gluten-free bread, you'll find that the large assortment of whole grain flours on the market enables gluten-free bakers to create a rich variety of multigrain loaves. I recommend using my bread flour mix and adding an additional whole grain flour, just like traditional bread bakers, who mix high-gluten bread flour with all-purpose whole wheat, rye, or pumpernickel flours to alter the taste and texture of their loaves. Although I was able to recreate the most true-to-wheat versions of classic artisan and sandwich breads using millet and sorghum in a ratio of half whole grain to half starch, I typically use teff, a darker, fiber and protein rich, nutty, whole grain flour for many of my multigrains. In addition to adding extra nutrition, teff will add color, texture, and flavor to the bread. I also like to use coarsely ground gluten-free rolled oats (use a blender or food processor) and oat flour; they are slightly sweeter and add an extra bit of chew to the loaf.

To make a multigrain loaf: I recommend that you add ¼ to ⅓ cup of whole grain flour (and no more than ½ cup) to replace an equal amount of the bread flour mix. If you prefer, you can add 2 tablespoons to ¼ cup of ground nut flour in addition to all the flour in a recipe, in order to enhance the flavor and texture of your breads.

Take note: Your breads will become denser and heartier when you add additional whole grain flour or ground nut flour to the dough. The more you add, the denser they become. In gluten-free bread baking, less is more, unless you want to make a brick.

How to Purchase and Store Gluten-Free Flours

Whole Grain Flour

Brown rice, millet, and sorghum flours are whole grain flours and must be stored carefully. The two flour mixes (detailed above) can be stored at room temperature for about four months in tightly sealed plastic or glass containers. If your house is hot and humid, or if you will not be baking for long periods of time, store them in the refrigerator. Store open packages of brown rice flour, millet flour, and sorghum in the refrigerator.

It is best to purchase all these flours from grocery stores, local natural food stores, or online sellers that have a lot of turnover so you can be sure you are getting fresh packages. Do not purchase millet and sorghum too far in advance of when you're making your flour mix (more than four months). However, Authentic Foods brown rice flour (and their sorghum and other whole grain flours) are so well packaged that they are shelf stable for longer periods when kept at an average temperature of 65° to 75°F.

When you open a new bag of flour, make sure it does not have a strong odor, an indication that it is rancid or old. Millet flour in particular (just like whole-wheat flour) tends to get rancid and bitter-tasting if it is old or not stored properly by the distributor, at the store, or in your home. In fact, all the whole grain flours should have a pleasant, grainy, nutty smell and taste.

Take note: If you purchase any Bob's Red Mill whole grain flour (but his brown rice and millet in particular), be aware that you should always check the flour for freshness as soon as you get home because his flours are packaged in thin, clear plastic that can cause faster degradation of the flour than foil or other heavier, opaque packaging.

Keep opened and unopened bags of teff flour, gluten-free oat flour, and any other whole grain flour you use in the refrigerator to preserve freshness. I recommend you open the bags soon after you buy them in order to make sure they aren't rancid. It is usually not necessary to store gluten-free rolled oats in the refrigerator unless your home is hot and humid or you don't use them very often.

Although you may want to keep a small container of sweet rice flour in your pantry at room temperature, I recommend that you keep the rest of the open bag in the refrigerator so it remains fresh for long-term storage; even though it isn't a whole grain, it takes a long time to use up a big bag.

Starches

Potato starch, tapioca flour, and corn starch brands are fairly interchangeable and consistent in quality. They can be stored at room temperature for about a year or more and, as a result, can be purchased in advance of when you will be using them to make the flour mixes. Both newly opened packages and packages that have been opened and tightly sealed should have almost no discernable taste or smell. In fact, it is rare to come across rancid potato starch, tapioca flour, or corn starch, but it can happen. Moreover, there have been occasional reports of "sour" tapioca flour (often used in Brazilian cheese bread) being mistakenly packaged in regular tapioca flour packages. Be aware that the tapioca flour you need to use in this mix does not have a sour taste or smell.

How to Measure and Mix Gluten-Free Flours

I recommend that you prepare batches of the Brown Rice Flour Mix and Bread Flour Mix whenever you run low, so that you'll always have them available. If you have easy access to baking flour, you are more likely to bake when the urge strikes.

Using Volume Measure: Flour scooping versus spooning

Everyone measures flour a difference way: some people scoop, some sift, some spoon, and some dump it into the cup. But the amount of flour you end up with in that one-cup measure can vary depending on the method you use, and it can vary a lot—by one tablespoon, more or less. So I have tried to narrow the variables that can go wrong. By specifying a specific method and describing it to the best of my ability, I am trying to make sure that your cupcake or muffin comes out as well as the ones I make in my own kitchen. I suggest you spoon flour into the measuring cup. If you scoop your flour, you may inadvertently add 1 tablespoon or more flour and make a heavier, denser cupcake. Perhaps you might not notice it unless you test side by side—

as I always do. But along with great taste, texture, and appearance, my goal also includes consistency: You should be able to make the best possible version of the recipe every single time.

To measure flour for making flour mixes: Use a soup spoon to spoon each flour from the package into the measuring cup, or pour flour from the package into the measuring cup over a bowl (my favorite method), then use a knife (or the handle of the spoon) to level the top. *Do not scoop* gluten-free flours out of the package with the measuring cup. Empty the measured flour into a plastic or glass container large enough to leave four to five inches free to the top. Shake the container vigorously to mix the flours. I usually make 12 cups of brown rice flour mix at a time and store and shake it in a 21-cup container.

To measure flour for use in recipes: Shake container vigorously to mix and aerate the flours *(shake and bake)*. Use a soup spoon to spoon the flour from container into the measuring cup, then use a knife (or handle of the spoon) to level the top. Do not scoop gluten-free flours out of the container with the measuring cup.

Using Weight Measurements

To measure flour for making flour mixes: Use the weights given above to make the desired amount of Brown Rice Flour Mix or Bread Flour Mix. Empty the measured flour into a container large enough to leave four to five inches free to the top. Shake the container vigorously to mix the flours.

To measure flour for use in recipes: Use weight measurement below or volume measurement from *"Using Volume Measure—To measure flour for use in recipes"* above.

1 cup Brown Rice Flour Mix = 125 grams (4.4 ounces)

1 cup Bread Flour Mix is between 121 grams (4.25 ounces) and 128 grams ounces (4.5 ounces). The difference between the two numbers amounts to about one tablespoon of the flour mix, and is dependant which brand of millet and sorghum you use.

Most Frequently Asked Questions about the Flour Mixes

Can you replace the brown rice flour in my mix with white rice flour?

Yes, but your baked goods will dry out faster and won't stay fresh as long, they won't be as nutritious, and they will have that notorious gluten-free "empty" taste.

Is there a good replacement for brown rice flour in your recipes?

No, not really. In truth, my recipes are finely calibrated to work with extra finely ground brown rice flour, and it is a full two-thirds of the flour mix. However, if you need to leave out the rice flour, the best replacement to use in my recipes is the most finely ground sorghum you can buy. Authentic Foods makes extra finely ground sorghum flour. Bob's Red Mill sorghum has a much larger grind that is perfect for bread, but it makes a slightly grittier cupcake. The grind of King Arthur's sorghum flour falls between these two. You will have to reduce the amount of liquid and/or fat in the recipe (or increase the flour), but there is no across-the-board reduction amount because it depends on what you are trying to make and what is in it. You may have to increase the amount of xanthan gum (explained in more detail in the next chapter) just a bit to improve the structure, but this will depend on the other ingredients in the recipe.

Why do you use potato starch, tapioca flour, and corn starch in the mixes?

Potato starch (not potato flour) contributes to a delicate crumb and rich mouth feel. Tapioca flour (also called tapioca starch) helps lighten baked goods and give them a fine texture. Corn starch helps add a bit of added structure and tenderness to the breads.

Can you use potato flour instead of potato starch in my brown rice flour mix?

In gluten-free baking, potato flour adds moisture but doesn't lighten. It is a flour made from the whole potato, whereas potato starch is made only from the starchy parts.

To illustrate: If you make one of my muffin recipes using my brown rice flour mix made with *potato starch*, they will be light and tender. If you make muffins using my flour mix made with *potato flour* (by mistake or on purpose), it will make a muffin that you could throw against the wall and it would stick there for eternity (well, maybe only a week. But you get the idea).

Is there a good substitute for potato starch?

Option 1: Replace all the potato starch with more tapioca flour. This will give you a light baked good but without that "certain something" in the way of richer mouth-feel that the potato starch gives. It will also be a little softer, and much mushier in texture. Ultimately, it will be less likely to hold as much of its rise.

Option 2: Replace 1 cup potato starch with ½ cup more tapioca flour and ½ cup corn starch first in a simple recipe. Then replace that 1 cup of potato starch with ½ cup tapioca starch, ¼ corn starch, and ¼ cup sweet rice four, make the same recipe, and see which version you like best.

Option 3: One enterprising baker on the West Coast created his own concoction for his son with my mix: He divides the total amount of potato starch in half and uses half arrowroot and half extra finely ground sweet rice flour. So when the mix calls for 1 cup potato starch, use ½ cup arrowroot and ½ sweet rice flour. But arrowroot is expensive (at least where I live). So if you want to try a less expensive version of this arrowroot/sweet rice flour option, replace 1 cup potato starch with ¾ cup tapioca (which is much like arrowroot) and ¼ sweet rice, and adjust from there (or ½ cup tapioca and ½ cup sweet rice and see which you like best).

Is there a good substitute for tapioca flour?

Option 1: Replace all the tapioca flour with 1 cup arrowroot starch (which is usually more expensive). This will give you a slightly denser (and slightly wetter, depending on the recipe) baked good.

Option 2: Replace 1 cup tapioca flour with ½ cup potato starch and ½ cup corn starch. This will give you a slightly denser, firmer baked good.

Option 3: Replace 1 cup tapioca flour with ⅓ potato starch and ⅔ corn starch; then try ⅔ potato and ⅓ tapioca, and see which version you prefer in terms of texture.

Is there a good substitute for corn starch?

What I usually recommend is that you first try Option 1 (below) in an easy recipe, like the rustic flat bread, to see if you like it. Then try Option 2 to see which you like better (recipe in *Gluten-Free Baking Classics* and on mygluten-freetable.com).

Option 1: Replace 1 cup corn starch with ½ cup potato starch and ½ cup tapioca flour.

Option 2: Replace 1 cup corn starch with ⅓ potato starch and ⅔ tapioca flour.

Is there a good replacement for millet flour in your recipes?

I have tested many variations to replace millet flour and the best tasting, most wheat-looking replacement uses 1 cup sorghum flour, 1 cup gluten-free oat flour, 1 cup potato starch, and 1 cup tapioca starch. *If you use this mix, you will have to increase the liquid in each recipe by 1 tablespoon* (the oat flour absorbs a lot of liquid). The breads do not freeze quite as well because the oat flour tends to dry out more quickly and gets a bit more crumbly, but the loaves are delicious. If you use this combination and you plan to make one of my multigrain bread recipes, consider using teff flour as the additional whole grain flour, because the combination works really well.

Is there a good replacement for sorghum flour in your recipes?

Substitute 1 cup gluten-free oat flour for 1 cup sorghum flour in the bread flour mix. It may be necessary to add up to 1 tablespoon more liquid to each recipe, depending on the brand of millet you use. How will you know? If the bread has very small, tight air holes and seems very firm, try adding that extra tablespoon of liquid.

Can I grind my own flour?

Many people who use grain mills will swear by them, and in fact, they can work well for the millet and sorghum flours in my bread flour mix. But it is more difficult to grind your own extra finely ground brown rice flour, especially since you won't be able to stabilize it or put it through the very fine industrial sieves used by Authentic

Foods (many brands of brown rice flour are not stabilized, so they can be sold more inexpensively). My understanding from several made-for-home grain mill owners and from people who, *for convenience and/or price reasons*, buy brown rice flour with a large grind, is that you may need to give the grain a further whirl in a blender to get rid of the grit. To make doubly sure after that, you can also sift it through a fine sieve to get really powdery flour like the one from Authentic Foods.

If you attempt to grind your own brown rice flour, try to do a side-by-side comparison with either Authentic Foods extra finely ground brown rice flour or one with the finest grind you can find, so that you can get a good understanding of what your end product is really like. It is best to know as much as possible about the flour you are making and using in the brown rice flour mix; a very large grind may require a different amount of liquid in a recipe.

What do you think about the argument that you need a different flour mix depending on what you are trying to make?

I don't agree. Once you have a flour mix that you know and understand, it is easier to know what you have to do to tweak a recipe if it doesn't work. You can work your way up your learning curve in a more manageable way.

Authentic Foods 800-806-4737 (www.authenticfoods.com)
Bob Red Mill 800-349-2173 (www.bobsredmill.com)
King Arthur Flour Company 800-827-6836 (www.kingarthurflour.com)

3

GLUTEN-FREE BAKING FUNDAMENTALS: OTHER BASICS

The Secrets of Xanthan Gum and Guar Gum

THE GLUTEN IN WHEAT, RYE, AND BARLEY HELPS HOLD BAKED GOODS TOGETHER AND GIVES them structure and elasticity. When we use gluten-free flours, we need to add back the elasticity, and give baked goods the support they need to rise and to hold together. The best and most commonly used way to do this is to use xanthan gum (and sometimes guar gum) in the recipe. In fact, xanthan gum is a proven workhorse for gluten-free baking, and almost all of the recipes I develop use it. In side-by-side tests, however, I've found that guar gum provides a better, more tender result in my recipes for chiffon, sponge, and angel food cakes.

Both xanthan and guar gum are water-soluble; technically they are called hydrocolloids. They provide elasticity and improve mouth feel, build viscosity (help retain moisture), encapsulate flavors, extend shelf life, and stabilize baked goods so that they can be successfully frozen and thawed.

Typically, xanthan gum is blended with the other dry ingredients in gluten-free baking (at least for small-batch home bakers). It hydrates relatively quickly and evenly, which helps prevent lumping during the critical initial mixing stage. This even hydration aids in the uniform distribution of moisture in the batters, which in turn helps stabilize the fine air cells formed during the mixing process. The stabilization of air cells improves volume and symmetry in the finished baked good.

If you use too little xanthan or guar gum, your baked goods will fall apart and turn out brittle and hard. If you use too much, your baked goods will condense and shrink after you bake them, growing ever tighter and smaller as the gum works its magic for days after. Xanthan gum will actually take time to set up in some recipes. In particular, you will find that pie crusts, tart crusts, and certain cookies can be a bit crumbly when you eat them right out of the oven; but after "resting" for several hours, or after being chilled in the refrigerator, the texture becomes "normal."

The amount of xanthan gum needs to be re-calibrated for each recipe based on the type and amount of flour mix used; the liquids and flavorings that are added; the number of eggs, if any; and the desired texture of the baked good you are trying to make. Based on extensive testing (and contrary to the advice of many gluten-free cookbook writers), I do not believe there is a one-size-fits-all rule for xanthan gum in gluten-free baking. I strongly recommend you avoid flour mixes that include it as an ingredient because it is difficult to adjust for it when it is already in the mix.

For an illustration of exactly how little xanthan gum is needed to make a difference, see the Pumpkin Roll recipe on page 83.

Background details: Xanthan gum is produced by a fermentation process using the bacterium *Xanthomonas campestris*. In fact, this bacteria grow on plants found in the cabbage family, where the gum was discovered. Xanthan gum is actually the cell wall surface of the bacteria that is separated by a complex enzymatic process. During the fermentation process the bacteria are fed simple sugars (like glucose syrup) and minerals. When completed, the mixture is pasteurized to kill the bacteria. The gum is then separated by precipitating it using an alcohol substance. The gum is then washed, dried, and milled to a fine powder.

Guar gum is extracted from the guar seed *(Cyanosis tetragonoloba)*, which comes primarily from India and Pakistan.

Heads up about xanthan gum: always check the date on the package of any xanthan gum you buy; it gets old after several years. In addition, it can be improperly stored at the distributor or store. The result is that your baked goods might not rise or hold together as well.

Moreover, although this is rare, I feel compelled to warn you that, every now and then, you can get a bad bag of xanthan gum, by which I mean the gum might work like it's been supercharged with Viagra. I was the unlucky buyer of such a bag of higher-than-"normal"-grade gum (packaged by a well-known company). After I opened it for the first time, I used it to make my pizza crust (a recipe that appeared in *Gourmet* magazine in November 2005, and in my first book, *Gluten-Free Baking Classics*). The crust is typically tender with a bit of chew and crunch. But the crust I made with my newly purchased "bad bag" of xanthan gum was tough and had the texture of rubber. I carefully made it again and got the same result. I'd made this recipe more than a hundred times over the years, and I knew the only difference was the new bag of xanthan gum. When I tried using it again in my vanilla cupcakes, they came out unusually small in size, with a chewy, rubbery texture and tight, small air pockets. You could have used them to play paddle ball. I contacted the manufacturer. They denied they had a problem. I bought another bag and it worked perfectly. Buyer beware.

Baking Pans

I recommend that you use good-quality baking pans if you intend to do a lot of gluten-free baking; it can really make a difference in the quality of your baked goods. Less expensive pans do not conduct heat well, and baked goods can rise too fast or become dry and over-browned. Your pans do not have to be professional quality, however. I use good, made-for-home bakeware that is readily available in stores everywhere, online, or in catalogs.

Gluten-free batters and doughs bake up best in lighter-colored, medium-weight metal baking pans. Dark pans bake faster because the dark surfaces absorb more of the radiant heat coming from the oven walls (as compared to pans with lighter, shiny surfaces, which tend to reflect, rather than absorb, radiant energy). You can end up with a baked good that rises too fast, and then falls and cracks, or one that is too brown on the outside and underdone on the inside. If you have dark metal pans, you may have to lower the oven temperature by 25°F and/or decrease the baking time to compensate.

My experience has also shown that super thick, heavy bakeware can cause problems for many gluten-free home bakers (at least with my recipes): Cookie dough melts before it bakes, and the outer crust on sandwich breads and cakes can become too thick. The exceptions to this are traditional Bundt cake pans (by Nordic Ware®); my Bundt cake recipes in this book are specifically designed for a thick, heavy pan (the Nordic Ware® Bundt pan is the best).

I typically use glass pie pans in most of my pie recipes because I like the way finished pies look in a glass pan. However, my pie and tart crusts work equally well in metal and ceramic pans, especially French metal tart pans with removable sides (which I use to make all my tarts). Take note: I *do not lower* the temperature by 25°F when using a glass or ceramic pie pan, as wheat bakers sometimes do. My pie recipes typically pre-bake and/or par-bake the crust at a lower temperature than those used for wheat.

At the beginning of each chapter, I list the specific bakeware, including dimensions, used in each of the recipes that follow. Bakeware details are also included in each recipe.

How to measure ingredients for recipes in this book

Not all measuring cups and measuring spoons are created equal. I found this out the hard way: I've seen plastic dry-ingredient measuring cups that weren't precisely correct, and I've seen liquid glass measuring cups with lines painted on in the wrong place on the glass. In both cases, they were inexpensive, imported ones. Always double-check for accuracy whenever you buy any new dry or liquid measuring cup or set of measuring spoons.

Measure dry ingredients in dry measure nesting cups of 1, ½, ⅓, and ¼ cup capacity. Spoon ingredients into the measuring cup, fill to the brim, and then level them off with the edge of a knife or the back of the spoon you used to transfer the ingredients.

Measure small amounts of dry ingredients in measuring spoons the same way (typically 1 tablespoon, and ¼, ½, and 1 teaspoon). Take care to be accurate. For instance, as much as ⅛ teaspoon too much xanthan gum can affect certain baked goods.

Measure liquids in glass or Pyrex heatproof measuring cups with a spout. These typically come in 1-, 2- and 4-cup sizes. Check the level of your liquids at eye level when you measure them.

Other Frequently Asked Questions

Is it possible to use milk substitutes?

Yes. You can use rice, soy, or almond milk in all of my recipes that call for milk. Rice and almond milk add less of an aftertaste, unless you like the taste of soy. Remember that the gluten-free flours are a bit transparent in flavor. In fact, I prefer using rice milk because it has the least taste and doesn't have an adverse effect on the texture. Coconut milk adds a noticeable coconut taste and affects the texture and appearance of my recipes.

You can use Earth Balance®Buttery Spread *or* Buttery Sticks (not the Shortening Sticks) to replace the butter in my recipes (my dairy-free testers have done this; I myself have only done so in some recipes). Several bakers have also written to tell me that they like to use butter-flavored shortening in my pie crust and biscuits, but I prefer the Earth Balance.

Is it possible to use egg substitutes?

Eggs add richness, texture, color, and structure. But it is possible to replace them in many of my recipes. What you use depends on what you are making and what function the egg has in the recipe.

Ener-G-Replacer: 1 ½ teaspoons Ener-G Egg Replacer mixed with 2 tablespoons water = 1 egg. This can produce a good *but not always ideal result* in some recipes. When using this egg substitute, try to use milk higher in fat in order to compensate for not having yolks. It will improve mouth feel and help keep the baked good fresh.

Flax Egg: 1 tablespoon flax seed meal mixed with 3 tablespoons warm water = 1 egg. Allow to sit for 15 minutes to "set up" before using in the recipe. Although I sometimes use flax seed gel as an egg replacer when I bake for people who have egg allergies, it really is better suited to helping hold things together (as an emulsifier). Flax gels are weak structure builders because they don't have the relatively strong protein network of eggs to reinforce dough and batters. As a result, fully baked cakes, muffins, and breads won't be as light and airy when using flax seed gels to replace eggs.

World War II option: Add 1 teaspoon baking soda to the dry ingredients and 1 teaspoon distilled white vinegar to the liquid ingredients. Only combine the dry and liquid right before you put the baked good in the oven.

Is it possible to use sugar alternatives?

The recipes in this book were based on traditional, classic baked goods made with wheat. They were not based on wheat recipes for special diets or restricted dietary needs. Sugar acts as a liquid in baking, and since sugar substitutes contain varying amounts of liquid, each recipe would have to be re-calibrated for dry/wet proportions, cooking time, and maybe even baking temperature, based on the substitute you use. That said, you could try substituting with the sugar alternative of your choice based on your own knowledge base of how to make substitutions.

If you are interested in reducing the sugar in my recipes, it is possible—but not always easy. I don't recommend taking out more than 1 tablespoon if a recipe uses less than ½ cup total sugar, or more than a ¼–⅓ cup if the recipe uses 1 cup or more sugar. Depending on the recipe, you may have to adjust liquid (more) and baking time (less), or you will have a dry baked good.

What yeast do you use?

I use Red Star Active Dry Yeast to develop my yeast-based recipes because it has been a consistently reliable product that produces the best rise in my baked goods (for both my field testers and for me), and it is sold in grocery stores everywhere across the country. I use Red Star Quick Rise Instant Dry Yeast for baked goods that do not need a high rise (pizza, bread sticks, and flat breads). You can use other yeast, but I recommend trying a recipe first with Red Star, so you can see what it's supposed to look like. Take note: SAF Instant Yeast has not produced a really good rise in my bread recipes for field testers or me.

Can I make the bread recipes without yeast?

Yes, however, the breads will not look or taste the same. Use about 2 ½ teaspoons of baking powder per cup of my Bread Flour Mix to replace the yeast in my bread recipes. Use 4 teaspoons for an artisan bread using 1 ½ cups of flour mix, and 5 teaspoons for a sandwich bread recipe using 2 cups of flour mix. I have tried this myself, and I know of several other bakers who have been successful using this formula.

Is it possible to use a substitute for xanthan gum or guar gum?

Although I've tested various combinations of ground flax seeds, psyllium husk, chia seeds, and pectin, I've never been able to recreate a vanilla cupcake, a muffin, biscuit, sandwich bread, or artisan bread that had the more "classic" texture, appearance, and, in many cases, taste of gluten-free baked goods made with xanthan gum. The baked goods not made with xanthan gum all seemed a little more like. . .well, like gluten-free baked goods. They were a bit denser, or wetter, or off color, or they had an after-taste (often bitter), or they had less structure, or they dried out more quickly. *At the present time*, I am unable to offer what I'd consider to be a fool-proof substitute for xanthan gum to make classic gluten-free baked goods. (See the Chapter 10 section entitled *"Psyllium husk to replace xanthan gum and/or add fiber,"* on page 191, for more information).

What can be used to replace gelatin in the sandwich breads?

The sandwich breads call for gelatin in order to add a little bit of extra body and structure. If you can't use gelatin or don't like it, add an extra egg yolk or leave it out entirely.

Do you use a particular brand of baking cocoa in your recipes?

I've used many kinds of baking cocoa, and I don't really have a favorite. It may be my palate, but I've been hard- pressed to tell the difference in side-by-side tests of chocolate baked goods. Many years ago I did a test for my chocolate sponge cake (from *Gluten-Free Baking Classics*) because I figured, of all my recipes, the type of baking cocoa would matter most there, but it just wasn't that noticeable and certainly not worth the extra cost (I compared an expensive import from a fancy gourmet store that a friend had given me as a present against Hershey baking cocoa from my local grocery store).

When I develop recipes, I try to use commonly available ingredients that people can buy in any local supermarket (*except for the flour and xanthan gum*). As a result, I've used Hershey's baking cocoa to develop all my recipes. It is not Dutch processed. That said, you can use any other natural cocoa powder you prefer.

Do I need a special kind of mixer to make your recipes?

No. I developed all my recipes using a basic home Kitchen Aid mixer (read: least expensive model), but any home mixer will do. One problem I discovered, though, is that newer models of many home mixers run faster than the older models. In other words, "medium speed" on a brand-new Kitchen Aid mixer is faster than it was on an old Kitchen Aid mixer. I have found this to be true with Kitchen Aid specifically, but I've also noticed it with other brands (including hand-held models). My evidence has come from bakers across the country who've written to me, my field testers, and my own experiences with a new Kitchen Aid mixer I bought only recently; it runs faster and less smoothly than my old one, which I had for 25 years (i.e., I miss my old Kitchen Aid mixer).

Beware of using *a professional-size mixer* with the recipes in this book. I've found that home bakers have a tendency to overbeat my recipes when they use professional-sized mixers, particularly Kitchen Aid, to make them. The recipes in this book make "home-sized" baked goods. What happens is that the mixing bowl on the mixer is too large for the amount of batter, so home bakers tend to compensate by overbeating the batter without realizing it.

Why don't you include nutritional information for each recipe?

I have considered adding nutritional information for all my baking books, but always end up deciding against it. I think baked goods should be a very small part of our daily diet. I believe in getting nutrients and fiber from fresh (when possible) vegetables, fruit, beans, legumes, nuts, seeds, meat, poultry, fish, and dairy. You won't find any kale in my brownie recipes. There is nothing remotely healthy about baked goods—not even when cookbook writers try to dress them up as low-fat or low-sugar or low-carb. And so, philosophically, I am opposed to trying to pretend that they should ever be considered good for our bodies. They exist to make us happy—not healthy.

To elaborate, baked goods can have an important role in our lives—but I don't think it's good to eat a lot of them. When I'm not testing recipes, I generally eat only small amounts of sweet baked goods on the weekend, and I limit eating bread, pizza, and pasta to a couple of times a month. I believe sweets are treats, and that even bread should be eaten sparingly. But when I do indulge, I don't want to know how much fat, or how many calories and carbs, are in my chocolate fudge cake or lemon squares. I just want them to be fabulous. A baking book is not a health book or a diet book, and I don't want to pretend that it is.

Do you have recommendations for baking at high altitudes?

Although there are no definitive adjustments I can give for any one recipe, I can give some guidelines based on feedback from a few of my field testers. But do I think it's important to understand what is actually happening when you bake at higher altitudes: The lower air pressure found there means liquids will have a lower boiling point, which means they will evaporate faster; the low air pressure, combined with the low humidity found at higher altitudes, not only dries out baking flour but can lead to dry, crumbly baked goods; the lower boiling point also means it can take longer to bake foods because at that (lower) boiling point, chemical and physical reactions slow down; and finally, the lower air pressure can make cakes, breads, and muffins rise too rapidly, or over-rise, and then fall.

Be aware that many recipes do not require much, or any, adjustment. Try a new recipe to see if it works before making any changes; if it's too dry or doesn't rise well, or collapses, or it sinks or is under-baked in the middle, make the changes one at a time.

- Decrease leavening by $1/4$ to $1/2$ teaspoon in order to prevent baked goods from over-proofing, and/or rising too fast or over-rising in the oven. In particular, yeast breads will rise faster and need to be watched so they don't over-proof.
- Increase liquids 1 to 4 tablespoons if the finished baked good is too dry.
- Decrease sugar 1 to 3 tablespoons per cup. The increased evaporation of liquid in the air concentrates the sugar in your baked good; sugar can weaken the structure and cause your baked good to fall, or your cookies to flatten.

- Increase the baking temperature 15° to 25°F to help set the cell structure. You may need to shorten the baking time (by about 20 percent).
- If the structure isn't strong enough to hold the rise (cake, bread, muffins), or your cookies flatten, you may need to add flour 1 tablespoon at a time.
- Don't overbeat eggs. In some cases, you might want to try extra large eggs in order to add extra protein, which will help with the structure and help improve moisture retention. If using only egg whites, beat until soft rather than firm peaks.
- Reduce fat 1–2 tablespoons at a time.

Some other basic recommendations for high altitude baking:
- Keep flours in airtight containers in order to prevent them from drying out.
- Try not to over-beat cakes, muffins, and sweet breads; this can cause them to rise too fast and then fall.
- Make sure to grease pans well, because baked goods tend to stick to the sides of the pan at higher altitudes (except for angel food and sponge cakes, which are baked in ungreased pans).
- Don't overfill muffin and quick bread pans, in order to allow more room for the batter to expand.

Gluten-Free Baking Pantry

Non-Refrigerated
Authentic Foods GF Classic Blend(my brown rice flour mix already mixed up)
Extra finely ground brown rice flour (I only use Authentic Foods)*
Extra finely ground sweet rice flour (I only use Authentic Foods)*
Millet (I use Arrowhead Mills and Bob's Red Mill)*
Sorghum (I use Bob's Red Mill and Authentic Foods)*
Potato starch (not potato flour)
Tapioca flour (also called tapioca starch)
Cornstarch
Teff flour (I use Bob's Red Mill)*
Gluten-free rolled oats
Gluten-free oat flour (I use Bob's Red Mill)*
Stone ground cornmeal
Xanthan gum (I use Bob's Red Mill)
Guar gum
Granulated sugar
Confectioners sugar
Dark brown sugar

Store open packages of whole-grain flour in refrigerator.

Powdered cocoa
Semisweet chocolate morsels
Semisweet baking chocolate
Unsweetened baking chocolate
German sweet chocolate
Pure vanilla extract
Other pure extracts you use often: chocolate, almond, lemon, etc.
Baking soda
Baking powder (I use Davis or Clabber Girl)
Cream of tartar
Iodized salt
Sea salt
Variety of dried spices, including allspice, cardamom, cinnamon, ground cloves, ground ginger, and nutmeg,
Variety of seeds to use in multigrain breads, including caraway, poppy, sesame, flax, and sunflower

Refrigerated

Milk (I use fat-free for most recipes, but you can use 1% or 2%) or Rice milk
Heavy cream
Large fresh eggs (make sure you are getting large eggs and that there aren't extra-large or medium mixed in because some of the large eggs were broken and replaced)
Unsalted butter (for dairy free baking use Earth Balance®Buttery Spread or Buttery Sticks)
Fresh lemons (grated zest can be stored in freezer)
Prepared pesto (can be stored in freezer) for quiches, tarts
Bottled key lime juice
Assorted nuts for baking including walnuts, almonds, and pecans

Chapter Notes: G. Sworn, Monsanto (Kelco Biopolymers, Tadworth) (2000) "Xanthan gum" in *Handbook of Hydrocolliods*, eds. Glyn Owain Phillips, Peter Athony Williams. Woodhead Publishing Limited, Cambridge, England, pp. 103-115.

4

HOW TO
CONVERT A RECIPE

I F YOU WERE TO ENROLL IN AN ACCREDITED COOKING SCHOOL IN ORDER TO LEARN HOW TO bake with wheat, you would be taught very exact, time-tested methods for making pastry, breads, cakes, and cookies. Ingredients would be uniform; standards for what constitutes a good rise, a perfect crust, or a sought-after texture would be explained in detail. You would learn exactly what a chocolate fudge cake batter should look like before you pour it into the pan, and exactly how to handle the dough for your whole grain sandwich bread. Your training would provide a solid foundation for more learning and creativity for years to come.

If you choose to learn by reading the cookbooks of renowned bakers, the ingredients, techniques, and lessons would be similar within categories across a wide array of recipes. All purpose flour in one cookbook is the same as all purpose flour in another, and once you understood how it behaves, you would be better able to tweak and create your own recipes.

But if you were newly diagnosed with celiac or non-celiac gluten intolerance, you might go to a local bookstore or an online bookseller and peruse the culinary landscape for baking lore. You would probably also scan the hundreds of gluten-free websites and blogs on the Internet. And what would you find? An intellectual free-for-all. To your great dismay you would discover literally dozens of cookbook writers, all giving different instructions, using different flour mixes (or no flour mix at all), and having different opinions about what makes the best gluten-free baked goods. The result? If you were to trust fate and randomly select one of the thousands of recipes available in cookbooks or online, and then take the time to buy the ingredients and make it, the chances are good, not only that you would be able to tell it was gluten-free, but that it wouldn't be as good as you wanted it to be.

And therein lies the challenge: How do you start to make sense of it all and, ultimately, be able to convert your own recipe? You need two things: a flour mix that you know well, and a good recipe.

Guidelines for Converting a Recipe with the Two Flour Mixes Detailed in this Book

Start with a good-quality wheat version of the recipe you want to make. A well-written recipe details the ingredients, procedures, oven temperature, and baking times; it will become your starting place for the conversion. Take note: These are not guidelines for no-sugar, no-fat, low-carb, "healthy," or high-fiber baked goods.

Option 1: You have a trusted, much-loved wheat recipe that you've made and eaten before.

It can be a recipe that you created, or one that came from family or friends, or it can come from a cookbook writer or blogger. *The important thing is that you've either made it or you've eaten it before, that the recipe works well, and that you like it.* In my first book, *Gluten-Free Baking Classics*, most of the recipes were based on wheat recipes that I had been making for years, so I was very familiar with what the taste, texture, and appearance of the finished product was supposed to be like. Moreover, many of the people who write me to ask for my help converting a treasured family recipe know exactly what they are trying to recreate. I typically write back and ask for a very detailed description of the taste and texture in order to understand what they are looking for. Then it's all a matter of explaining to them the ingredient combinations I would test, the steps I would take, exactly what I would start with, and how I would tweak it if it needs adjustment.

1.Recipe size: If the recipe is for a double or triple batch or more, reduce it to a single. If you can, make half the recipe when testing.

2. Flour for sweet baked goods: It is important to understand that my brown rice flour mix is not a cup-for-cup flour replacement for wheat flour, because xanthan gum or guar gum is added separately. I typically start with the same amount of flour as the wheat-based recipe for the first round of testing (downsized to a single batch and cut in half, if possible).

If you want to add finely ground nuts and/or cocoa powder to a recipe that doesn't already contain it, you will most likely have to remove an amount of the brown rice flour mix equal to whatever amount of ground nuts or cocoa you add. Finely ground nuts will add texture, flavor, and character. Cocoa powder will add density, texture, and depth of chocolate flavor (whether added alone or along with melted chocolate).

When a baked good has to be firm yet tender, like pie crust or an ice cream sandwich cookie, it may require a small amount of sweet rice flour, typically two to four tablespoons, depending on the recipe. The amount of sweet rice flour used will replace an equal amount of the brown rice flour mix. (My brown rice flour mix does not include sweet rice flour, because not all recipes require its special purpose: additional tenderness.) See Chapter 2 for more information about Sweet Rice Flour.

Why don't I use potato flour in any of my recipes? Potato flour is most often used to add moisture to gluten-free flour mixes that are made up mostly of white rice flour or other starch-based flours. See Chapter 2 for more information about Potato Flour.

3. *Flour for breads:* I typically match the wheat recipe to a similar recipe from my book, *Gluten-Free Baking Classics*, as a starting place whenever possible. The proportion of bread flour mix to liquid, yeast, fat, and eggs (when eggs are included) is stable within a small range in my recipes. Once you are familiar with it, it is much easier to tweak the base recipes to create new breads; there is no need to recreate the wheel each time you want to convert a bread recipe.

When extra whole-grain flour is added to a bread recipe, it usually means you will have to remove an equal amount of the bread flour mix. Extra-added whole-grain flour adds flavor, color, and character, and makes the bread slightly more tightly textured and dense.

The addition of finely ground nuts to a bread recipe usually means you will have to remove an equal amount of the bread flour mix, but not if it's only a small amount (1 to 4 tablespoons). Finely ground nuts will add texture, flavor, color, and character to the bread.

4. *Sugar:* Depending on the recipe, it should be possible to reduce the sugar, unless the recipe has only a couple of tablespoons to begin with. But if it has a cup or more of sugar for 2 to 3 cups of flour mix, then you might be able to take out some and still not negatively impact the taste, moisture, and lightness. As noted in Chapter 2, I don't recommend taking out more than 1 tablespoon if a recipe uses less than ½ cup total sugar, or more than ¼ to ⅓ cup if the recipe uses 1 cup or more sugar. Depending on the recipe, you may have to adjust liquid (more) and baking time (less), or you will have a dry baked good.

I have found that many older recipes, particularly those from the last 30 years, tend to have a lot of sugar—more, in fact, than recipes from 50 to 100 years ago. Baked goods (and processed food in particular) started getting sweeter in the 1970s. But the relative transparency of the gluten-free starch-based flours in gluten-free flour mixes allows sweetness and other flavors to shine through. I try to tweak my recipes so the other flavors aren't overshadowed by the sweetness. When you bite into one of my baked goods, you might notice that it's sweet, but you'll notice the lemon or the chocolate or the vanilla flavor more. Many gluten-free baked goods taste more "sweet" than anything else, and you have to really work at noticing the other flavors.

5. *Yeast:* The amount of active dry yeast used in gluten-free bread recipes is usually larger than the amount that would be used in a wheat bread. It is also important to make sure the dough has a nice, slow rise in order to allow the xanthan gum time to "set"; a fast rise will contribute to an unstable bread or a yeast-based cake that is likely to fall.

The amount of quick-rise dry yeast is also typically increased over the amount that would be used in a wheat recipe. I typically recommend quick rise for baked goods that do not have to rise very high, such as pizza, flat breads, pretzels, and bread sticks.

6. *Baking powder and baking soda:* The amount of baking powder and baking soda is often increased by as little as $\frac{1}{4}$ teaspoon to as much as 1 $\frac{1}{2}$ times, depending on the recipe.

For example: 2 teaspoons might become 2 $\frac{1}{4}$ teaspoons.

Or, if you need even more leavening, 1 $\frac{1}{2}$ times 2 teaspoons = 3 teaspoons (or 1 tablespoon).

However, I've found it's best not to increase the leavening at all in the first round of testing for cake recipes *that only contain baking soda*. This is because the recipe will typically contain a strong acid in the form of a liquid that will propel the baking soda into action quickly when you combine the wet and dry ingredients; this will often be enough to get the cake to rise well. If it does need to rise more, I've found that it's easier to add more baking soda in the second test round than it is to clean up the oven after the cake explodes out of the pan.

When recipes contain both baking powder and baking soda, I've had more success when I raise only the baking powder on the first round of testing; I add more baking soda on the second round if it needs more lift.

Remember, too much leavening (*and/or overbeating and/or a too hot oven and/or dark pans*) can cause your baked goods to rise too fast *and/or* too high, and then fall in the middle. If your baked good rises well and then falls, or rises too high and then falls, you'll have to try to figure out whether you overbeat the batter, or your oven is too hot, or your dark pans were the culprit, before you adjust the leavening. Occasionally, cakes or sweet breads may fall slightly in the middle if you inadvertently added a bit less flour than necessary (because you spooned the flour into the measuring cup too lightly).

7. *Salt:* The amount of salt can usually be slightly reduced, because it tends to stand out against the more transparent flavors of the flours (in particular, the starches).

8. *Xanthan gum:* When I first started converting recipes, I'd test multiple levels of xanthan gum within categories of recipes using $\frac{1}{4}$-teaspoon increments. I now look for a similar recipe of mine that I've already converted to gluten-free, and use the amount of xanthan gum in that recipe *as a starting amount*. The recipe should have a similar amount and/or similar proportions of flour, liquid (including sugar, which acts like a liquid in baked goods), fat, and eggs.

How will you know if there is too little xanthan gum in your recipe? If, for example, you've converted a wheat muffin recipe to gluten-free (a recipe that you knew worked well with wheat), and you take the muffin out of the muffin pan and put it on the rack, and it starts to slowly sink and, as it cools, gets really hard or brittle, then there is a good chance you might need to add a bit of xanthan gum for the next round. The gum will help give the muffin the structure it needs to maintain its rise, and it will provide a bit of elasticity and "springy-ness" to the texture.

If on the other hand, you take the muffin out of the pan and it stays up, but then, as it cools, slowly contracts or shrinks in size—on all sides—and gets tight and rubbery, you've probably added a bit too much xanthan gum. If you remove a bit of gum in the next round, the muffin will be better able to maintain its air pockets and tenderness.

9. *Flavoring for sweet baked goods:* If possible, increase the amount of extracts, spices, and other flavorings a little; usually you'll need to add 1½ times as much as you would use in a wheat version of the recipe (1 teaspoon vanilla extract becomes 1½ teaspoons); sometimes, you'll need even more (you would double it to 2 teaspoons). The goal is twofold: to accentuate the delicious flavors of the recipe, so you won't notice the lack of wheat; and to cover up as much of the brown rice flavor as you can.

10. *Flavorings for breads:* You probably never thought about how much flavor wheat really has until you had to give it up. As a result, you may not realize that that is one of the things you actually miss most. In gluten-free bread and pizza recipes, I recommend compensating for the lack of wheat flavor by using some of the more richly flavored whole grain flours like millet, sorghum, and teff. They have a delicious, nutty flavor and can help you to make bread that has a real grain taste when used along with other more transparent flours like tapioca, cornstarch, and potato starch. I also like to enhance the flavor of some of my breads with add-ins like nuts and seeds (and sometimes raisins).

11. *Eggs:* Although there seem to be more than a few gluten-free cookbook writers and bloggers who recommend adding an extra egg or egg white to help improve the structure of gluten-free baked goods, I've found that it can make the texture more gooey looking and/or tougher than it needs to be. That extra egg is usually used to compensate for a less-than-ideal combination of flours (often the absence of whole grain flour), an incorrect balance of fat and liquid to dry ingredients, or an incorrect amount of xanthan gum.

I find it useful to start with the exact same amount of eggs for the first round of testing. In reality, I've never had to add an extra egg in over ten years of gluten-free baking. If something seems out of whack on the recipe, I'm more likely to tweak the balance of wet to dry, because I've found I can get a more wheat-like appearance and texture by adjusting that, rather than simply throwing in another egg or egg white.

12. *Liquid:* The amount of liquid (and fat) in the original wheat-based recipe often has to be decreased slightly, but not always. Wheat flour absorbs relatively more liquid than *finely ground brown rice flour*, millet, and sorghum when they are combined with the starches used in my two flour mixes (potato, tapioca, and corn). A baked good that contains too much liquid will have a denser texture and look a little as if it has collapsed in on itself. It also might have a dense area along the bottom where the air pockets are compacted together. When this occurs, I find it simpler to decrease the liquid in the recipe first, instead of adding flour.

13. Fats: I often replace butter with canola oil in my recipes because it tends to produce a lighter gluten-free baked good and adds less flavor. I've also found that I'm often able to reduce the amount of fat in the recipe by 1 to 3 tablespoons, but not always.

A baked good that has too much fat will seem kind of soggy, a little softer than normal, and it won't rise well; it may sink a little in the middle or be smaller than normal, with a kind of flat top. It might also have smaller-than-normal air pockets that seem to have a dampness to them.

Option 2: You know what you want to make, but you don't have a wheat recipe for it that you know well or like.

Although cultural and individual palates differ, serious bakers (and state fair judges!) recognize *the relatively narrow range* of attributes *within categories* that excellent baked goods exhibit. So I hope it's safe to say that there seems to be a general consensus about what makes a really good-quality, classic baked good. Because you don't want to waste your time, money, and energy converting a poor-quality recipe, you should try to find a good one. And to do that, you'll need to take a "recipe road trip" to survey the landscape.

Compare wheat versions of the recipe you want from several of the most well-respected *wheat cookbook writers,* and you'll notice there are common elements. You'll want to incorporate these common elements into your gluten-free version. Ultimately, you might be able to narrow your choice down to the *one* best representative version, or you may have to carefully create a composite that includes the ingredients and techniques from several.

I have a collection of cookbooks going back over 100 years, and I've come to understand that many of the recipes you find in today's cookbooks and magazines are merely tweaked versions of the same recipes published in earlier times. Moreover, recipes you find on the Internet (both wheat and gluten–free) are often tweaked versions of the tweaked versions. It's a good idea to pare down a recipe to its essentials before you try to convert it. Strip away the extra flourishes: the whole wheat flour added to try to make it a "healthy" cake, the liquor that was added to make it a little different, the extra raisins that never should have been there to begin with, the two extra different spices that over-complicate the flavor, the extra sugar that was added in the 1980s, and the extra butter or heavy cream used to make it seem more indulgent than it needs to be.

Once you have written down your newly converted gluten-free version of the recipe for your first test, it's a good idea to compare it to gluten-free recipes in the same category that you know well, in order to look for similarities. In other words, if you are trying to create a new cake, compare the ingredients and proportions to other gluten-free cake recipes you know well to make sure nothing looks out of kilter. Then you can proceed as above to adjust the recipe before you do a first round test.

Considerations for Converting a Recipe without the Two Flour Mixes Detailed in this Book

If you plan to use another flour mix (store bought or from a recipe), you should bake with it across a wide range of existing recipes first. Make sure to use recipes that are specifically designed to work with it. Your goal will be to learn how the flour mix works with different ingredients. Each time you find a recipe that works well, one that you really like, compare it to a good wheat version. Your goal will be to see what changes were necessary to allow the flour mix to work well. As you develop a solid repertoire of recipes and an understanding of how the flour mix works in each of them, you'll be better able to develop your own recipes.

But if you want to be what I call a "free-style baker" (i.e., you want to use a different combination of flours for different recipes using a ratio), then I recommend you learn about how different flours behave by using them in flour mixes in a lot of different kinds of recipes first. Make sure the recipes work well, and then start switching out one flour at a time to see what happens. Remember, the quantity of each flour or starch you use in a recipe will make a difference, and it needs to be considered in relation to the other ingredients and their respective quantities.

However, based on my own experience and on letters from aspiring gluten-free recipe converters, I think it's easier to convert a classic-style recipe when you have a flour mix that you know and understand, versus just throwing in whatever you have in the cabinet based on a ratio. Why?

A general ratio rule for using different types of flour and weights to create flour mixes glosses over the nuances of gluten-free baking, and it will be hard for you to understand what you're doing right and wrong as you fine-tune the recipe. Ratios for wheat baking were developed only after standardized ingredients like all-purpose flour became available. *But there are no standardized flours or mixes available to gluten-free bakers. One hundred grams of sorghum flour is not equal to one hundred grams of brown rice flour, or one hundred grams of millet flour, in a recipe; they do not behave the same way when mixed with the other ingredients and will not produce a vanilla cupcake that looks, tastes, or feels the same in your mouth.* One hundred grams of Bob's Red Mill brown rice flour isn't even equal to one hundred grams of Authentic Foods brown rice flour. The rice flour particles are of different sizes, and therefore have different densities; they will absorb liquid differently, and the texture and appearance will therefore be affected.

In addition, the larger grind (Bob's Red Mill) leaves a slightly gritty texture in the baked good.

Over time, if you use a different combination of flours for every recipe you develop, then when a new recipe doesn't work the first time, you can't know whether you need to increase the xanthan gum, add or delete some of the liquid or fat, add or delete some of the flour in the mix, leave out one of the flours entirely, or add a new, different flour. You can start over and tweak the recipe, but you can't really learn a lot about how to make that general category of recipes better when something goes wrong. You'll only end up knowing how to make that one recipe. "Free-style" gluten-free baking will not help you to build a foundation of usable knowledge for creating your own classic-style gluten-free baked goods.

Another important consideration is that, if you decide to use hearty, whole-grain flours like millet and teff in sweet baked goods (like cakes and cookies), those baked goods will look and rise differently than ones made with all purpose wheat. Depending on the amount of millet or teff flour used, the end product can wind up looking and tasting more like a heavier whole wheat baked good. Many whole-grain gluten-free flours, except brown rice flour, have a strong enough taste to stand out and signal "gluten-free". Moreover, some, like amaranth and quinoa, have such a distinct after-taste that they cannot be covered up with other flavoring. I'm not saying that baked goods made with these flours won't be good; I'm saying that they're less likely to resemble classic wheat baked goods and more likely to taste and/or look like a gluten-free baked good.

If you decide to use bean flours, or coconut, almond, or seed flours, it's important to remember that bean flours leave a strong after-taste that gets even stronger on the second day or after freezing, and that almond, coconut, and seed flours each has a very distinct flavor that stands out and can be difficult to cover up. Moreover, they produce baked goods that have a *totally non-traditional texture* as compared to classic wheat baked goods, even if they taste good.

A final consideration: If you create recipes using only white rice and starch flours, your baked goods will lack even a mild flour flavor. The result is an "empty taste" that is characteristically "gluten-free". The baked goods will also dry out more quickly because they lack protein and fiber, which, besides adding nutrients, helps to keep them fresher longer.

5

Muffins, Sweet Breads, and Scones

Oatmeal Raisin Muffins

Pecan Spice Muffins with Pecan Streusel Topping

Cherry Almond Muffins

Lemon Almond Muffins

Chocolate Muffins

Orange Walnut Muffins

Date Nut Bread

Zucchini Bread

Eggnog Teacakes

Lemon Ginger Scones

Lemon Scones with Lemon Glaze

Cranberry Orange Scones

Cinnamon Roll Scones

T HERE'S NOTHING BETTER THAN STARTING THE MORNING WITH SOMETHING SPECIAL BAKING up hot and fresh in the oven. Even though many of us may save the bulk of our breakfast baking efforts for more leisurely weekends and holidays, this chapter offers some delicious choices for any time the mood strikes: hearty Cherry Almond or Oatmeal Raisin muffins studded with fruit and nuts, delicate scones filled with bright lemon zest and candied ginger, tender Eggnog Teacakes brushed with a glittery rum glaze, fresh-from-the-garden Zucchini Bread, and delectable Cinnamon Roll Scones laced with brown sugar and cinnamon. They're all so good you may want to try every one of them.

I like to prep the dry and wet ingredients for muffins the night before I'm going to make them. I put the dry ingredients in a tightly sealed container on the counter; I put the wet ingredients (milk, oil, eggs, and extracts) in a tightly sealed container in the refrigerator (I put grated lemon and orange rind, if I'm using them, in a separate container in the refrigerator, too). In the morning, I only have to preheat the oven and mix the ingredients together.

Dairy substitutes: My butter substitute of choice for most of the baked goods in this chapter is Earth Balance® Buttery Spread or Buttery Sticks (not the Shortening Sticks). My milk substitute of choice is rice milk.

This chapter uses the following pans:
- 12-cup muffin pan
- Three 5 x 3-inch loaf pans
- Large baking sheet (not insulated or heavy, thick bakeware, like Calphalon)

Try to use lighter-colored, shiny metal pans. Unless you lower the heat in the oven by 25°F, dark pans may cause your muffins and sweet breads to over-brown. The extra heat absorbed by dark pans can also cause your muffins and sweet breads to rise too quickly and then fall a bit. Take note: Extra heavy muffins pans will give you a nice, even rise, but you may have to bake your muffins a little longer than indicated in the recipe.

The Last Word on Muffins
- Set up before starting the recipe: Assemble all ingredients.
- Measure carefully.
- Use the right size pan.
- Preheat the oven to the proper temperature (make sure the oven is calibrated correctly).

- Do not open the oven door more than necessary.
- Use a timer in case you get distracted.
- Once you mix the liquids into the dry ingredients, you need to get your muffins, sweet breads, or scones into the oven quickly. The baking powder leaps into action once it is combined with the liquid, so make sure your oven is preheated and your pans are prepared; it will make a difference in the texture and lightness of your baked goods. Davis and Clabber Girl are double-acting, slow-acting baking powders and you won't need to rush quite as much. However, Rumsford is a fast-acting baking powder that releases about two-thirds of its gas when moisture is added to it in the bowl (i.e., run like crazy). Please see the introduction to the scone recipes on page 53 for more information about baking powder.

OATMEAL RAISIN MUFFINS

These cinnamon-scented muffins have a wholesome goodness that's hard to beat. Whole grain rolled oats team up with sweet, tender raisins to make a hearty, slightly chewy muffin that's guaranteed to get you out of bed and down to the breakfast table. Team them with a bowl of yogurt and fresh fruit, and you'll have the fuel you need to get through the morning. They keep well in the refrigerator for several days, and they're so delicious, you may have to make extra if you decide you want to put some in the freezer for another week.

½ cup gluten-free rolled oats
⅔ cup dark brown sugar, lightly packed
1 ½ cups Brown Rice Flour Mix (188 grams)
1 tablespoon baking powder
1 teaspoon baking soda
¾ teaspoon xanthan gum
¼ teaspoon salt
1 teaspoon ground cinnamon
¾ cup golden raisins
¾ cup chopped walnuts
½ cup skim or lowfat milk
½ cup canola oil
2 large eggs
1 teaspoon pure vanilla extract
Cinnamon sugar* for garnish

1. Preheat oven to 350°F. Position rack in center of oven. Grease 12-cup muffin pan with cooking spray.

2. Combine oats and brown sugar together in a food processor and process until oats are coarsely ground.

3. Mix flour, oat-sugar mixture, baking powder, baking soda, xanthan gum, salt, and cinnamon in large mixing bowl. Add raisins and walnuts; stir to coat evenly.

4. Combine milk, oil, eggs, and vanilla in small bowl. Add liquids to flour mixture and stir until just blended

5. Fill muffin pan. Sprinkle tops with cinnamon sugar. Bake 18–22 minutes until light golden. Remove from oven and cool in pan for 3 minutes. Remove muffins from pan and cool slightly on a plate or rack before serving.

Makes 12 muffins

Muffins can be stored in a tightly sealed plastic container in refrigerator for three days, or covered with plastic wrap and then with foil and stored in freezer for up to three weeks. Best when eaten within three days of baking. Rewarm briefly in microwave.

* To make cinnamon sugar, combine 2 teaspoons granulated sugar and ¼ teaspoon ground cinnamon (or more to taste) in a small bowl.

PECAN SPICE MUFFINS
with Pecan Streusel Topping

Makes 12 muffins

Muffins can be stored in a tightly sealed plastic container in refrigerator for three days, or covered with plastic wrap and then with foil and stored in freezer for up to three weeks. Best when eaten within three days of baking. Rewarm briefly in microwave.

*To make cinnamon sugar, combine 2 teaspoons granulated sugar and ¼ teaspoon ground cinnamon (or more to taste) in a small bowl.

These delicate muffins have a touch of spice and just enough plump, golden raisins and sweet, nutty pecans to keep you coming back for more. I added the warm, irresistible flavors of allspice and cinnamon, the scent of which will beckon to you as they bake in the oven. They're perfect for breakfast, a teatime treat, or a festive autumn brunch after a big morning of apple picking. I like to make them with the Pecan Streusel Topping below, but you can sprinkle on some cinnamon sugar instead. Really though, the streusel topping is delicious—so try it. You know you want it.

2 cups Brown Rice Flour Mix (250 grams)
⅔ cup granulated sugar
1 tablespoon baking powder
1 teaspoon baking soda
¾ teaspoon xanthan gum
¼ teaspoon salt
1 teaspoon ground allspice
½ teaspoon ground cinnamon
¾ cup golden raisins
¾ cup chopped pecans
½ cup skim or lowfat milk
½ cup canola oil
2 large eggs
1 teaspoon pure vanilla extract
Pecan Streusel Topping (recipe below) or cinnamon sugar*
    for garnish

1. Preheat oven to 350°F. Position rack in center of oven. Grease 12-cup muffin pan with cooking spray.

2. Mix flour, sugar, baking powder, baking soda, xanthan gum, salt, allspice, and cinnamon in large mixing bowl. Add raisins and pecans; stir to coat evenly.

3. Combine milk, oil, eggs, and vanilla in small bowl. Add liquids to flour mixture and stir until just blended.

4. Fill muffin pan. Top with Pecan Streusel (recipe below) or sprinkle with cinnamon sugar. Bake 18–25 minutes, until muffins are light golden brown. Remove from oven and cool in pan for 3 minutes. Remove muffins from pan and cool slightly on a plate or rack before serving.

PECAN STREUSEL TOPPING

½ cup Brown Rice Flour Mix (63 grams)
⅓ cup dark brown sugar, lightly packed
¼ finely chopped pecans
½ teaspoon ground cinnamon
¼ teaspoon xanthan gum
3 tablespoons unsalted butter, melted

1. Combine flour, brown sugar, pecans, cinnamon, and xanthan gum in a small bowl; stir to blend. Pour in butter and stir until all dry ingredients are moistened. Break into small pieces with spoon.

CHERRY ALMOND MUFFINS

Makes 12 muffins

Muffins can be stored in a tightly sealed plastic container in refrigerator for three days, or covered with plastic wrap and then with foil and stored in freezer for up to three weeks. Best when eaten within three days of baking. Rewarm briefly in microwave.

*Dried cherries come in sweet and tart versions. I prefer the sweet dried cherries in this muffin, but several testers preferred the tart. Choose depending on your own preference.

Fragrant with almond and colorfully studded with bright red cherries, these muffins will brighten up your morning. In the summer when fresh cherries are in season, you can get out your trusty cherry pitter and turn heads at your next summer brunch. But if your home is like mine, fresh cherries are never around long enough to use for baking. So most of the time, I make my muffins with dried cherries, which are conveniently pitted, have a deep cherry flavor, and are available all year round.

1 ⅓ cups Brown Rice Flour Mix (167 grams)
⅔ cup finely ground almonds
⅔ cup granulated sugar
1 tablespoon baking powder
1 teaspoon baking soda
¾ teaspoon xanthan gum
¼ teaspoon salt
1 ½ cups dried cherries* (or fresh pitted fresh cherries, washed and well dried)
⅔ cup slivered almonds
½ cup skim or lowfat milk
½ cup canola oil
2 large eggs
1 teaspoon pure vanilla extract
1 teaspoon pure almond extract
⅓ cup slivered almonds and granulated sugar for garnish

1. Preheat oven to 350°F. Position rack in center of oven. Grease 12-cup muffin pan with cooking spray.

2. Mix flour, finely ground almonds, sugar, baking powder, baking soda, xanthan gum, and salt in a large mixing bowl. Add cherries and slivered almonds; stir to coat evenly.

3. Combine milk, oil, eggs, vanilla extract, and almond extract in small bowl. Add liquids to flour mixture and stir until just blended.

4. Fill muffin pan. Sprinkle tops with slivered almonds and granulated sugar. Bake 18–25 minutes until light golden. Remove from oven and cool in pan for 3 minutes. Remove muffins from pan and cool slightly on a plate or rack before serving.

LEMON ALMOND MUFFINS

Omit dried cherries and vanilla extract. Add 1 packed tablespoon grated lemon rind in Step 2 and mix well. Add 1 cup slivered almonds instead of ⅔ cup in Step 2. Add ½ teaspoon pure lemon extract in addition to the 1 teaspoon of pure almond extract in Step 3.

CHOCOLATE MUFFINS

Makes 12 muffins

Muffins can be stored in a tightly sealed plastic container in refrigerator for three days, or covered with plastic wrap and then with foil and stored in freezer for up to three weeks. Best when eaten within three days of baking. Rewarm briefly in microwave.

Everyone needs a good, simple chocolate muffin recipe in their baking repertoire, and this one fits the bill. These muffins are easy to make, and they have a rich chocolate flavor and a light, tender texture that makes it hard to stop eating them. Even though you'll find there's nothing quite like the allure of chocolate in the morning, they're also perfect for afternoon snacks.

1 ⅔ cups Brown Rice Flour Mix (208 grams)
⅔ cup unsweetened cocoa powder
⅔ cup granulated sugar
¼ cup dark brown sugar
1 tablespoon baking powder
1 teaspoon baking soda
¾ teaspoon xanthan gum
¼ teaspoon salt
1 cup chocolate chips (regular or mini)
⅔ cup skim or lowfat milk
½ cup canola oil
2 large eggs
1 ½ teaspoons pure vanilla extract
1 teaspoon pure chocolate extract
Granulated sugar for garnish

1. Preheat oven to 350°F. Position rack in center of oven. Grease 12-cup muffin pan with cooking spray.

2. Mix flour, cocoa powder, granulated sugar, brown sugar, baking powder, baking soda, xanthan gum, and salt in a large mixing bowl. Add chocolate chips and stir to coat evenly.

3. Combine milk, oil, eggs, vanilla extract, and chocolate extract in small bowl. Add liquids to flour mixture and stir until just blended.

4. Fill muffin pan (it will almost be filled to the top) and smooth the tops of the batter with the back of a spoon or a spatula. Sprinkle tops with granulated sugar. Bake 18–20 minutes, until cooked through and a toothpick comes out clean (not including the melted chocolate chips). Remove from oven and cool in pan for 3 minutes. Remove muffins from pan and cool slightly on a plate or rack before serving.

ORANGE WALNUT MUFFINS

Add a little sunshine to your day! I like to make these delicious muffins as a treat for weekend brunches or weekday coffee breaks. The recipe combines the bright flavor of oranges with omega-rich crunchy walnuts to create a tender muffin that will perk up everyone around your table. They're especially nice in the dark days of winter, because the delicate aroma of sweet oranges will fill your kitchen as they bake.

2 cups Brown Rice Flour Mix (250 grams)
$2/3$ cup granulated sugar
1 tablespoon baking powder
1 teaspoon baking soda
$3/4$ teaspoon xanthan gum
$1/4$ teaspoon salt
1 packed tablespoon grated orange rind
1 packed teaspoon grated lemon rind
1 $1/2$ cups chopped walnuts
$2/3$ cup orange juice
$1/2$ cup canola oil
2 large eggs
Granulated sugar for garnish

1. Preheat oven to 350ºF. Position rack in center of oven. Grease 12-cup muffin pan with cooking spray.

2. Mix flour, sugar, baking powder, baking soda, xanthan gum, and salt in large mixing bowl. Mix in orange and lemon rind. Add walnuts and stir to coat evenly.

3. Combine orange juice, oil, and eggs in small bowl. Add liquids to flour mixture and stir until just blended.

4. Fill muffin pan. Sprinkle tops with sugar. Bake 18–25 minutes until light golden. Remove from oven and cool in pan for 3 minutes. Remove muffins from pan and cool slightly on a plate or rack before serving.

Makes 12 muffins

Muffins can be stored in a tightly sealed plastic container in refrigerator for three days, or covered with plastic wrap and then with foil and stored in freezer for up to three weeks. Best when eaten within three days of baking. Rewarm briefly in microwave.

DATE NUT BREAD

Makes three 3x5-inch loaves

Store bread covered tightly with plastic wrap in refrigerator for up to four days. Can be covered with plastic wrap and then with foil and stored in freezer for up to four weeks. Best when eaten within four days of baking. Rewarm briefly in microwave.

You can find recipes for date nut bread going all the way back to the turn of the last century. Most of them are pretty basic and uncomplicated. In fact, many allow the sweet goodness of chopped dates and crunchy walnuts or pecans to shine through without any other flavoring; others add a touch of spice. I opted for layering my loaves with a little pizazz. My gluten-free version uses cinnamon, nutmeg, and hints of molasses from dark brown sugar to enhance the dates. I also added a touch of vanilla to round out the flavor. The fragrant loaves are delicious warm from the oven, but they freeze well and can be easily rewarmed in the microwave. I like to buy whole pitted dates and chop them up in a food processor. It's a little more work, but they taste better than the packaged pre-chopped dates available in stores near me.

2 cups (about 8 ounces) chopped dates (use dried, not fresh dates)
½ cup plus 3 tablespoons skim or lowfat milk, separated
2 cups Brown Rice Flour Mix (250 grams)
⅔ cup dark brown sugar, lightly packed
1 tablespoon baking powder
1 teaspoon baking soda
¾ teaspoon xanthan gum
¼ teaspoon salt
1 ½ teaspoons ground cinnamon
½ teaspoon ground nutmeg
½ cup chopped walnuts
½ cup canola oil
2 large eggs
1 teaspoon pure vanilla extract

1. Preheat oven to 350°F. Position rack in center of oven. Grease three 3 x 5-inch loaf pans with cooking spray.

2. Place chopped dates in a small bowl with 3 tablespoons of the milk and stir to combine. Set aside to allow all the liquid to be absorbed by the fruit, about 10 minutes.

3. Mix flour, brown sugar, baking powder, baking soda, xanthan gum, salt, cinnamon, and nutmeg in large mixing bowl (or in large mixing bowl of electric mixer, whichever is easier). Make sure to break up pieces of brown sugar. Add nuts and stir to coat evenly.

4. Combine milk and oil in small bowl. Beat in eggs and vanilla. Add liquid mixture and dates to flour and nut mixture and mix on low speed or stir until just blended.

5. Fill loaf pans with batter. Bake about 35 minutes until golden and toothpick comes out clean. Cool for 8 minutes on a rack and then remove from pan. Cool another 30 to 45 minutes on rack before serving. Cut using a serrated knife with a sawing motion. Serve warm or at room temperature.

ZUCCHINI BREAD

Makes three 3x5-inch loaves

Store bread covered tightly with plastic wrap in refrigerator for up to four days. Can be covered with plastic wrap and then with foil and stored in freezer for up to four weeks. Best when eaten within four days of baking. Rewarm briefly in microwave.

*To make cinnamon sugar, combine 2 tablespoons sugar and ½ teaspoon ground cinnamon in a small bowl.

Zucchini bread recipes have been handed down in families for more than half a century. Interestingly, they seem to vary greatly in terms of sugar and spice. Some have so much sugar that they look like they really should be called "cake," not bread. Some are loaded with add-ins like coconut, raisins, and nuts. Some have absolutely no spice and rely on just the zucchini and sugar for flavor. And some have so much cinnamon, nutmeg, ginger, or allspice that they seem more like a gingersnap or a pumpkin pie. I took the middle ground and added some chopped walnuts and just enough cinnamon to liven up the flavor. The end result? My little gluten-free zucchini breads are fragrant, light textured, a bit green, and best of all, delicious.

2 cups Brown Rice Flour Mix (250 grams)
⅔ cup granulated sugar
1 tablespoon baking powder
1 teaspoon baking soda
¾ teaspoon xanthan gum
¼ teaspoon salt
1 teaspoon ground cinnamon, or to taste
1 ⅓ to 1 ½ cups shredded zucchini
½ cup finely chopped walnuts
½ cup skim or lowfat milk
½ cup canola oil
2 large eggs
½ teaspoon pure vanilla extract
Cinnamon sugar* for garnish

1. Preheat oven to 350°F. Position rack in center of oven. Grease three 3 x 5-inch loaf pans with cooking spray.

2. Put shredded zucchini in a small bowl and pat dry with paper towels.

3. Mix flour, sugar, baking powder, baking soda, xanthan gum, salt, and cinnamon in large mixing bowl. Add zucchini and nuts; stir to coat evenly.

4. Combine milk and oil in small bowl. Beat in eggs and vanilla. Add liquids to zucchini nut mixture and stir until just blended.

5. Fill loaf pans with batter. Sprinkle top with cinnamon sugar, if desired. Bake 35-40 minutes, until light golden and toothpick comes out clean. Cool for 8 minutes on a rack and then remove from pan. Cool another 30 to 45 minutes on rack before serving. Cut using a serrated knife with a sawing motion. Serve warm or at room temperature.

EGGNOG TEACAKES

Inspired by a recipe from cookbook writer Flo Baker that I'd made years ago in my wheat-baking days, these delicate teacakes will become a welcome holiday standby. They have a tender texture, a subtle eggnog flavor, and a frosted rum sugar glaze that adds a bit of crunch and glittery glamour to the outer coating. You might want to make several batches to give as hostess gifts and party favors, or to serve when friends stop by.

⅓ cup dried currants
1 tablespoon dark rum
1 ⅔ cups Brown Rice Flour Mix (208 grams)
1 ½ teaspoons baking powder
½ teaspoon xanthan gum
¼ teaspoon salt
¼ teaspoon ground nutmeg
Generous pinch ground cinnamon
Generous pinch ground allspice
2 large eggs
⅔ cup granulated sugar
½ cup canola oil
½ cup fresh, eggnog (lowfat can be used)*
1 teaspoon pure vanilla extract
Frosted Rum Glaze (recipe follows)

1. Combine dried currants and dark rum in a small dish and set aside.

2. Preheat oven to 350°F. Position rack in center of oven. Grease three 5 x 3-inch loaf pans with cooking spray.

3. Mix flour, baking powder, xanthan gum, salt, ground nutmeg, cinnamon, and allspice in medium bowl. Set aside.

4. Beat eggs in large bowl of electric mixer until lemon-colored. Slowly add sugar, a little at a time, and beat until mixture turns pale yellow and thick. Add flour mixture, oil, eggnog, and vanilla, scrape sides and bottom of bowl, then mix at low speed for 1 more minute. Stir in currants and rum.

5. Pour batter into prepared pan. Place in center of oven and bake 35–40 minutes for small loaves, until knife inserted in center comes out clean. Cool bread for 8 minutes on a rack and then remove from pans.

Makes three 5x 3-inch loaves. Recipe can be doubled

Store bread covered tightly with plastic wrap in refrigerator for up to five days. Can be covered with plastic wrap and then with foil and stored in freezer for up to six weeks. Best when eaten within four days of baking.

*I used an organic low-fat eggnog because all the regular grocery store brands had a lot of stuff in them that shouldn't be in eggnog. Low-fat eggnog made a slightly lighter teacake than full-fat. I tried two non-dairy eggnogs: Coconut milk eggnog tasted delicious—but it had a strong coconut taste. I didn't use it in the cake. The soy eggnog tasted more "eggnoggy," and it worked fine.

6. Arrange loaves so they aren't touching on the rack, and place rack over a piece of wax paper. Brush top and sides with prepared Frosted Rum Glaze. Cool completely on rack before serving or wrapping for storage. Serve at room temperature.

Frosted Rum Glaze

> ½ cup granulated sugar
> 2 tablespoons dark rum
> 1 tablespoon boiling water

1. Combine sugar, dark rum, and boiling water in a small (microwave-proof) bowl; stir until well combined. Use immediately. If the glaze gets too firm, rewarm very slightly in microwave. *The sugar crystals should not melt completely because the glaze is supposed to appear frosted.*

A Word About Scones

AFTER DEVELOPING A GLUTEN-FREE VERSION OF TRADITIONAL, ROUND BRITISH SCONES FOR my first cookbook, I turned my attention to their sweeter, triangle-shaped American cousins. Cookbook writers and food journalists have offered up a smorgasbord of variety for me to consider over the years. In truth, many were a far stretch from the original concept and came fully loaded with icing, chocolate, bacon, fresh fruit, or whole grains. I also found that recipe developers couldn't agree on the "best way" to make them. Wheat recipes called for buttermilk or heavy cream or half and half, or whole milk; more butter or less butter; 1 egg, 2 eggs, or no eggs; more flour or less flour; oven temperatures of 375°F, 400°F, or 425°F; dough placed close together, or not close at all, on the baking sheet. But a lot can go wrong in a simple scone recipe, especially a gluten-free one. I tried more combinations than I thought possible and finally created a scone that was lightly crisp on the outside and slightly crumbly on the inside. Finally, I had a starting point for my own variations—and for yours.

I will caution you to use a double-acting, slow-acting baking powder like Davis or Clabber Girl for the scone recipes in this book. Slow-acting baking powders contain an acid like sodium aluminum sulfate, which only dissolves at a high temperature (and thus starts to work) once your dough or batter is in the oven. Actually, Davis and Clabber Girl contain both sodium aluminum sulfate and monocalcium phosphate, so about two-thirds of the gas is released in the oven. This gives you time to pat out and cut the dough before the carbon dioxide gas is released.

Baking powders that only contain an acid that dissolves at a low temperature, like monocalcium phosphate, release about two-thirds of their gas before your batter or dough gets into the oven. Rumsford is a fast-acting baking powder that releases about two-thirds of its gas when moisture is added to it in the bowl. Do not use it for the following scone recipes.

LEMON GINGER SCONES

Makes 12 scones

Store leftover scones in an airtight container in refrigerator for three days, or cover scones with plastic wrap, and then with foil, and store in freezer for up to three weeks. Best when eaten within three days of baking. Rewarm in a preheated 350°F oven for about 10 minutes, or for several seconds in a microwave.

*If you plan to use a butter substitute, measure it first and then chill it until it is very cold. Do not use shortening or margerine in this recipe.

These richly flavored scones have a lively lemon flavor and warm, spicy undertones that come from ground ginger and cardamom. But they don't stop there. Chopped crystallized ginger adds a certain sparkle to make them completely addictive. The recipe creates twelve delicately sized scones that will disappear in a flash whenever you serve them. If you're lucky enough to be able to set some aside, however, you'll find they freeze well and taste almost as good as new when reheated.

2 cups Brown Rice Flour Mix (250 grams)
¼ cup granulated sugar
4 teaspoons baking powder (see Cook's Note below)
¾ teaspoon xanthan gum
½ teaspoon baking soda
½ teaspoon salt
½ teaspoon ground ginger
¼ teaspoon ground cardamom
2 packed teaspoons grated lemon rind
½ cup cold unsalted butter, cut into small pieces*
⅔ cup crystallized ginger chopped into small pieces
    (about ¼ inch)
1 large egg
¾ cup half-and-half
1 large well beaten egg, to brush on top of scones
Granulated sugar to garnish, optional
Rice flour, for shaping dough

1. Preheat oven to 400°F. Position rack in center of oven. Line heavy baking sheet with parchment paper.

2. Combine flour, sugar, baking powder, xanthan gum, baking soda, salt, ginger, cardamom, and grated lemon rind in large bowl of electric mixer. With mixer on low, cut butter into flour mixture until it resembles a coarse meal. Add candied ginger; mix until combined. Put mixture into a small bowl and set aside.

3. Beat egg in the same large bowl of electric mixer until very light and foamy. Add flour mixture and start the mixer on low speed, then pour the half-and-half on top of the flour; mix at medium-low speed for about 30 seconds, until the dough just comes together.

4. Use rice flour to lightly flour hands, and then gently pat out the dough into two 6-inch thick rounds on a floured surface (dough will be sticky, and you may need to lightly coat it with some excess rice flour). Use a sharp knife or pizza cutter to cut each circle in half and then cut each half into three pie-shaped wedges. Put scones 1 inch apart on prepared baking sheet. Brush tops, but not the cut sides, with beaten egg. Sprinkle small amount of granulated sugar over the top, if desired.

5. Place scones in center of oven. Bake 15 to 20 minutes, until very dark golden and cooked through. Cool 10 minutes on a rack. Serve warm with butter or preserves.

Cook's Note: use a double-acting, slow-acting baking powder like Davis or Clabber Girl. This gives you time to pat out and cut the dough before the carbon dioxide gas is released.

LEMON SCONES with Lemon Glaze

Omit ground ginger, ground cardamom, and crystallized ginger.

Add 2 packed tablespoons grated lemon rind (instead of 2 packed teaspoons) in Step 2 above.

Add 1 teaspoon pure vanilla extract in Step 3 above after you beat the egg.

Omit optional granulated sugar to sprinkle on top.

After scones have finished baking (Step 5 above), cool on a rack for 10 minutes and then drizzle Lemon Glaze (recipe follows) across the tops.

Lemon Glaze

½ cup confectioners' sugar
1 tablespoon lemon juice
1 tablespoon unsalted butter, melted

1. Combine confectioners' sugar, lemon juice, and melted butter in a small bowl, and stir until smooth and creamy.

CRANBERRY ORANGE SCONES

Makes 12 scones

Store leftover scones in an airtight container in refrigerator for three days. Or cover them with plastic wrap and then with foil and store in freezer for up to three weeks. Best when eaten within three days of baking. Rewarm in a preheated 350°F oven for about 10 minutes, or for several seconds in a microwave.

*If you plan to use a butter substitute, measure it first and then chill it until it is very cold. Do not use shortening or margerine in this recipe.

I first thought about making these scones over the holidays when bags of fresh cranberries started to arrive in my local grocery store. But food processor-chopped fresh cranberries didn't make the final cut of this recipe. I found I had to add too much sugar to compensate for the sharply acidic fresh fruit, and the extra moisture weighed down the scone instead of allowing it to rise well. After a bit of testing, I found that the uniquely tart yet slightly sweet taste of dried cranberries was perfect. Combined with a touch of orange zest, they made a colorful, fragrant scone that delivered festive flavors to my holiday table.

¾ cup half-and-half
¾ cup dried sweetened cranberries
2 cups Brown Rice Flour Mix (250 grams)
¼ cup granulated sugar
4 teaspoons baking powder (see Cook's Note below)
¾ teaspoon xanthan gum
½ teaspoon baking soda
½ teaspoon salt
1 packed tablespoon grated orange rind
½ cup cold unsalted butter, cut into small pieces*
1 large egg
1 ½ teaspoons pure vanilla extract
¼ teaspoon pure lemon extract
1 large well beaten egg, to brush on top of scones
Granulated sugar for garnish,optional
Rice flour, for shaping dough

1. Preheat oven to 400°F. Position rack in center of oven. Line heavy baking sheet with parchment paper.

2. Combine half-and-half and cranberries in glass measuring cup and set aside.

3. Combine flour, sugar, baking powder, xanthan gum, baking soda, salt, and orange rind in large bowl of electric mixer. With mixer on low, cut butter into flour mixture until it resembles a coarse meal. Put mixture into a small bowl and set aside.

4. Beat egg in the same large bowl of electric mixer until very light and foamy. Add vanilla extract and lemon extract. Add flour mixture and start the mixer on low speed, then pour the half-and-half and cranber-

ries on top of the flour; mix at medium-low speed for about 30 seconds, until the dough just comes together.

5. Use rice flour to lightly flour hands, and then gently pat out the dough into two 6-inch thick rounds on a floured surface (dough will be sticky and you may need to lightly coat it with some excess rice flour). Use a sharp knife or pizza cutter to cut each circle in half, and then cut each half into three pie-shaped wedges. Put scones 1 inch apart on prepared baking sheet. Brush tops, but not the cut sides, with beaten egg. Sprinkle small amount of granulated sugar over the top if desired.

6. Place scones in center of oven. Bake 15 to 20 minutes, until dark golden and cooked through. Cool 10 minutes on a rack. Serve warm with jam or preserves.

Cook's Note: Use a double-acting, slow-acting baking powder like Davis or Clabber Girl. This gives you time to pat out and cut the dough before the carbon dioxide gas is released.

CINNAMON ROLL SCONES

Makes 8 scones

Breakfast doesn't get better than this. This recipe combines the swept-off-your-feet romance of a light, delicate scone with the down-home goodness of a tender cinnamon roll. The dough is enriched with half-and-half and egg, and has the crisp outer crust and slightly crumbly texture of a good scone. The magic comes after the dough is patted out into a rectangle; you brush it with a bit of melted butter, sprinkle on some cinnamon sugar, and then roll it up and slice it to make "cinnamon rolls." They puff up beautifully in the oven, their buttery sweetness and spice beckoning even before you drizzle the finishing touch of vanilla-scented glaze over the top. This mouth-watering pastry is easy to make and will surely become a favorite in your home.

Store leftover scones in an airtight container in refrigerator for three days. Or cover them with plastic wrap and then with foil and store in freezer for up to three weeks. Best when eaten within three days of baking. Rewarm in a preheated 350°F oven for about 10 minutes, or for several seconds in a microwave.

*If you plan to use a butter substitute, measure it first, and then chill it until it is very cold. Do not use shortening or margerine in this recipe.

Filling

> ⅓ cup packed dark brown sugar
> ¾ teaspoon ground cinnamon
> ¼ teaspoon ground nutmeg, optional

Dough

> 2 cups Brown Rice Flour Mix (250 grams)
> ¼ cup granulated sugar
> 4 teaspoons baking powder (see Cook's Note below)
> ¾ teaspoon xanthan gum
> ½ teaspoon baking soda
> ½ teaspoon salt
> ½ cup cold unsalted butter, cut into small pieces*
> 1 large egg
> 2 teaspoons pure vanilla extract
> ¾ cup half-and-half
> 1 tablespoon unsalted butter, melted
> Rice flour, for shaping dough

Glaze

> ¾ cup confectioners' sugar
> 1 – 2 tablespoons milk or half and half
> ½ teaspoon pure vanilla extract

1. *To make Filling:* Combine brown sugar, cinnamon, and nutmeg (optional) in a small bowl and set aside.

2. *To prepare Dough:* Preheat oven to 400°F. Position rack in center of oven. Line heavy baking sheet with parchment paper.

3. Combine flour, sugar, baking powder, xanthan gum, baking soda, and salt in large bowl of electric mixer. With mixer on low, cut cold butter into flour mixture until it resembles a coarse meal. Put mixture into a small bowl and set aside.

4. Beat egg in the same large bowl of electric mixer until very light and foamy. Add vanilla and combine. Add flour mixture and start the mixer on low speed, then pour the half-and-half on top of the flour; mix at medium-low speed for about 30 seconds, until the dough just comes together.

5. Liberally spread rice flour over surface of a wooden board and lightly flour hands. Use a spatula to move dough out of the bowl onto the wooden board in a ball shape. Dough will be sticky. Roll dough around in the rice flour until it is lightly covered. Gently press into a 12 x 8-inch rectangle with your hands.

6. Lightly brush melted butter over top of rolled dough and sprinkle with brown sugar and cinnamon mixture. Starting with 8-inch side, carefully roll dough jellyroll fashion. Try to gently pinch the dough together along the outside end of the roll to seal the cylinder so it doesn't uncoil when baking. Use a very sharp, pointy, thin serrated knife to cut the rolled up dough into eight 1-inch slices. Coat the knife with rice flour if dough is sticking to it.

7. Carefully arrange slices on prepared baking sheet so that they are 1 ½ to 2 inches apart on all sides (be sure the end of the seam is pinched tightly to the rest of the dough so it doesn't unravel). Place in center of oven, and bake about 25 minutes until light brown and cooked through. Cool on a rack for 5 minutes.

8. *To make Glaze:* Combine confectioners sugar, milk, and vanilla in a small bowl, and stir until smooth and creamy. Drizzle over top of scones. Cool on a rack for 10 more minutes. Serve warm.

Cook's Notes: Use a double-acting, slow-acting baking powder like Davis or Clabber Girl. This gives you time to pat out and cut the dough before the carbon dioxide gas is released.

6

Cakes

Red Velvet Cake

Marble Pound Cake

Chocolate Pound Cake

Applesauce Cake

Pineapple Upside Down Cake

Banana Pecan Crunch Cake

Plum Torte

Coconut Cheesecake

Chocolate Custard Cake with Berries

Pumpkin Bars

Pumpkin Roll with Cream Cheese Filling

Orange Chiffon Cake

Chocolate Bundt Cake

Apple Walnut Bundt Cake

Pumpkin Spice Bundt Cake

Lemon Buttermilk Bundt Cake

Old Fashioned Buttermilk Bundt Cake

Old Fashioned Chocolate Chip Bundt Cake

CAKES HAVE A WAY OF TURNING EVERYDAY MOMENTS INTO A CELEBRATION. AND THE cakes in this chapter will help you to celebrate all kinds of happy, everyday moments: coffees with friends, Sunday brunch, pot luck suppers, informal dinner parties, birthdays, and even a few holidays. You'll find recipes for comforting, old-fashioned Bundt cakes, pumpkin "bars," a quick and easy applesauce cake, an iconic plum torte, and a head-turning orange chiffon cake. You'll find old favorites and, possibly, a few new ones. Even though cakes require more time and thought than baking up a batch of cookies or a pan full of muffins, they really do help to make people feel special. When you bake a cake, people typically exclaim, "Wow, you've made a cake!" and follow it with a big, cheerful smile. So plan a simple little celebration and bake up one of these smile-inducers as soon as you can. You'll be glad you did.

Dairy substitutes: My butter substitute of choice for most of the baked goods in this chapter is Earth Balance® Buttery Spread or Buttery Sticks (not the Shortening Sticks). My milk substitute of choice is rice milk.

This chapter uses the following pans:
- 9-inch round cake pan
- 8-inch square cake pan
- 9-inch round springform pan
- 12-cup muffin pan
- Three 5 x 3-inch loaf pans
- Angel Food cake pan or 10-inch tube pan with removable bottom (not non-stick)
- Medium 10 cup Bundt pan (9 inches across the top x 2 ½ inches)
- Large 12 cup Bundt cake pan (10 inch across the top x 3 ½ inches)
- Kugelhopf crown-shaped mold or a fluted ring mold (9-inch across the top; holds 8 to 10 cups filled to the top rim)
- 9-inch Glass (Pyrex) or ceramic deep-dish pie pan
- 15 ½ x 10-inch baking jelly roll pan

Try to use lighter colored, shiny metal pans. Unless you lower the heat in the oven by 25°F, dark pans may cause your cakes to over-brown. The extra heat absorbed by dark pans can also cause your cakes to rise too quickly and then fall a bit. I do not recommend using silicone cake pans for any of these recipes.

The Last Word on Cakes

• Set up before starting the recipe: Assemble all the ingredients.
• Measure carefully.
• Use the right size pan.
• Preheat the oven to the proper temperature (make sure the oven is calibrated correctly).
• Do not open the oven door more than necessary.
• Use a timer in case you get distracted.
• Separate eggs when they are cold, and then let them warm to room temperature.
• Once you mix the liquids into the dry ingredients, you need to get your cakes into the oven fairly quickly. The baking powder leaps into action once it is combined with the liquid, so make sure your oven is preheated and your pans are prepared; it will make a difference in the texture and lightness of your baked goods. Davis and Clabber Girl are double-acting, slow-acting baking powders, so you won't need to rush quite as much. However, Rumsford is a fast-acting baking powder that releases about two-thirds of its gas when moisture is added to it in the bowl.
• Follow the beating directions carefully. When a recipe says to beat the eggs until foamy, or add sugar to the eggs (or butter) a little at a time, or beat eggs until thick and lemon colored, or beat butter until light and fluffy, or do not over beat, these instructions are given to help ensure a good result.

Double Checking

I sometimes receive emails from people wondering why their cake rose and then fell, or why it cracked, or why it sank in the middle. The answer is often because it rose too fast. The most common reasons the cakes in this chapter might rise too fast are:

• Your oven is running hot—check it with an oven thermometer.
• You used dark pans and didn't reduce the oven temperature to compensate. Dark pans require lower temperatures because they absorb more radiant heat. Try lowering your oven temperature by 25°F.
• You overbeat your cake batter. This is particularly important for the heavier cakes (Banana Crunch Cake, Pound Cakes and Bundt Cakes), but it applies to all of them. Check your mixing time and the speed of the mixer. See Chapter 3, page 25, the section entitled *"Do I need a special kind of mixer to make your recipes?"*

But it can also be for several other reasons:
• You spooned the flour into the measuring cup too lightly. Too little flour can create a sunken cake.
• You used old or bad xanthan gum, and it didn't work to help give structure to the cake.
• You measured the baking powder or baking soda incorrectly; you may have used too much.

RED VELVET CAKE

There is a famous legend about Red Velvet Cake that involves a woman who was served a piece while she dined at the Waldorf Astoria in New York City in the 1940s. She loved the unique taste, texture, and color so much that she asked for the recipe. The chef graciously wrote it down—and then charged her $100.00 for it! True or not, my gluten-free version is moist and velvety, and will make you a legend with your family and friends. It even has a bit of the authentic "tang" of the wheat version, due largely to the true-to-the-original addition of buttermilk and vinegar. I've also included a non-buttermilk version (below) for days when you don't have any real buttermilk (or buttermilk powder) in the house; it's still delicious, although it's missing the "tang," so it's slightly sweeter. Frost your cake with cream cheese icing (recipe below) or any other vanilla frosting you like. Take note: you can leave out the signature "red" food coloring without affecting the taste or texture.

Makes two 9-inch rounds or 24 cupcakes

Serve slightly chilled or at room temperature. Can be made a day ahead. Store frosted cake in refrigerator. Unfrosted cake layers can be covered tightly with plastic wrap and stored in refrigerator for one day. Unfrosted cake layers can be covered with plastic wrap and then with foil, and stored in freezer for up to three weeks. Best when eaten within three days of baking.

*Substitute 1 cup water and ¼ cup buttermilk powder for 1 cup fresh lowfat buttermilk.

2 cups granulated sugar
4 large eggs
2 ½ cups Brown Rice Flour Mix (313 grams)
3 tablespoons unsweetened cocoa powder
2 teaspoons baking powder
1 teaspoon baking soda
1 teaspoon xanthan gum
½ teaspoon salt
1 cup canola oil
1 cup lowfat buttermilk* (dairy free instructions below)
2 teaspoons pure vanilla extract
1 tablespoon red food coloring (optional)
1 teaspoon distilled white vinegar
Cream Cheese Frosting (recipe below)

1. Preheat oven to 350°F. Position rack in center of oven. Line two round 9-inch layer cake pans with parchment paper or waxed paper and grease lightly with cooking spray.

2. Beat sugar and eggs in large bowl of electric mixer at medium speed for one minute. Add flour, cocoa powder, baking powder, baking soda, xanthan gum, salt, oil, buttermilk, vanilla, red food color, and vinegar; beat at medium-low speed for one minute.

3. Pour batter into prepared pans. Place in center of oven and bake about

35 minutes (18-20 minutes for cupcakes) or until center springs back to touch and cake has pulled away from sides of the pan.

4. Cool cake layers in the pans on a rack for 5 minutes. Use a small knife to cut around pan sides to loosen cake. Invert cake layers onto a rack, peel off parchment paper, and cool completely.

5. Place one cake layer on a platter. Spread 1 cup of frosting over top and sides. Place second layer on top. Spread remaining frosting over entire cake.

Dairy-free Buttermilk: Combine 1 cup rice or soy milk with 1 tablespoon lemon juice or distilled vinegar. Use only 1 cup of the combined liquid in this recipe.

Buttermilk-Free Red Velvet Cake: Omit 1 cup buttermilk, 1 teaspoon baking soda, and 1 teaspoon vinegar. Add 1 cup milk and 3 teaspoons baking powder (instead of 2 teaspoons).

Cream Cheese Frosting

½ cup unsalted butter, at room temperature
½ cup low-fat cream cheese, at room temperature
3 cups confectioners' sugar, sifted if lumpy
3 tablespoons milk
2 teaspoons pure vanilla extract

1. Beat butter and cream cheese in large bowl of electric mixer until light and fluffy.

2. Add 1 cup confectioners' sugar, milk, and vanilla, and beat at low speed until well blended. Add remaining sugar and beat at high speed until light and creamy.

MARBLE POUND CAKE

Marble pound cake always makes me smile because it transports me back to summer nights when I was a child. I remember eating it alongside ice cream topped with chocolate fudge sauce after dinner on the patio. Simple yet intricate—that's the beauty of a slice of cake that incorporates two distinctly different flavors and colors into one. The trick is getting enough chocolate flavor into the chocolate swirl, but that's where the magic of chocolate extract comes in. If you want this cake to be at its best, it's worth looking for the extract at the store or online. This is a fun-to-eat classic that you won't want to miss.

2 ounces semisweet chocolate chopped
1 ½ cups Brown Rice Flour Mix (188 grams)
2 ½ teaspoons baking powder
½ teaspoon xanthan gum
¼ teaspoon salt
3 large eggs
1 cup granulated sugar
1 cup plain whole-milk yogurt
⅓ cup canola oil
1 tablespoon pure vanilla extract
½ teaspoon pure chocolate extract*
¼ teaspoon baking soda
Chocolate Ganache Glaze (recipe follows)

1. Preheat oven to 350°F. Position rack in center of oven. Grease a 10-cup Bundt pan (9-inches across the top) or kugelhopf mold with cooking spray.

2. Melt chocolate in small, heavy saucepan over low heat, stirring constantly. Remove from heat and cool until lukewarm.

3. Whisk flour, baking powder, xanthan gum, and salt in a small bowl. Set aside.

4. Beat eggs in large bowl of electric mixer at medium-high speed; gradually add sugar 1 tablespoon at a time, and beat until pale yellow and thick. Add flour mixture, yogurt, oil, and vanilla, and beat at medium-low speed for 30 seconds (do not add chocolate extract or baking soda in this step).

Makes one 9-inch Bundt-shaped cake (see Cook's Note)

Serve at room temperature. Can be made a day ahead. Store cake tightly covered with plastic wrap in refrigerator. Pound Cake can be covered with plastic wrap and then with foil and stored in freezer for up to three weeks. Best when eaten within four days of baking.

*I recommend Nielsen-Massey Pure Chocolate Extract

5. Scoop out ⅓ of the vanilla batter into a small mixing bowl. Mix melted chocolate, chocolate extract, and baking soda into the bowl, and stir until well combined. Set aside.

6. Evenly spread ⅔ of the remaining vanilla batter into prepared pan. Lightly spread ⅔ of the chocolate batter on top of the vanilla. Spread the remaining vanilla batter over the chocolate batter; then spread the remaining chocolate batter on top the last layer of the vanilla batter.

7. Take a table knife and cut through the middle of the batter making a wide "S" from side to side all around the cake pan until the batter is nicely marbled. Place cake in center of oven and bake about 50 minutes (a toothpick inserted in center of cake should come out clean). Do not open oven for first 45 minutes of baking time.

8. Cool cake in the pan on a rack for 10 minutes. Carefully remove cake from pan and cool slightly on rack. Spoon warm Chocolate Ganache Glaze (recipe below) over top of cake and let it drip down the sides. Allow cake to cool completely before moving to a cake plate.

Cook's Note: Use a 9-inch (across top) kugelhopf crown-shaped mold or a fluted ring mold that holds 8 to 10 cups filled to the top rim. If you use a 9 x 5-inch loaf pan, cake will be denser. Do not use a 9-inch flat-bottomed tube pan or you will have a 1-inch high cake. You can use mini Bundt pans, but you will need to adjust baking time.

Chocolate Ganache Glaze

2 ounces semisweet chocolate, chopped
2 tablespoons heavy cream
1 tablespoon light corn syrup
½ teaspoon pure vanilla extract

1. Combine chocolate, heavy cream, and corn syrup in a small, heavy saucepan; cook over low heat, stirring constantly, until chocolate melts and mixture is smooth. Remove from heat, add vanilla, and stir to blend.

CHOCOLATE POUND CAKE

One day I started to crave chocolate pound cake. I hadn't had a good one for years, but I kept seeing them in food magazines and on food blogs, and the pictures called out to me. I started with my vanilla pound cake recipe (from *Gluten-Free Baking Classics*) and added unsweetened cocoa powder, melted semisweet chocolate, and mini chocolate chips to create a deliciously pleasing cake that is dense, dark, and very chocolaty. I had to make it several times, because it kept disappearing out of the refrigerator before I could test it to see how long it would last. In fact one night, more than half a cake went missing after being left alone in the house with two teenage boys. So if you've been longing for a good chocolate pound cake, try this one and see how long it lasts in your house.

4 ounces good quality semisweet chocolate, chopped
1 ¼ cups Brown Rice Flour Mix (155 grams)
¼ cup unsweetened cocoa powder (not Dutch processed)
2 teaspoons baking powder
1 teaspoon baking soda
½ teaspoon xanthan gum
½ teaspoon salt
3 large eggs
1 cup granulated sugar
2 teaspoons pure vanilla extract
1 teaspoon pure chocolate extract*
1 cup plain whole-milk yogurt
⅓ cup canola oil
¾ cup good quality mini semi-sweet chocolate chips
Chocolate Ganache Glaze (recipe follows)

1. Preheat oven to 350°F. Position rack in center of oven. Grease a 10-cup Bundt pan (9-inches across the top) or kugelhopf mold with cooking spray.

2. Melt chocolate in small, heavy saucepan over low heat, stirring constantly. Remove from heat and cool until lukewarm.

3. Whisk flour, cocoa, baking powder, baking soda, xanthan gum, and salt in a small bowl. Set aside.

4. Beat eggs in large bowl of electric mixer at medium-high speed; gradually add sugar 1 tablespoon at a time, and beat until pale yellow and thick. Add melted chocolate, vanilla extract, and chocolate extract into

Makes one 9-inch Bundt-shaped cake (See Cook's Note) or three 5 x 3-inch loaves

Serve slightly chilled or at room temperature. Can be made a day ahead. Store cake covered tightly with plastic wrap in refrigerator. Pound Cake can be covered with plastic wrap and then with foil and stored in freezer for up to three weeks. Best when eaten within four days of baking.

* I recommend Nielsen-Massey Pure Chocolate Extract

the batter, and mix until well combined.

5. Add flour mixture, yogurt, and oil; beat at medium-low speed for 30 seconds. Stir in mini chocolate chips.

6. Evenly spread batter into prepared pan. Place cake in center of oven and bake 45 to 50 minutes (a toothpick inserted in center of cake should come out clean). Do not open oven for first 45 minutes of baking time.

7. Cool cake in the pan on a rack for 10 minutes. Carefully remove cake from pan and cool slightly on rack. Spoon warm Chocolate Ganache Glaze (recipe below) over top of cake and let it drip down the sides. Allow cake to cool completely before moving to a cake plate.

Cook's Note: Use a 9-inch (across top) kugelhopf crown-shaped mold or a fluted ring mold that holds 8 to 10 cups filled to the top rim. If you use a 9 x 5-inch loaf pan, cake will be dense and heavy. Do not use a 9-inch flat-bottomed tube pan, or you will have a 1-inch-high cake. You can use mini Bundt pans, but you will need to adjust baking time.

Chocolate Ganache Glaze

2 ounces semisweet chocolate, chopped
2 tablespoons heavy cream
2 teaspoons light corn syrup
½ teaspoon pure vanilla extract

1. Combine chocolate, heavy cream, and corn syrup in a small, heavy saucepan; cook over low heat, stirring constantly, until chocolate melts and mixture is smooth. Remove from heat, add vanilla, and stir to blend.

APPLESAUCE CAKE

You'd think it would be simple to find a classic recipe for applesauce cake, but it's not. There is a wide variety, and they each seem to call for different amounts and combinations of ingredients: applesauce from a jar versus homemade (and chunky versus smooth); three or four different spices (almost like a spice cake) versus no spice whatsoever versus just cinnamon alone; white sugar versus brown sugar versus some combination of both; raisins and nuts versus no add-ins; slices of apple on top or chunks of apple thrown into the batter versus no apple. And then, to really complicate matters, cookbooks from before World War II used eggs, but during the war, rationing led to versions made without eggs and no other substitutes. I tried them all. The final result? My applesauce cake has a tender texture and a delicate flavor that is almost honey cake-like. Make it when you want an uncomplicated, home-style cake that isn't overly sweet. It goes really well with a nice cup of tea. See Cook's Notes for variations below.

Makes one 8-inch square cake

Serve warm, slightly chilled, or at room temperature. Can be made a day ahead. Store cake in refrigerator tightly covered with plastic wrap. Can be covered with plastic wrap and then with foil, and stored in freezer for up to two weeks. Best when eaten within three days of baking.

*Use homemade or jarred, no-sugar-added applesauce; do not use chunky style.

1 large egg
⅔ cup granulated sugar
⅓ cup loosely packed dark brown sugar
1 ½ cups Brown Rice Flour Mix (188 grams)
2 teaspoons baking soda
2 teaspoons ground cinnamon
½ teaspoon xanthan gum
¼ teaspoon salt
1 cup unsweetened applesauce*
⅓ cup canola oil
1 teaspoon pure vanilla extract
¾ cup chopped walnuts
½ cup golden raisins
Confectioners' sugar

1. Preheat oven to 350⁰F. Position rack in the center of oven. Lightly grease an 8-inch square baking pan with cooking spray.

2. Combine egg and both sugars in large bowl of electric mixer, and beat 1 minute. Add the flour, baking soda, cinnamon, xanthan gum, salt, applesauce, oil, and vanilla, and beat at medium speed for about 30 seconds until well combined. Add the walnuts and raisins and mix well.

3. Bake about 35 minutes until middle springs back and a toothpick in-

serted in center of cake comes out clean (be careful about over-baking because crumb is very soft and may stick to toothpick anyway). Cool cake on a rack for 5 minutes. Use a small knife to cut around pan sides to loosen cake if necessary, and then invert onto a rack. Cool about one hour before serving. Place on a cake plate (top side up) and sprinkle with confectioners' sugar.

Cook's Notes: You can reduce the sugar if you want, but if you take out more than ⅓ cup in total it will be more like a sweetbread and not a cake.

Variations:

• Increase/decrease amount of cinnamon and/or add nutmeg, cloves, or ginger to taste.

• Sprinkle cinnamon sugar* on top before it goes in the oven to add additional sweetness, more cinnamon flavor, and a bit of crunch.

• Arrange thinly sliced apples across the top before baking to add a bit more pure apple flavor.

*To make cinnamon sugar, combine 1 ½ tablespoons granulated sugar and cinnamon to taste.

PINEAPPLE UPSIDE DOWN CAKE

Pineapple upside down cake is old-fashioned comfort food that looks complicated but is really very simple to make. Yellow cake batter is poured over a thin layer of melted butter, brown sugar, and sliced pineapple; you bake it and then turn it bottom side up to create an impressive looking cake that will make those around your table feel special. It is slightly decadent and very delicious and makes the perfect dessert when you want to end your meal with something a little out of the ordinary.

2 tablespoons unsalted butter, melted
½ cup packed dark brown sugar
7 rings of sliced pineapple (canned or fresh)
1 cup granulated sugar
2 large eggs
1 ¼ cups Brown Rice Flour Mix (155 grams)
1 ½ teaspoons baking powder
½ teaspoon xanthan gum
¼ teaspoon salt
½ cup canola oil
½ cup skim or lowfat milk
1 teaspoon pure vanilla extract

1. Preheat oven to 350°F. Position rack in center of oven. Grease bottom and sides of 9-inch layer cake pan with cooking spray.

2. Spread melted butter over the bottom of prepared cake pan. Sprinkle brown sugar over the top and pat it down into the butter. Place pineapple slices on several paper towels and pat dry, then arrange them in the cake pan (six slices around the outside, one in the middle).

3. Beat sugar and eggs in large bowl of electric mixer at medium speed for 1 minute. Add flour, baking powder, xanthan gum, salt, oil, milk, and vanilla; beat at medium speed for 1 minute.

4. Pour batter into prepared pan. Place in center of oven and bake for about 40 minutes, or until center springs back when touched and cake is very lightly browned.

5. Cool on a rack for 5 minutes, then invert onto the rack. Cool about one hour more and then place on a cake plate.

Makes one 9-inch round cake

Serve warm, slightly chilled, or at room temperature. Cut cake using a serrated knife with a sawing motion. Can be made one day ahead. Cake can be covered tightly with plastic wrap and stored in refrigerator for up to three days. Best when eaten within three days of baking and not frozen.

BANANA PECAN CRUNCH CAKE

Makes one 9-inch round cake

Serve warm, slightly chilled, or at room temperature. Cut with a sawing motion with a serrated knife. Can be made a day ahead. Store cake in refrigerator tightly covered with plastic wrap. Can be covered with plastic wrap and then with foil and stored in freezer for up to two weeks. Best when eaten within three days of baking.

*Bananas should be at room temperature.

My family didn't make banana cake when I was growing up, but I had the delicious memory of one I'd tasted at a local specialty store more than ten years ago stuck in my head. It lingered in my mind until I finally decided to try to recreate it with what little I could remember: it was a caramel-hued, banana-scented cake with a touch of rum and some crunch on the top. I felt confident that I would know it when I tasted it, so I set to work. I added pecans, some dark brown sugar, and a bit of vanilla to create a truly delectable dessert—Banana Pecan Crunch Cake. Oh my, this is a good cake. It's so good that it's hard to stop yourself from slicing another sliver and then another. Try it, and you'll see. It could very well become your family's banana cake. I know it became mine.

Crumb Topping (recipe follows)
1 ½ cups Brown Rice Flour Mix (188 grams)
½ cup very finely ground pecans
2 teaspoons baking powder
1 teaspoon baking soda
¾ teaspoon xanthan gum
½ teaspoon salt
2 large eggs
½ cup loosely packed dark brown sugar
⅓ cup granulated sugar (see Cook's Note)
1 ½ cups very ripe mashed bananas (about 3 medium bananas)*
3 tablespoons dark rum
2 teaspoons pure vanilla extract
¼ cup canola oil

1. Prepare Crumb Topping (recipe follows).

2. Preheat oven to 350°F. Position rack in center of oven. Lightly grease a 9-inch springform pan with removable bottom with cooking spray.

3. Whisk flour, ground pecans, baking powder, baking soda, xanthan gum, and salt in a small bowl. Set aside.

4. Beat eggs in large bowl of electric mixer until lemon colored. Add sugars and beat until pale yellow and thick. Add bananas, rum, and vanilla, and mix until well combined. Scrape bowl. Add flour mixture and oil, and beat at medium-low speed for about 30 seconds. Do not overbeat.

5. Spread batter into prepared pan. Top with Crumb Topping (recipe follows). Place in center of oven and bake about 55 minutes, or until a

toothpick inserted in the center of cake comes out clean. Do not open oven for first 45 minutes.

6. Cool cake on a rack for 8 minutes. Remove sides of pan and cool on rack. To remove cake from bottom, use two pancake turners to lift cake onto a cake plate. It is easier to remove the cake from the pan if it is cold.

Cook's Note: This cake is not overly sweet. Instead, I tried to create a balance among the sweet bananas, the sweet pecans, and the sugar, so you can taste them all. If, after you make it the first time, you decide you'd like to make it slightly sweeter, you can increase the granulated sugar from ⅓ to ½ cup. If that still isn't sweet enough, increase the granulated and dark brown sugar by one more tablespoon each.

Crumb Topping

¾ cup Brown Rice Flour Mix (95 grams)
½ cup coarsely chopped pecans
⅓ cup packed dark brown sugar
2 tablespoons granulated sugar
½ teaspoon xanthan gum
4 tablespoons unsalted butter, melted
½ teaspoon pure vanilla extract

1. Combine flour, pecans, brown sugar, granulated sugar, and xanthan gum in a small bowl; stir to blend. Pour in butter and vanilla and stir until all dry ingredients are moistened. Gently break into medium and small (the size of M&Ms®) crumb pieces with spoon.

PLUM TORTE

Makes one 9-inch round cake

Serve room temperature or chilled. Store torte tightly covered with plastic wrap in refrigerator. Can be made a day ahead. Can be covered with plastic wrap and then with foil and stored in freezer for up to two weeks. Best when eaten within three days of baking.

*To make Cinnamon sugar combine 1 ½ tablespoons granulated sugar and ½ teaspoon ground cinnamon.

The original version of this beloved plum cake recipe was made popular by Marian Burros back in the 1980s when it first appeared in her column in the *New York Times*. One late summer day, I started seeing mounds of small Italian "prune" plums at the grocery store and farmers market, and visions of her torte came roaring back into my mind. I thought about how much I really missed it, so I bought a bunch of ripe plums and recreated it with gluten-free flours. Burros' original plum torte recipe converted beautifully. In fact, you might have thought it was always gluten-free. Make it when you want a delicious fruit-based dessert to top off a casual summer barbecue or a leisurely weekend brunch. When plums are out of season, you can make the torte with peeled and thickly sliced apples or pears.

¾ cup granulated sugar
½ cup unsalted butter
1 cup Brown Rice Flour Mix (125 grams)
1 ¼ teaspoons baking powder
½ teaspoon xanthan gum
Pinch of salt
2 large eggs
1 teaspoon pure vanilla extract
24 halves pitted Italian "prune" plums (or small purple plums)
Cinnamon sugar for topping*

1. Preheat oven to 350°F. Position rack in lower third of oven. Lightly grease a 9-inch springform pan with cooking spray.

2. Cream the sugar and butter in large bowl of electric mixer. Add flour, baking powder, xanthan gum, salt, eggs, and vanilla, and beat well, about 2 minutes at medium speed.

3. Spoon the batter into prepared springform pan. Place the plum halves skin side up on top of the batter. Sprinkle lightly with cinnamon sugar.

4. Bake about 55 minutes, until golden brown and toothpick comes out clean from the center. Remove and cool on rack before moving to a cake plate.

COCONUT CHEESECAKE

I usually make two or three different kinds of cheesecake over the course of a year for various holidays or celebrations. But this one has become so loved in my home that we started to invent celebrations as an excuse for me to make it. I created it one day when I felt like eating cheesecake and coconut cream pie and I couldn't decide which to make. When the friends around my table and I all took our first tentative bite, I knew I had a winner: People just kept eating and smiling. No one put their fork down. The only trouble was that everyone had a second piece, and the cake was almost completely gone by the end of dinner. I had to remake it in order to test how long it would last in the refrigerator and freezer. Darn. If you love coconut and cheesecake, go ahead and make this cake, so you can find out how fast it disappears at your table.

Crust

    1 cup Brown Rice Flour Mix (125 grams)
    ¼ cup granulated sugar
    1 teaspoon xanthan gum
    5 tablespoons unsalted butter

Cream Cheese Filling

    4 8-oz. packages cream cheese (not low fat)
    ¾ cup granulated sugar
    2 teaspoons pure vanilla extract
    1 teaspoon coconut extract
    4 large eggs
    1 cup Coco Lopez Cream of Coconut*
    1 ½ cups toasted sweetened flaked coconut, for garnish

Coconut Whipped Cream Topping

    1 cup heavy cream
    ⅓ cup very cold Coco Lopez Cream of Coconut
    2 tablespoons confectioners' sugar (or to taste)

1. **To make crust:** Preheat oven to 350°F. Position rack in center of oven. Grease bottom of 9-inch round springform pan with cooking spray. Dust lightly with rice flour.

Makes one 9-inch round cake

Remove from refrigerator 30 minutes to one hour before serving. Store in refrigerator for up to five days. Whole cake or sections can be tightly covered with plastic wrap and then with foil, and stored in freezer for up to one month (freeze unwrapped on a plate until firm and then wrap).

*Puree contents of can in a blender until just combined before measuring.

2. Combine flour, sugar, and xanthan gum in large bowl of electric mixer. Add butter, and mix on low speed until crumbly. Press lightly into bottom of springform pan.

3. Bake in center of oven for 12 minutes. Remove from oven and set aside. Turn oven control up to 475°F.

4. *To make cheesecake:* Beat cream cheese until smooth in bowl of electric mixer at medium speed. Reduce speed and slowly add sugar, vanilla extract, and coconut extract. Beat in eggs one at a time. Scrape bowl and beaters. Add cream of coconut and mix until well blended.

5. Pour cream cheese batter into pan. Bake in center of oven for 10 minutes; turn oven control down to 200°F and bake 65 minutes more. Turn off oven, but do not open door; leave cake in oven for another 15 minutes. Cool cake on wire rack and refrigerate. When cold, remove sides and slide cheesecake off bottom onto a platter.

6. *To make coconut garnish:* Spread sweetened flaked coconut in a thin layer on a small baking sheet. Bake in a preheated 350°F oven, stirring every few minutes until light golden brown. This will only take a few minutes: don't leave the oven. Set aside to cool.

7. *To make topping:* Combine heavy cream, cream of coconut, and confectioners' sugar in large bowl of electric mixer; beat until stiff peaks form.

8. *To finish cake:* Cover top and sides of cake with Coconut Whipped Cream Topping. Sprinkle toasted coconut over top and sides and pat into the topping. Refrigerate until ready to serve.

CHOCOLATE CUSTARD CAKE
with Berries

Quick and easy and perfect for springtime, here's a chocolaty twist on clafouti that you can make in a snap. I've added fresh-picked berries, cocoa powder, and a touch of Kahlua to enrich this classic custard-like cake. All you have to do is mix it up in a bowl, pour it into a deep-dish pie pan to bake, and then sprinkle the top with some finely chopped semi-sweet or milk chocolate when it's done. You can also make a delicious dairy-free version using rice milk or another non-dairy substitute (see directions below).

1 cup fresh raspberries or strawberries
½ cup Brown Rice Flour Mix (63 grams)
½ cup packed dark brown sugar
2 tablespoons unsweetened cocoa powder
⅛ teaspoon salt
4 large eggs
2 cups whole milk minus 1 tablespoon
1 tablespoon Kahlua Liqueur or strong coffee
2 teaspoons pure chocolate extract*
1 teaspoon pure vanilla extract
3-4 ounces semisweet chocolate or milk chocolate,
     very finely chopped
Confectioners' sugar for garnish

1. Wash and carefully dry the berries. If using strawberries, hull them and cut them in half.

2. Preheat oven to 375°F. Position rack in center of oven. Grease a 9-inch round glass (Pyrex) or ceramic deep-dish pie pan with cooking spray and dust lightly with rice flour. Arrange berries on bottom of pie pan.

3. Whisk flour, dark brown sugar, cocoa powder, and salt in a large bowl (try to incorporate the brown sugar as much as possible).

4. Break eggs into center of flour mixture and whisk until smooth. Add milk, Kahlua, chocolate extract, and vanilla extract, and whisk until smooth (this will take about 30 seconds, so the brown sugar is fully mixed into the batter).

5. Pour batter into prepared pan. Put pan in center of oven and bake about 55 minutes (a knife inserted into center of cake should come out clean). Do not open oven for first 45 minutes of baking time.

Makes one 9-inch cake

Serve warm or at room temperature. Can be made a day ahead, but is especially nice when slightly rewarmed (although there are die-hard fans of cold clafouti). Store cake tightly covered with plastic wrap in refrigerator. Best when eaten within three days of baking.

*I recommend Nielsen-Massey Pure Chocolate Extract.

6. Sprinkle chopped chocolate across the top of the cake. Cool cake in the pan on a rack for about 1 ½ hours. Sift confectioners' sugar over top.

Cook's Note: For a dairy-free version use rice milk, almond milk, or coconut milk and one extra tablespoon of Brown Rice Flour Mix (½ cup plus 1 tablespoon Brown Rice Flour Mix). Depending on dairy substitute, cake may take less time to bake.

PUMPKIN BARS

Several years ago, I helped a reader who was searching for a way to make "Pumpkin Bars" with gluten-free flours. She sent me the wheat recipe she'd been using, and when I researched it, I found it in food magazines, a wide assortment of cookbooks, and all over the Internet. Interestingly, several Junior League cookbooks called the exact same recipe "Pumpkin Sheet Cake." The only difference was that it was baked in an 11 x 17-inch baking pan instead of one slightly smaller (10 x 15 inches). I came to realize that "Pumpkin Bars" had been around for a long time, though I'd never had one.

When I started comparing recipes, I realized they were all almost identical, with only minor variations in spice, oil, and sugar. The recipes also made *a lot* of pumpkin squares because they called for a 10 x 15-inch pan. I decided that I wanted to make a smaller amount, so I cut the recipe in half and used an 8 x 8-inch pan. I kept the cinnamon but increased the amount, and I left out all the various add-ins that bakers had used to make the recipe their own: nutmeg, cloves, nuts, and raisins. Almost all the versions had a simple cream cheese frosting made with a combination of butter and cream cheese and a lot, or a little, sugar. Some had vanilla extract, and some were strangely (at least to me) without it. I wanted something more in my frosting, so I added a touch of allspice along with the vanilla, but you can easily leave it out. Perhaps you've had a hankering for pumpkin bars and want a quick fix? Try my gluten-free version. They're so good you won't miss the wheat.

Makes one 8-inch square cake

Serve chilled or at room temperature. Bars can be made a day ahead. Store in refrigerator for up to four days. Bars can be wrapped with plastic wrap and then with foil and stored in freezer for up to two weeks.

2 large eggs
¾ cup granulated sugar
⅓ cup plus 2 tablespoons canola oil
¾ cup plus 2 tablespoons pumpkin puree
1 cup Brown Rice Flour Mix (125 grams)
2 teaspoons ground cinnamon
1 teaspoon baking powder
½ teaspoon baking soda
¼ teaspoon xanthan gum
¼ teaspoon salt
Cream Cheese Frosting (recipe follows)

1. Preheat oven to 350°F. Position rack in center of oven. Grease bottom of 8-inch square baking pan with cooking spray.

2. Beat eggs, sugar, oil, and pumpkin in large bowl of electric mixer for 1 minute at medium speed. Add flour, cinnamon, baking powder, baking soda, xanthan gum, and salt, and mix at low speed until well combined and smooth.

3. Spread batter in prepared pan and bake in center of oven 25–30 minutes until puffed and cooked through (toothpick inserted into center should come out clean). Cool in pan on rack.

4. Spread Cream Cheese Frosting (recipe follows) over the top when completely cool and refrigerate, covered, until cold. Cut cake into bars and serve.

Cream Cheese Frosting

4 ounces low-fat cream cheese, room temperature
¼ cup unsalted butter, room temperature
1 cup confectioners' sugar, sifted if lumpy
1–2 tablespoons milk
1 ½ teaspoons pure vanilla extract
½ teaspoon ground allspice (optional)

1. Beat cream cheese and butter in large bowl of electric mixer until light and fluffy.

2. Add confectioners' sugar and milk, and beat at low speed until well blended. Add vanilla and allspice; beat until smooth.

PUMPKIN ROLL
with Cream Cheese Filling

I've had many requests for a gluten-free pumpkin roll recipe over the years. People typically ask me to help them convert their treasured family recipe for it right around mid-October. I didn't catch on at first because the requests trickled in a little at a time, but after about six years, I finally noticed a distinct pattern—almost every recipe was the same. The quantity and combination of spices in the cake changed slightly, as did the amount of butter and vanilla in the cream cheese filling, but it was pretty clear that I was helping to convert a basic recipe that had been tweaked by friends and family.

After testing three of the most commonly submitted spice combinations, I choose a pretty classic blend of cinnamon, ginger, and nutmeg; it was universally liked by my tasters. The second-place combination was 1 teaspoon cinnamon and 1 teaspoon allspice (a cinnamon and clove rendition was nice, but not as popular as the more classic blend).

The hardest part was getting the amount of xanthan gum right, and the lesson clearly illustrates the magic it plays in gluten-free baking and how little is needed to make a difference. I started with ¼ teaspoon of xanthan gum, which gave me a tender, delicate crumb, but a surface appearance that was a little unruly (a bit "open-crumbed"). As is my obsessive way, I increased the amount of xanthan gum to ½ teaspoon and tried it again. The cake had a smoother surface appearance, but the texture was tighter, more "sponge-like" and bit chewy. The xanthan gum had done its job—a bit too well. And just ¼ teaspoon had made a big difference. (Imagine the large amounts of xanthan gum people innocently and unnecessarily add to their baked goods when they use flour mixes that contain it!). I decided to go with taste and texture, and stayed with ¼ teaspoon. Luckily, I found that, after a good long chill in the refrigerator, the cake looked prettier and was easy to slice.

I went middle-of-the-road for the Cream Cheese Filling. Reader-submitted versions varied from 2 tablespoons to 6 tablespoons of butter, and from no vanilla extract to 2 teaspoons. My recipe has 4 tablespoons butter and 1 ½ teaspoons of vanilla. It tastes delicious. Some versions contained chopped nuts; others had pieces of toffee or candied ginger. My recipe specifies chopped nuts as an option, but you can add whatever you think will make those around your table happiest.

So maybe you were thinking about making a pumpkin roll for the holidays? And even if you weren't, now you can. It's really easy to make, it looks impressive, and it tastes really good.

Makes one 15-inch x approx. 4-inch roll. Serves 8 to 10

Serve chilled or at room temperature. Can be made a day ahead. Store in refrigerator for up to four days.

¾ cup Brown Rice Flour Mix (95 grams)
¾ teaspoon baking powder
1 teaspoon ground cinnamon
1 teaspoon ground ginger
½ teaspoon ground nutmeg
½ teaspoon baking soda
¼ teaspoon xanthan gum
¼ teaspoon salt
3 large eggs, room temperature
1 cup granulated sugar
⅔ cup pumpkin puree
1 teaspoon pure vanilla extract
Confectioners' sugar
Cream Cheese Filling (recipe follows)
1 cup chopped walnuts or pecans (optional)

1. Preheat oven to 350°F. Position rack in center of oven. Line a 15 ½ x 10 ½-inch baking pan with parchment paper. Lightly spray parchment paper and sides of pan with cooking spray. Spread a clean, thin cotton dish towel on a flat surface and sprinkle with about ⅓ cup confectioners' sugar (the sugar will help to keep cake from sticking to the towel; you will use the towel to roll up the cake after it is finished baking).

2. Place flour, baking powder, cinnamon, ginger, nutmeg, baking soda, xanthan gum, and salt in a small bowl; whisk until thoroughly combined.

3. Beat eggs and sugar in large bowl of electric mixer at high speed for 5 minutes until pale yellow and thick. Add pumpkin puree and vanilla and mix until well combined. Turn mixer speed to low and slowly add the flour mixture; mix until just combined.

4. Spread batter in prepared pan and bake in center of oven about 18 minutes, until puffed and cooked through (toothpick inserted into center should come out clean and cake will spring back when pressed lightly; color will turn a darker golden brown).

5. Remove cake from oven and immediately invert onto the prepared dish towel. Peel off parchment paper. With a light touch, roll cake and towel together into a roll (starting at the narrow end), and place on a rack to cool completely.

6. Gently unroll cake and spread Cream Cheese Filling over the entire surface. If using, sprinkle nuts over Filling and gently pat them into place. Reroll the cake and transfer it to a large cake plate or serving platter. Cover with plastic wrap or foil and refrigerate at least six hours (this will make it easier to slice). Dust with confectioners' sugar just before serving. Cut cake into slices with a long thin knife.

Cream Cheese Filling

8 ounces cream cheese, room temperature
¼ cup unsalted butter, room temperature
1 cup confectioners' sugar, sifted if lumpy
1 ½ teaspoons pure vanilla extract

1. Beat cream cheese and butter in large bowl of electric mixer until light and fluffy.

2. Add confectioners' sugar and vanilla and beat at low speed until well blended.

ORANGE CHIFFON CAKE

The story of chiffon cake goes back to the 1920s, when insurance salesman Harry Baker created a flavorful, moist cake for his catering business and it developed a cult-like following. In 1947, he sold the secret recipe to General Mills, and "Chiffon Cake" was introduced to America the following year. It was one of the first published dessert recipes to use vegetable oil instead of butter, and it was light and delectable. Harry separated his eggs and folded stiffly beaten whites into his batter to create a beautiful, tender cake. Modern versions, while fairly similar, seem to vary in the number of egg yolks and whites used (typically between 5 and 8). I took the middle ground when I created my gluten-free version and used six yolks and seven whites. It made a gorgeous, tall cake. You can put on a glaze or frosting, if you want, but this cake tastes so good you could leave it plain or simply sift a bit of confectioners' sugar over the top.

2 cups plus 2 tablespoons Brown Rice Flour Mix (265 grams)
1 tablespoon baking powder
½ teaspoon guar gum or xanthan gum if guar gum is unavailable
½ teaspoon salt
6 large eggs, separated*, plus 1 large egg white, at room temperature
1 ½ cups granulated sugar, divided
½ cup canola oil
¾ cup orange juice
1 tablespoon packed freshly grated orange rind
1 ½ teaspoons pure orange extract
1 teaspoon pure vanilla extract
Orange Glaze (recipe follows) or confectioners' sugar for garnish

1. Preheat oven to 350°F. Position rack in center of oven. Have ready a clean angel food cake pan or 10-inch tube pan with a removable bottom. Do not use a non-stick angel food pan for this cake. Do not grease the pan.

2. Combine flour, baking powder, guar gum, and salt together in small bowl. Set aside.

3. Beat egg whites in large bowl of electric mixer. Start mixer at medium speed and beat until whites are foamy. Gradually increase speed to high. Add ½ cup of the sugar, 2 tablespoons at a time, beating until sugar

Makes one 10-inch cake

Serve slightly chilled or at room temperature. Cut cake using a serrated knife with a sawing motion. Can be made a day ahead. Store cake in refrigerator. Cake can also be covered with plastic wrap and then with foil and stored in freezer for up to three weeks. Best when eaten within three days of baking.

*Separate eggs when they are cold, and then let them warm to room temperature.

dissolves and whites form stiff and glossy peaks. Do not scrape bowl while beating. Set aside.

4. Beat egg yolks in large bowl of electric mixer until lemon-colored. Gradually add remaining 1 cup of sugar, 2 tablespoons at a time, and continue to beat until pale yellow and thick. Add oil and mix until well incorporated. Add orange juice, grated orange rind, orange extract, and vanilla extract, and beat until just combined at medium speed about 30 seconds. Add flour mixture, and mix until smooth on medium speed about 1 minute.

5. Fold ⅓ of the beaten egg whites into the batter to lighten it; gently fold in remaining egg whites. Pour batter into cake pan and place in center of preheated oven. Bake 45-50 minutes until cake springs back when lightly touched.

6. Invert cake in pan on large metal funnel or narrow-necked bottle (an empty wine bottle is perfect); cool completely. Loosen cake with sharp knife and remove from pan onto a serving plate. Drizzle Orange Glaze (recipe below) over the top of the cake or sprinkle with confectioners' sugar.

Orange Glaze

3 tablespoons unsalted butter
2 tablespoons orange juice
1 tablespoon heavy cream
1 cup confectioners' sugar

1. Melt butter in a small, heavy saucepan and then remove from heat. Stir in orange juice and heavy cream; add confectioners' sugar in two additions; whisk until very smooth. Cool to lukewarm before drizzling over cake (cool glaze until it has thickened but is still pourable).

Cook's Note: If you put the cake on a rack before you put on the glaze, any extra glaze that drips down under the rack can be scraped up, rewarmed, and drizzled back over the cake to make a thicker topping.

CHOCOLATE BUNDT CAKE

This rich chocolate Bundt cake is filled with the deep chocolate flavor that comes from layering unsweetened cocoa powder, melted semi-sweet chocolate, and chocolate chips all together in one cake. Your mouth will water even when it's baking in the oven because it smells so good. I used a classic Bundt pan, which allows the cake to rise slowly and develop a crusty outside and a tender, dense inside. It's easy to make and perfect for parties and entertaining because it's large enough to feed a crowd of dessert aficionados. Bake one for the chocolate cake lovers in your life.

¼ cup water
1 tablespoon instant espresso-coffee powder
3 ounces good quality semisweet chocolate, chopped
2 cups Brown Rice Flour Mix (250 grams)
½ cup unsweetened cocoa powder (not Dutch processed)
3 tablespoons buttermilk powder* (dairy-free instructions below)
2 teaspoons baking soda
2 teaspoons baking powder
¾ teaspoon xanthan gum
½ teaspoon salt
1 cup canola oil
¾ cup water*
4 large eggs
2 cups granulated sugar
2 teaspoons pure vanilla extract
1 teaspoon pure chocolate extract**
1 ¼ cups semisweet chocolate chips
Chocolate Ganache Glaze (recipe follows)

1. Preheat oven to 350°F. Position rack in center of oven. Lightly grease a large 12-cup Bundt pan (10-inches across the top) with cooking spray.

2. Bring ¼ cup water to a simmer in a small saucepan. Turn off heat. Add espresso powder and stir until dissolved. Add chopped chocolate and whisk until smooth. Remove from heat and cool until lukewarm.

3. Put flour, cocoa powder, buttermilk powder (if using), baking soda, baking powder, xanthan gum, and salt in medium bowl, and whisk until thoroughly combined. Set aside. Combine oil and water in a glass measuring cup. Set aside.

Makes one 10-inch cake

Serve slightly chilled or at room temperature. Can be made a day ahead. Store cake covered tightly with plastic wrap in refrigerator (this cake also holds up well for two days at room temperature). Bundt cake can be covered with plastic wrap and then with foil and stored in freezer for up to three weeks. Best when eaten within four days of baking.

* Or substitute ³⁄₄ cup fresh lowfat buttermilk for ³⁄₄ cup water and 3 tablespoons buttermilk powder.

** I recommend Nielsen-Massey Pure Chocolate Extract.

4. Beat eggs in large bowl of electric mixer until lemon-colored. Slowly add sugar 2 tablespoons at a time, and beat until mixture turns pale yellow and thick. Beat in melted chocolate-coffee mixture, vanilla extract, and chocolate extract.

5. Add flour mixture alternately with oil and water mixture in two additions; scrape sides and bottom of bowl, then mix at low speed for 1 more minute. Do not overbeat. Stir chocolate chips into the batter, then pour batter into prepared pan. Place cake in center of oven and bake 50-55 minutes, or until a toothpick inserted in the center comes out clean (do not open door for first 45 minutes).

6. Cool cake in the pan on a rack for 10 minutes. Carefully remove cake from pan and cool slightly on rack. Spoon warm Chocolate Ganache Glaze (recipe follows) over top of cake and let it drip down the sides. Allow cake to cool completely before moving to a cake plate.

Dairy-free Buttermilk: Combine ¾ cup rice or soy milk with 2 teaspoons lemon juice or distilled vinegar. Use only ¾ cup of the combined liquid in this recipe (do not add ¾ cup water or buttermilk powder).

Chocolate Ganache Glaze

3 ounces semisweet chocolate, chopped
3 tablespoons heavy cream
1 tablespoon light corn syrup
1 teaspoon pure vanilla extract

1. Combine chocolate, heavy cream, and corn syrup in a small, heavy saucepan; cook over low heat, stirring constantly, until chocolate melts and mixture is smooth. Remove from heat, add vanilla, and stir to blend. Cool slightly before drizzling over cake (cool glaze until it has thickened but is still pourable).

Cook's Note: Extra glaze that drips down under the rack can be scraped up, rewarmed, and drizzled back over the cake to make a thicker topping.

APPLE WALNUT BUNDT CAKE

Like many rustic cakes made with fruit and nuts, this Apple Walnut Cake is moist, flavorful, and delicious. Cinnamon, nutmeg, and allspice team up with apples, walnuts, and a touch of rum to create a fragrant cake that will keep everyone coming back for seconds. It makes the perfect dessert for a simple dinner or casual brunch with friends, and if you're lucky enough to squirrel some away, you'll be able to savor it with a cup of coffee the next day.

2 ½ cups Brown Rice Flour Mix (313 grams)
1 tablespoon baking powder
1 teaspoon baking soda
1 tablespoon buttermilk powder* (dairy-free instructions below)
2 teaspoons ground cinnamon
¾ teaspoon xanthan gum
½ teaspoon ground nutmeg
½ teaspoon ground allspice
½ teaspoon salt
3 large eggs
1 cup granulated sugar
½ cup loosely packed dark brown sugar
¾ cup canola oil
3 tablespoons dark rum or apple juice
⅓ cup water*
2 teaspoons pure vanilla extract
3 cups peeled, cored and chopped *Granny Smith Apples*
   (about ½-inch dice)**
1 cup coarsely chopped walnuts
Caramel Glaze (recipe follows) or confectioners' sugar

1. Preheat oven to 350°F. Position rack in center of oven. Lightly grease a 12-cup Bundt pan (10-inches across the top) with cooking spray.

2. Whisk flour, baking powder, baking soda, buttermilk powder, cinnamon, xanthan gum, nutmeg, allspice, and salt in a small bowl. Set aside.

3. Beat eggs in large bowl of electric mixer until well blended. Add sugars and beat until creamy (about 1 minute); scrape bowl. Add flour mixture, oil, rum, water, and vanilla, and mix at low speed for 1 minute until well combined. Do not overbeat. Mix in apples and walnuts.

Makes one 10-inch cake

Serve warm, slightly chilled, or at room temperature. Cut cake using a serrated knife with a sawing motion. Can be made a day ahead. Store cake covered tightly with plastic wrap in refrigerator. Cake can be covered with plastic wrap and then with foil and stored in freezer no longer than two weeks. Best when eaten within three days of baking.

* Substitute ⅓ cup fresh lowfat buttermilk for ⅓ cup water and 1 tablespoon buttermilk powder

** Apples should be at room temperature. Do not use overripe apples.

4. Spread batter into prepared pan. Place in center of oven and bake 50-55 minutes, or until a toothpick inserted in the center of cake comes out clean. Do not open oven for first 45 minutes.

5. Cool cake on a rack for 8 minutes. Carefully remove cake from pan and cool slightly on rack. Spoon Carmel Glaze (recipe follows) over top of cake and let it drip down the sides (or sift confectioners' sugar over top of cake once it is no longer warm). Allow cake to cool completely before moving to a cake plate.

Dairy-free Buttermilk: Combine ⅓ cup rice or soy milk with 1 teaspoon lemon juice or distilled vinegar. Use only ⅓ cup of the combined liquid in this recipe (do not add ⅓ cup water or buttermilk powder).

Caramel Glaze

⅓ cup dark brown sugar
3 tablespoons unsalted butter
3 tablespoons heavy cream
1 teaspoon pure vanilla extract
⅔ cup confectioners' sugar

1. Combine brown sugar and butter in a small, heavy saucepan; cook over medium-high heat until butter melts and sugar dissolves. Stir in heavy cream, bring to a low, gentle boil, and cook for 1 minute. Remove from heat, and add vanilla and then confectioners' sugar in two additions; whisk until very smooth. Cool until lukewarm before drizzling over cake (cool glaze until it has thickened but is still pourable).

Cook's Note: Extra glaze that drips down under the rack can be scraped up, rewarmed, and drizzled back over the cake to make a thicker topping. It can also be spooned over ice cream or used for dipping apple slices.

PUMPKIN SPICE BUNDT CAKE

Pumpkin cakes are hugely popular, especially around the holidays when you'll see them featured as a centerpiece dessert for buffets and brunches. Luckily, they're also really easy to make. Baked in a traditional Bundt pan, my Pumpkin Spice Cake has a moist, tender crumb and delicate outer crust. It's fragrant with cinnamon, allspice, nutmeg, and ginger, and will fill your house with a warm, comforting scent. I top it with a luscious Caramel Glaze that will make your mouth water, but you could also sprinkle it with confectioners' sugar or serve it with some cinnamon ice cream on the side for a special dessert.

2 cups Brown Rice Flour Mix (250 grams)
1 tablespoon baking powder
2 teaspoons ground cinnamon
1 teaspoon ground allspice
1 teaspoon baking soda
¾ teaspoon xanthan gum
½ teaspoon ground nutmeg
½ teaspoon ground ginger
½ teaspoon salt
4 large eggs
1 ½ cups granulated sugar
¾ cup plus 2 tablespoons canola oil
1 15-ounce can pumpkin puree (about 1 ¾ cups)
Caramel Glaze (recipe follows) or confectioners' sugar for garnish

1. Preheat oven to 350°F. Position rack in center of oven. Lightly grease a large 12-cup Bundt pan (10-inches across the top) with cooking spray.

2. Whisk flour, baking powder, cinnamon, allspice, baking soda, xanthan gum, nutmeg, ginger, and salt in a small bowl. Set aside.

3. Beat eggs in large bowl of electric mixer until lemon colored. Slowly add sugar 2 tablespoons at a time and beat until mixture turns pale yellow and thick. Add oil and pumpkin and beat at medium speed until well blended. Scrape bowl and beaters. Add flour mixture and mix at low speed for 1 minute until thoroughly combined. Do not overbeat.

4. Spread batter into prepared pan. Place in center of oven and bake 50-55 minutes, or until a toothpick inserted in the center of cake comes out clean. Do not open oven for first 45 minutes.

Makes one 10-inch cake

Can be made a day ahead. Store cake covered tightly with plastic wrap in refrigerator. Allow cake to come to room temperature before serving. Cake can be covered with plastic wrap and then with foil and stored in freezer for up to three weeks. Best when eaten within three days of baking.

5. Cool cake on a rack for 8 minutes. Carefully remove cake from pan and cool slightly on rack. Spoon Caramel Glaze (recipe follows) over top of cake and let it drip down the sides (or sift confectioners' sugar over top of cake once it is no longer warm). Allow cake to cool completely before moving to a cake plate. The flavor and texture of this cake are best when served at room temperature (not cold from refrigerator).

Caramel Glaze

⅓ cup dark brown sugar
3 tablespoons unsalted butter
3 tablespoons heavy cream
1 teaspoon pure vanilla extract
⅔ cup confectioners' sugar

1. Combine brown sugar and butter in a small, heavy saucepan; cook over medium high heat until butter melts and sugar dissolves. Stir in heavy cream, bring to a low, gentle boil, and then cook for 1 minute. Remove from heat, add vanilla and then confectioners' sugar in two additions; whisk until very smooth. Cool until lukewarm before drizzling over cake (cool glaze until it has thickened but is still pourable).

Cook's Note: Extra glaze that drips down under the rack can be scraped up, rewarmed, and drizzled back over the cake to make a thicker topping. It can also be spooned over ice cream or used for dipping apple slices.

LEMON BUTTERMILK BUNDT CAKE

This old-fashioned lemon buttermilk cake will quietly seduce you with its delicate lemon flavor and tender, moist texture. In fact, you'll probably find yourself secretly slicing another piece when no one is looking. It's the kind of cake that's perfect for a late morning coffee klatch, an afternoon tea, or a casual pot luck supper with friends. Classic in its simplicity, you can dress it up with fresh berries and ice cream or enjoy it on its own.

2 ½ cups Brown Rice Flour Mix (313 grams)
1 tablespoon baking powder
1 teaspoon baking soda
1 teaspoon xanthan gum
½ teaspoon salt
4 large eggs
1 ¾ cups granulated sugar
¾ cup plus 2 tablespoons canola oil
1 cup lowfat buttermilk* (dairy-free instructions below)
1 ½ teaspoons pure lemon extract
1 teaspoon pure vanilla extract
1 packed tablespoon grated lemon rind (see Cooks Notes below)
Lemon Glaze (recipe follows) or confectioners' sugar for garnish

1. Preheat oven to 350°F. Position rack in center of oven. Lightly grease a large 12-cup Bundt pan (10-inches across the top) with cooking spray.

2. Whisk flour, baking powder, baking soda, xanthan gum, and salt in a small bowl. Set aside.

3. Beat eggs in large bowl of electric mixer until lemon- colored. Add sugar 2 tablespoons at a time and beat until pale yellow and thick; scrape bowl. Add flour mixture, oil, buttermilk, lemon extract, vanilla extract, and grated lemon rind; mix at low speed for 1 minute until well combined. Do not overbeat.

4. Spread batter into prepared pan. Place in center of oven and bake 50-55 minutes, or until a toothpick inserted in the center of cake comes out clean. Do not open oven for first 45 minutes.

5. Cool cake on a rack for 8 minutes. Carefully remove cake from pan and cool slightly on rack. Spoon Lemon Glaze (recipe follows) over top of cake and let it drip down the sides (or sift confectioners' sugar over top of cake once it is no longer warm). Allow cake to cool completely before moving to a cake plate.

Makes one 10-inch cake

Serve slightly chilled or at room temperature. Can be made a day ahead. Cover tightly with plastic wrap and store in refrigerator. Cake can be covered with plastic wrap and then with foil and stored in freezer no longer than two weeks. Best when eaten within three days of baking.

*I prefer this cake with real lowfat buttermilk, but you can substitute 1 cup water and ¼ cup buttermilk powder for the 1 cup fresh lowfat buttermilk.

Dairy-free Buttermilk: Combine 1 cup rice or soy milk with 1 tablespoon lemon juice or distilled vinegar. Use only 1 cup of the combined liquid in this recipe.

Cook's Notes: Although this cake traditionally has a delicate lemon flavor, you can add 1 extra tablespoon of grated lemon rind to create a more vibrant lemon flavor.

Lemon Glaze

3 tablespoons unsalted butter
1 tablespoon heavy cream
2 tablespoons fresh lemon juice
¼ teaspoon pure lemon extract
1 cup confectioners' sugar

1. Melt butter in a small, heavy saucepan. Stir in heavy cream and bring to a simmer. Remove from heat, add lemon juice, lemon extract, and then confectioners' sugar in two additions; whisk until very smooth. Cool to lukewarm before drizzling over cake (cool glaze until it is thicker but is still pourable).

Cook's Note: Extra glaze that drips down under the rack can be scraped up, rewarmed, and drizzled back over the cake to make a thicker topping.

OLD-FASHIONED BUTTERMILK BUNDT CAKE

Omit lemon extract and grated lemon rind.
Add 1 tablespoon pure vanilla extract instead of 1 teaspoon.
Top with Vanilla Glaze (recipe follows).

Vanilla Glaze

3 tablespoons unsalted butter
3 tablespoons heavy cream
½ teaspoon pure vanilla extract
1 cup confectioners' sugar

1. Melt butter in a small, heavy saucepan. Stir in heavy cream and bring to a simmer. Remove from heat, add vanilla and then confectioners' sugar in two additions; whisk until very smooth. Cool to lukewarm be-

fore drizzling over cake (cool glaze until it is thicker but is still pourable).

Cook's Note: Extra glaze that drips down under the rack can be scraped up, rewarmed, and drizzled back over the cake to make a thicker topping.

OLD-FASHIONED CHOCOLATE CHIP BUNDT CAKE

In Step 4, pour ⅓ of the batter into the cake pan. Stir 1 ½ cups semisweet chocolate chips into the remaining batter, then pour the remaining batter into the pan (some of the chocolate chips will sink, but this way, they will be more evenly distributed throughout the cake).

If desired, top with Vanilla Glaze (above) or Chocolate Ganache Glaze from Chocolate Bundt Cake recipe (page 90), or confectioners' sugar.

Pies and Tarts

Alsatian Apple Tart

Classic Lemon Tart

Cherry Frangipane Tart

Blueberry Tart

Rustic Peach Tart

Rustic Pear Tart

Butterscotch Cream Pie

Lemon Cream Pie

Savory Harvest tart

Rustic Spinach and Mushroom Tart

Rustic Spinach and Feta Tart

Traditional Pie Crust

Tart Shell Crust

WHO DOESN'T LIKE PIE? BAKERS MAY DISAGREE OVER THE BEST way to make the perfect pie crust or how to thicken juicy fruit, but I don't think any of them would dispute how happy people look when you carry a freshly baked pie to the table. I've tried to create an interesting collection of recipes in the hope that you'll find some old favorites—or something new—to bake up in your own kitchen. Which pie will be the one *your* friends and family ask you to make over and over? The simple, elegant Alsatian apple tart? The luscious lemon cream pie? Or the addictive cherry frangipane tart? Perhaps the rustic spinach and mushroom tart will become *the one* you can't get out of your head. Grab a pie pan and some flour mix to find out.

Dairy substitutes: My butter substitute of choice for the classic pie crust and tart shell in this chapter is Earth Balance® Buttery Spread or Buttery Sticks (*not* the Shortening Sticks). Readers have also written me to tell me that they've been successful using butter-flavored Crisco. I've made my own side-by-side comparisons of all three and found that the texture and taste are best when the crusts are made with unsalted butter. However, when you want or need to use a substitute, use the Earth Balance® Buttery Spread or Sticks. It is best if the Earth Balance (or the butter) is very cold when you mix it into the flour (and don't put the salt in from the ingredient list if you use a butter substitute that contains a lot of salt).

One other consideration: Lard is a non-dairy butter alternative that is becoming popular again with chefs and bakers after being a nutritional outcast for many years. In the past several years, I've heard from several bakers who've written to tell me that my pie crust recipe comes out well using lard instead of butter.

This chapter uses the following pans:
• 8- or 9-inch pie pan (glass, metal or ceramic); I get my best results from Pyrex® glass
• 9- or 10-inch tart shell (metal)
• Large, lighter-colored, shiny heavy (but not insulated) baking sheet for the Rustic Tarts

The Last Word on Pie Crusts
• Set up before starting the recipe: Assemble all the ingredients.
• Use cold butter (or butter substitute).
• Measure carefully.
• Use the right size pan or adjust baking time to compensate.

- Preheat the oven to the proper temperature (make sure the oven is calibrated correctly).
- Do not open the oven door more than necessary.
- Use a timer in case you get distracted.

ALSATIAN APPLE TART

Makes one 9-inch tart

Can be made one day ahead. Store tightly covered in refrigerator. Best when eaten within two days of baking.

This Alsatian Apple Tart is elegant simplicity at its best. Remarkably easy to make, it combines sliced apples with luscious vanilla custard and a delicate pie crust to make a dessert that you and those around your table won't be able to stop eating. Serve it anytime—after a simple dinner, a festive holiday meal, a country picnic, or a Sunday brunch. It will disappear quickly and leave you looking for an excuse to make it again.

1 parbaked Traditional Pie Crust (see page 117) baked in a
    metal 9-inch tart pan with removable bottom (make sure
    sides are at least 1 ½ inches high)
1 – 1 ¼ pounds Golden Delicious Apples
2 large eggs
6 tablespoons granulated sugar
1 cup heavy cream
1 tablespoon milk
1 teaspoon pure vanilla extract
¼ teaspoon ground cinnamon, optional
Confectioners' sugar for garnish

1. Preheat oven to 375°F. Position rack in center of oven. Peel, core, and cut apples into ½-inch thick slices (you should have about 4 cups). Arrange apple slices in overlapping concentric circles on the parbaked crust in the tart pan (slices should fit tightly; they will shrink when baked). The slices in the center can be mounded slightly.

2. Combine the eggs and sugar in a medium-sized mixing bowl and whisk until well blended. Whisk in heavy cream, milk, vanilla, and cinnamon (if using). Pour over apples in the tart pan.

3. Bake in center of oven for 50-55 minutes, until apples are tender and filling has set in the center. Remove from oven and set aside to cool, about 1 hour. Place pan on top of a broad glass and carefully push down sides, then slide onto a serving plate (it will be easier to slide it off the metal bottom when it is cool). Sprinkle with confectioners' sugar. Serve warm or at room temperature.

Cook's Notes: You can make this tart with fresh peaches or blueberries when they are in season. Use thick slices (or halves) of washed, peeled and pitted peaches or 4 cups of washed and well-dried blueberries. You can also replace the cinnamon with nutmeg.

CLASSIC LEMON TART

Makes one 9-inch tart

*Can be made one day
ahead. Store tightly
covered in refrigerator.
Best when eaten within
three days of baking.*

The classic lemon tarts lined up in French pastry shops call out to lemon lovers everywhere, but they are almost never made with gluten-free ingredients. No matter. Here is a luscious lemon tart with a crunchy shortbread crust, a bright yellow color, and a cool, tangy taste. French versions tend to use less sugar, and American versions have more, but you can adjust the amount to suit your own taste based on the range I offer. This lemon tart is easy to make and perfect for holiday entertaining, but it is so good, you may end up making one just for yourself.

> 1 prebaked Tart Shell Crust (see page 119) baked in a metal
>   9-inch tart pan with removable bottom
> 2/3 cup fresh lemon juice
> 3/4 – 1 cup granulated sugar
> 4 large eggs
> 2 egg yolks
> 1 teaspoon grated lemon rind
> 1/2 teaspoon pure lemon extract
> 1/4 cup unsalted butter, cut into four pieces

1. Combine lemon juice, sugar, eggs, and egg yolks in a small saucepan. Cook, stirring constantly, over medium-low heat until filling has thickened and thickly coats the back of a wooden spoon (temperature should be about 175° F on an instant-read thermometer). Filling should not boil. This should take about 10 minutes.

2. Remove from heat and stir in lemon rind, lemon extract, and butter. Pour filling into small bowl and press plastic wrap directly onto surface to prevent hardening. Refrigerate until approximately lukewarm.

3. Pour lukewarm filling into prebaked tart shell. Refrigerate until well chilled. If using a tart pan with removable bottom, place pan on top of a broad glass and carefully push down sides of shell, then slide onto a serving plate (it will be easier to slide it off the metal bottom when it is cool). Serve cold.

CHERRY FRANGIPANE TART

I've found a lot of interpretations of frangipane tarts in the cookbook world, but none of them were exactly what I was looking for. Some didn't have enough filling. Some had a weird texture. More than a few had very little flavor. Or not enough cherries. Or too much sugar. Or not enough sugar. After a couple of failed attempts, I created my own recipe for a cherry frangipane tart that met all my criteria—tender crust, full-of-flavor fruit, just enough sweetness, rich almond flavor, and enough filling to satisfy the longing for filling. Although there are cookbook writers who swear you have to use almonds without skins, I've found that it didn't make a difference to the taste or texture. I've made it with fresh cherries when they were in season, and I've made it with frozen when they weren't. I've found that when I bought the best frozen cherries I could, they were just as good if not better than fresh ones because the fruit was more consistent—and they came pitted! So if you've been thinking about baking a frangipane tart but were befuddled by the hundreds of different variations, try this one! And be reassured, if you're not a cherry lover, the frangipane is also delicious with pears (poached or frozen), and fresh peaches or plums.

Makes one 9-inch tart

Can be made one day ahead. Store tightly covered in refrigerator. Best when eaten within two days of baking.

*I recommend Woodstock Organic Sweet Dark Cherries (www.woodstock-foods.com). Their frozen Organic Dark Sweet Cherries taste like perfectly ripened cherries, and the entire bag is filled with richly colored fruit that is already pitted.

1 prebaked baked and cooled Traditional Pie Crust (see page 117) baked in a metal 9-inch tart pan with removable bottom (make sure sides are at least 1 ½ inches high)
½ cup unsalted butter
½ – ⅔ cup granulated sugar (depending on sweetness of cherries)
1 large egg
1 cup finely ground almonds (almond meal)
1 tablespoon Brown Rice Flour Mix
1 tablespoon Amaretto (or dark rum)
1 teaspoon pure almond extract
3 cups fresh sweet cherries* (about 1 pound), washed, dried, and pitted; or 10-12 ounces (about 2 ½ cups) good-quality frozen cherries, thawed, drained, and gently patted dry with paper towel (See Cook's Note)

1. Preheat oven to 375⁰F. Position rack in center of oven. Beat butter and sugar in large bowl of electric mixer until pale and fluffy. Add egg, almonds, flour, Amaretto, and almond extract, and beat until smooth and creamy. Spread frangipane evenly over bottom of baked and cooled tart crust. *Do not put filling into a hot crust, or the butter will melt and*

separate; the crust can be lukewarm, but not hot. Then, spread pitted cherries across the top of the frangipane (try to place cherries smooth side up).

2. Bake tart in center of oven for 40–50 minutes until frangipane is puffed and light brown in color across the entire surface, including the middle. Remove from oven and set aside to cool about 1 hour. Place pan on top of a broad glass and carefully push down sides, then slide onto a serving plate (it will be easier to slide it off the metal bottom when it is cool). Serve tart warm or at room temperature.

Cook's Notes: Frozen cherries should be weighed and measured while frozen. Then you simply let the cherries defrost, pat them dry to the best of your ability, and then spread them over the filling.

BLUEBERRY TART

I love making this tart every summer when fresh blueberries are at their peak. It's a twist on tarts that feature uncooked fruit in a thickened, stove-cooked sauce. A couple of cups of the blueberries are mashed up and simmered along with the sugar for a few minutes before they are tossed in with the rest of the whole uncooked berries. Then the whole tart is baked. The result is one you are sure to enjoy—a juicy, richly hued tart full of flavor.

Makes one 9-inch tart

Can be made one day ahead. Store tightly covered in refrigerator. Best when eaten within two days of baking.

> 1 parbaked Traditional Pie Crust (see page 117) baked in a metal 9-inch tart pan with removable bottom (make sure sides are at least 1 ¼ inches high)
> 5 cups fresh blueberries, washed, dried, and picked over
> ½ cup granulated sugar
> 3 tablespoons water
> 2 tablespoons cornstarch
> ½ teaspoon ground cinnamon
> 1 tablespoon fresh lemon juice
> 2 tablespoons unsalted butter (or butter substitute)

1. Preheat oven to 375°F. Position rack in center of oven. Put three cups of blueberries in a large mixing bowl and set aside.

2. Combine remaining two cups of blueberries, sugar, and water in a medium-sized heavy saucepan. Coarsely mash blueberries with a potato masher and cook over medium-high heat until they break down a bit and the sugar dissolves (about three minutes). Stir in cornstarch, cinnamon, lemon juice, and butter. Spoon blueberry mixture into large mixing bowl containing blueberries, and stir until well combined. Pour into par-baked tart shell.

3. Bake in center of oven for about 40 minutes until filling is bubbling in the center and slightly golden. Remove from oven and cool on a rack. Place pan on top of a broad glass and carefully push down sides, then slide onto a serving plate (it will be easier to slide it off the metal bottom when it is cool). Serve at room temperature.

RUSTIC PEACH TART

Makes one 9-inch tart

Can be made one day ahead. Store tightly covered in refrigerator. Best when eaten within two days of baking.

This Rustic Peach Tart is a quick and delicious way to use some of those fresh peaches you found at the farm stand (see Cook's Note). It doesn't take a long time to make, and it bakes up quickly while you prepare the rest of your meal. The best part is that it doesn't take as long to cool as a traditional peach pie, so you'll be able to bring it to the table to enjoy with family and friends in no time.

Prepared Traditional Pie Crust dough (see page 117)
5 cups peeled ripe peaches, sliced 1 inch thick
¼ – ⅓ cup granulated sugar (or to taste)
1 tablespoon corn starch
½ teaspoon ground cinnamon (or more to taste)
¼ teaspoon ground ginger (or more to taste)
1 teaspoon lemon juice
1 tablespoon unsalted butter
1 large egg, beaten, to brush on crust
1 ½ tablespoons peach or apricot preserves, optional

1. Preheat oven to 400°F. Position rack in bottom third of oven. Line a large baking sheet with parchment paper.

2. Roll pie dough between two sheets of wax paper into a 12-inch round. Remove the top sheet and use your fingers to push dough in from the edges to make a perfect 11-inch round: The dough around the edges should now be thicker than the 9-inches across the center (this will make it easier for you to bake the tart the necessary time without the edges getting overdone). Turn the round of dough over onto the parchment paper on baking sheet and remove the other piece of wax paper.

3. Cut each peach slice into 2 or 3 large chunks and put into a large bowl. Add sugar, cornstarch, cinnamon, ginger, and lemon juice; stir until peaches are well coated. Spoon peaches over center of pie dough, leaving a 1-inch edge around the entire round. Carefully fold edges of dough over peaches and push down slightly, so the dough is well supported by the peaches. Patch any holes in the dough so juices don't leak out. Dot top of peaches with thin slices of butter. Generously brush crust with beaten egg (this will also help to keep in juices).

4. Place in center of rack and bake for 40–50 minutes, until crust is golden brown and peaches are tender. Cool slightly on a rack before serving.

5. Optional: Melt peach or apricot preserves in a small saucepan. While tart is cooling, brush melted preserves over top of peaches with a pastry brush.

Cook's Note: There are excellent flash-frozen peaches available in grocery stores for when peaches are out of season. The finished tart is not exactly the same as when you can get a pile of ripe, fragrant peaches from the farm stand, but it can still be a welcome treat in the dead of winter. If you use flash-frozen peaches, defrost and drain them completely before measuring. You also may have to add more sugar; check for sweetness. I recommend Woodstock Organic Frozen Peaches.

RUSTIC PEAR TART

Replace peaches with 5 cups firm ripe pears cut into medium chunks (peel, core, and slice pears into eight equal slices. Cut each slice into two equal chunks to make 5 cups).

While tart is cooling, brush with melted apple or red current jelly, optional.

BUTTERSCOTCH CREAM PIE

Makes one 9-inch pie

Can be made one day ahead. Store in refrigerator. Best when eaten within three days of baking.

Although the origins of the word "butterscotch" are debated, its first recorded use goes back to early 19th century England, when candy-maker Samuel Parkinson created what became a popular confectionery made with butter and brown sugar. (Carmel candy contains caramelized, or slightly burnt sugar, and has a different taste). History aside, butterscotch has come to mean the comforting taste of home to food lovers everywhere. I make my butterscotch cream pie the old-fashioned way, with fresh sweet butter, dark brown sugar, eggs, and milk. It has a rich, buttery taste with just enough molasses-tinged sweetness peeking through. Make this delicious treat soon to welcome home your own friends and family after a long week.

> 1 prebaked Tart Shell Crust (see page 119) baked in a 9-inch pie pan or 9-inch tart pan
> 2 large eggs
> ⅔ cup dark brown sugar
> ¼ cup corn starch
> ¼ teaspoon salt
> 2 cups whole milk
> 3 tablespoons unsalted butter
> 1 tablespoon pure vanilla extract

Whipped Cream Topping

> ¾ cup heavy cream
> 2 tablespoons confectioners' sugar
> 1 ½ teaspoons pure vanilla extract

1. Beat eggs in large bowl of electric mixer at medium-high speed until foamy. Gradually add sugar a little at a time and continue beating until the mixture is pale yellow and thick. Add the corn starch and salt, and beat until well blended.

2. Bring milk to a boil in a large heavy saucepan over medium-high heat while you are beating the eggs.

3. With the mixer on low, gradually add hot milk in a thin stream to egg mixture. Quickly scrap sides and bottom of bowl and mix at medium speed until well blended.

4. Pour the custard mixture back into the saucepan and cook it over medium-high heat, stirring constantly with a wire whisk, until it comes to a boil and thickens. Lower heat and cook for 1 minute more. Remove from heat and beat in butter and vanilla.

5. Pour filling into small bowl and press plastic wrap directly onto surface to prevent hardening. Refrigerate until lukewarm, and then pour into cooled, prebaked Tart Shell Crust. Chill at least 1 hour in refrigerator before putting on topping.

6. *To make Topping:* Combine heavy cream, confectioners' sugar, and vanilla in large bowl of electric mixer; beat until stiff peaks form. Use pastry bag to pipe sweetened heavy cream around edges of pie. Serve cold.

LEMON CREAM PIE

Makes one 9-inch pie

Can be made one day ahead. Store in refrigerator. Best when eaten within three days of baking.

Looking for comfort food and sunshine all on one plate? This lemon cream pie is the answer. It's not formal and perfectly formed like the Classic Lemon Tart. No, this is home style. There's no fussing or crust crimping— just a simple, crunchy shortbread crust. There's also a cool lemon pudding, imperfectly piped whipped cream, and a lick-your-fingers goodness that will have you looking forward to dessert as soon as you put it in the frig to chill. Lemon Cream pie won't take long to make, and it'll work it's magic with the very first bite.

1 prebaked Tart Shell Crust (see page 119) baked in a 9-inch
   pie pan
4 large egg yolks
$2/3$ cup granulated sugar
$1/4$ cup corn starch
$1/4$ teaspoon salt
2 cups whole milk
$1/4$ cup fresh lemon juice
2 packed teaspoons grated lemon rind
1 tablespoon unsalted butter
1 – 1 $1/2$ teaspoons pure lemon extract

Whipped Cream Topping

$3/4$ cup heavy cream
2 tablespoons confectioners' sugar
1 $1/2$ teaspoons pure vanilla extract

1. Beat egg yolks in large bowl of electric mixer at medium-high speed until foamy. Gradually add sugar a little at a time, and continue beating until the mixture is pale yellow and thick. Add corn starch and salt, and beat until well blended.

2. Bring milk to a boil in a large, heavy saucepan over medium-high heat while you are beating the egg yolks.

3. With the mixer on low, gradually add hot milk to egg mixture in a thin stream. Quickly scrape sides and bottom of bowl, and mix at medium speed until well blended.

4. Pour the custard mixture back into the saucepan and cook it over medium-high heat, stirring constantly with a wire whisk, until it comes

to a boil and thickens. Lower heat and cook for 1 minute more. Remove from heat and stir in lemon juice, lemon rind, butter, and lemon extract.

5. Pour filling into small bowl and press plastic wrap directly onto surface to prevent hardening. Refrigerate until lukewarm, and then pour into cooled, prebaked Tart Shell Crust. Chill at least 1 hour in refrigerator before putting on topping.

6. *To make Topping:* Combine heavy cream, confectioners' sugar, and vanilla in large bowl of electric mixer; beat until stiff peaks form. Use pastry bag to pipe sweetened heavy cream around edges of pie. Refrigerate until well chilled. Serve cold.

SAVORY HARVEST TART

Makes one 9-inch tart

Can be made a day ahead. Store tightly covered in refrigerator. Best when eaten within three days of baking. Bring to room temperature or warm slightly in the microwave.

Perfect for late summer picnics, fall tailgates, or a leisurely weekend lunch, this savory tart is flavorful and delicious. It's a great way to showcase some of that freshly picked zucchini you bought at the farmer's market (although you could easily substitute other vegetables). My traditional pie crust and an easy-to-make filling are topped with artfully arranged concentric circles of zucchini. It's a food masterpiece you can happily carry to your table.

1 parbaked Traditional Pie Crust (see page 117) baked in a
    metal 9-inch tart pan with removable bottom (make sure
    sides are at least 1 ¼ inches high)
1 tablespoon extra virgin olive oil
2 cups (about ¾ pound) thinly sliced zucchini
1 cup low fat ricotta cheese
1 package (5.2 oz.) Boursin cheese (or a similar soft, herb
    flavored cheese)
2 large eggs
2 tablespoons heavy cream
½ cup freshly grated Parmesan, separated
Salt and freshly ground pepper to taste

1. Preheat oven to 350°F. Position rack in center of oven.

2. Heat olive oil in large, heavy skillet over medium-high heat. Add zucchini slices and sauté until they are tender and very light golden (about 10 minutes). Season with salt and pepper to taste. Remove from heat and set aside in a small bowl.

3. Combine ricotta, Boursin, eggs, heavy cream, and ¼ cup Parmesan in a medium-sized bowl and mix well. Season with salt and freshly ground pepper to taste. Pour into the par-baked tart crust. Top with concentric circles of sliced zucchini and sprinkle remaining ¼ cup Parmesan over the top.

4. Bake in center of oven for 45-50 minutes until puffed and set. Remove from oven and set aside to cool. Place pan on top of a broad glass and carefully push down sides, then slide tart onto a serving plate (it will be easier to slide it off the metal bottom when it is very cool). Serve at room temperature or slightly warm.

RUSTIC SPINACH and MUSHROOM TART

Here's a delicious take on spanakopita made with a delicate pie crust, chopped spinach, thinly sliced mushrooms, and tangy feta cheese. This beautiful rustic tart is seasoned with basil and oregano, although dill or nutmeg would also work well. The mushrooms add a rich, earthy layer of flavor and texture, but if you prefer, you can leave them out and increase the spinach (see variation below). The recipe makes a relatively small tart that's perfect to feed about four people for lunch, brunch, or a light dinner. It also travels well for picnics.

Prepared Traditional Pie Crust dough (see page 117)
10 ounces frozen spinach
2 tablespoons olive oil
¾ cup chopped onion
8 ounces fresh mushrooms, sliced (white, wild, cremini, shiitake, or porcini)
1 teaspoon dried basil (or to taste)
1 teaspoon dried oregano (or to taste)
1 cup crumbled feta cheese
1 cup cottage cheese
1 large well-beaten egg
½ – ¾ teaspoon salt
¼ teaspoon freshly ground pepper
1 large egg, beaten, to brush on crust

1. Cook frozen spinach according to package directions. Squeeze spinach to remove as much liquid as possible (I put it into a fine sieve and press the liquid out with a large spoon). Set aside in a medium-sized mixing bowl.

2. Heat oil in a large, heavy frying pan over medium heat. Lightly sauté onion until soft, about 5 minutes. Add sliced mushrooms, basil, and oregano; cook, stirring frequently, until mushrooms release all their liquid. Stir onion and mushroom mixture into cooked spinach. (Filling can be prepared ahead of when you will bake tart; store it in a tightly covered container in the refrigerator. Rewarm in microwave when ready to proceed.)

3. Preheat oven to 400°F. Position rack in bottom third of oven. Line a large baking sheet with parchment paper.

4. Roll pie dough between two sheets of wax paper into a 12-inch round. Remove the top sheet and use your fingers to push dough in from the edges to make a perfect 11-inch round. The dough around the edges should now be thicker than the 9-inches across the center (this will

make it easier for you to bake the tart the necessary time without the edges getting overdone). Turn the round of dough over onto the parchment paper on baking sheet and remove other piece of wax paper.

5. Stir feta cheese and cottage cheese into spinach and mushroom mixture. Season to taste with salt and pepper. Add beaten egg and stir until well combined.

6. Spoon spinach mixture over center of pie dough; pat it into a 9-inch round, leaving a 1-inch edge around the outside. Carefully fold edges of dough over spinach filling and push down slightly, so the dough is well supported by the filling. Patch any holes in the dough so juices don't leak out. Generously brush beaten egg over the crust and filling.

7. Place in center of rack and bake for about 40 minutes, until crust is dark golden brown and filling is hot and cooked through. Cool slightly on a rack before serving.

RUSTIC SPINACH AND FETA TART

Use 16 ounces spinach instead of 10 ounces. Omit mushrooms.

TRADITIONAL PIE CRUST

Reprinted from Gluten-Free Baking Classics, 2006, 2008

Makes one 8- or 9-inch pie crust or one 10-inch tart crust. Recipe can be doubled.

This really is a fabulous pie crust, perhaps even better than those made with wheat. It stands up well to fruit fillings, custards, and even lemon meringue. It is probably the only pie crust you will ever eat that is as good the second day as it is the first. And it is easy to make in a mixer—no messy hands or time-consuming pastry cutters. You will become a pie-crust-making phenomenon in your own home. When you make the Traditional Pie Crust, be sure to use the sweet rice flour called for in the recipe. It will help give you a great crust. I recommend Authentic Foods finely ground sweet rice flour.

Take note: When you prebake this crust, do so at a lower temperature than is commonly used for pie crusts made with wheat (see directions below). This is to make sure the dough cooks before it browns. I also suggest that you partially bake the crust whenever you are making a fruit pie or quiche.

1 cup plus 2 tablespoons Brown Rice Flour Mix (140 grams)
2 tablespoons sweet rice flour
1 tablespoon granulated sugar
½ teaspoon xanthan gum
¼ teaspoon salt
6 tablespoons cold unsalted butter cut into 6 pieces (for butter substitutes see page 100)
1 large egg
2 teaspoons orange juice or lemon juice

1. Spray 9-inch pie pan or tart pan (with removable bottom) with cooking spray. Generously dust with rice flour.

2. Mix flours, sugar, xanthan gum, and salt in large bowl of electric mixer. Add butter and mix until crumbly and resembling coarse meal.

3. Add egg and orange juice. Mix on low speed until dough holds together but is not all in one big piece (it's better if it looks a little dry versus very damp, and it should not be sticky). Form dough into a ball using your hands, and place it on a sheet of wax paper. Top with a second sheet of wax paper and flatten dough to 1-inch thickness. Dough can be frozen at this point for up to 1 month; wrap in plastic wrap and then use foil as an outer wrap.

4. Roll out dough between the two sheets of wax paper. If dough seems tacky, refrigerate for 15 minutes before proceeding. Remove top sheet

of wax paper and invert dough into pie pan. Remove remaining sheet of wax paper, and crimp edges for single-crust pie. Dough can also be frozen at this point for up to 1 month; line pie shell with wax paper, wrap in plastic wrap, and use foil as an outer wrap.

To prebake a bottom pie crust:

Preheat oven to 375°F. Gently prick pastry in three or four places with a fork. Bake pastry for about 25 minutes or until golden and cooked through. You should be able to smell it in the oven. *The crust may take more than 25 minutes to cook through if the dough is very cold when you put it in the oven and/or if you use a metal or ceramic pie pan instead of glass.* Remove from oven and cool completely on a wire rack. If the dough rises up too much while baking in the first 15-20 minutes, you can very gently press it down with your hand (or a large spoon) while it is in the oven. Prebaked pie shells can be stored in airtight plastic containers or plastic wrap in refrigerator for 3 days. For longer storage, wrap in plastic wrap and then in foil, and store in freezer for up to 2 weeks.

To partially bake a bottom pie crust:

Preheat oven to 375°F. Depending on how thin you rolled the dough, bake pastry 15 minutes for a glass pan and 15–20 minutes for a metal or ceramic pan. The crust should be starting to turn golden and appear dryer and no longer raw. You should be just starting to smell it in the oven. *The crust may take even more time than indicated above if the dough is very cold when you put it in the oven.* Remove pie crust from oven; fill and bake as per recipe. If the dough rises up too much while baking, you can very gently press it down with your hand (or a large spoon) while it is in the oven. It tends to deflate fully once it comes out, but if not, you can press it down at that time.

Why don't you blind-bake this crust?

In multiple side-by-side comparisons, the crust that was not held down and covered with foil and "baking beans" (or pie weights) emerged lighter textured, more tender, and better cooked after the pie was finished and served (i.e., blind baking does not improve this particular crust).

TART SHELL CRUST

Reprinted from Gluten-Free Baking Classics, 2006, 2008

Gluten-free flours make great tart shells. They're crunchy and delicious, and they stay that way for days. This crust is actually a little like the best cookie-crumb crust you ever had—but better. You can make it in minutes and then let your imagination go: fruit tarts, key lime tart, lemon curd tart, chocolate cream tart, coconut cream tart, banana cream tart—just dream it up, and you can make it. You can also use this crust for the bottom of cheesecakes (prebake 12 minutes at 350°F); it doesn't get soggy like graham cracker crumbs. Take note: The crust is more fragile just after it is baked, but it firms up perfectly after it is chilled in the refrigerator.

1 cup Brown Rice Flour Mix (125 grams)
¼ cup granulated sugar
1 teaspoon xanthan gum
5 tablespoons cold unsalted butter, cut into 5 pieces
1 teaspoon pure vanilla extract

1. Preheat oven to 350°F. Position rack in center of oven. Grease 9-inch pie pan or tart pan (with removable bottom) with cooking spray. Generously dust with rice flour.

2. Combine flour, sugar, and xanthan gum in large bowl of electric mixer (or food processor). Add butter and mix (or pulse) on low speed until crumbly. Add vanilla and mix well. Gently press into bottom and up sides of pie or tart pan (if you pack the dough too densely, the crust will be hard to get out of the pan. If you pack it too loosely, the crust will be a bit crumbly).

3. Bake in center of oven for about 18 minutes or until light golden. Cool on rack in pan. For a tart, place pan on top of a broad glass and carefully push down sides, then slide onto a serving plate (it will be easier to slide it off the metal bottom when it is cool). For best results, remove pan sides and bottom once tart shell is filled and chilled.

Makes one 9-inch pie crust or one 9-inch tart crust. Recipe can be doubled.

Cover with plastic wrap and store in refrigerator. Best when eaten within three days of baking.

8

Cookies

Chocolate Mint Cookies

Snickerdoodles

Thumbprints

Peanut Butter Cookies

Lemon Tea Cookies

Moravian Spice Cookies

Anise Sesame Cookies

Lemon Sandwich Cookies

Chocolate Brownie Cookies

Old-fashioned Pumpkin Cookies

Chocolate Whoopie Pies

Pumpkin Whoopie Pies

Ladyfingers

Madeleines

Lemon Madeleines

Orange Walnut Biscotti

T RENDY COOKIES COME AND GO, BUT WE PASS OUR FONDNESS FOR THE CLASSICS DOWN from one generation to the next. We lovingly arrange them on holiday tables, tuck them into school lunch boxes, carry them to the office to share with co-workers, and snatch them from the cupboard or refrigerator to have with a late af-ternoon cup of tea. Many of the cookies in this chapter will be familiar to you. Who hasn't enjoyed a Chocolate Mint Girl Scout cookie or bitten into a fresh-from-the-oven Snickerdoodle fragrant with cinnamon? But perhaps you have yet to taste the delicate, sponge cake-like madeleine that Proust wrote of so wistfully, or enjoyed an orange walnut biscotti with your morning coffee. The nicest part about this collec-tion of old-time favorites is how well they converted to gluten-free. You'd be hard pressed to even notice the absence of wheat. In fact, these cookies are as good and sometimes better than the original. Try them and see.

Dairy substitutes: When the recipe doesn't specify shortening, my butter substitutes of choice for the cookies in this chapter are Earth Balance® Buttery Spread or Buttery Sticks (not the Shortening Sticks). My milk substitute of choice is rice milk.

This chapter uses the following pans:
• Large, shiny cookie sheets (or baking sheets) of medium to heavy weight. For best results, I do not recommend super-thick, insulated, or dark metal cookie sheets for my recipes; they tend to melt the cookie dough before it can bake up, and you end up with flat, spread out cookies.

The Last Word on Cookies
• Set up before starting the recipe: Assemble all the ingredients.
• Measure carefully.
• Preheat the oven to the proper temperature (make sure the oven is calibrated correctly).
• Do not open the oven door more than necessary.
• Use a timer in case you get distracted. Test for doneness at the first time given in the recipe, then continue baking, if necessary, until the cookie is fully cooked. Make a note of the total baking time for the next time you make the recipe.
• Do not put cookie dough on a hot cookie sheet (only use cool cookie sheets).

Double Checking

Why are my cookies spreading too much? Why are my cookies so thin?

- Your butter or shortening was too warm when you beat it with the sugar, so the sugar didn't get incorporated into the fat well. When a recipe specifies butter at room temperature, it should still be firm and not soft.
- The dough was too warm when you put the cookies into the oven. If your dough is too warm (this can happen if your home is warm), your cookies will spread more, and they may also take less time to bake. When the dough is cooler, your cookies will take longer to bake, they'll have more time to "set," and they'll be less likely to flatten out. If you notice that your cookie dough is getting warm, you can chill it in the refrigerator before and/or after forming the cookies (depending the recipe), but before you put it in the oven.
- You didn't beat the sugar and the butter/shortening until it was light and creamy, so the sugar didn't get incorporated into the fat well.
- Your oven wasn't calibrated correctly; if it's too low, it will melt the dough before it can bake.
- You used a dark cookie sheet and didn't adjust the oven temperature down by 25°F.
- You used one of those super-thick or insulated cookie sheets that really just melts the dough before it bakes.
- You were trying to be so careful not to spoon too much flour into the measuring cups that you spooned in too little, so the cookies had less flour to hold them together.
- You used butter or margarine when the recipe called for shortening (you might need to add a bit more flour to keep them from spreading).
- You used rice flour with a large grind, and it didn't react with the liquid and fat in the recipe the way fine rice flour does.
- You used old or bad xanthan gum, and it didn't work to help give structure to the cookies.

CHOCOLATE MINT COOKIES

Makes about 70 cookies

Cookies can be kept in refrigerator for two weeks or frozen for up to one month. Unbaked dough can be stored in refrigerator for up to three days or frozen for up to two months. To freeze, wrap plastic-wrapped log of dough in foil.

These cookies are delicious. People will reach for a second before they've finished swallowing their first. Like the famously addictive Girl Scout cookie sold once a year in communities around the country, this gluten-free version has a crunchy chocolate mint cookie coated with rich semi-sweet chocolate. It will be a very welcome addition to your cookie-baking repertoire.

¾ cup unsalted butter
1 cup granulated sugar
1 large egg
1 ½ teaspoons pure peppermint extract
½ teaspoon pure vanilla extract
1 ½ cups Brown Rice Flour Mix (188 grams)
¾ cup unsweetened cocoa powder (not Dutch processed)
1 teaspoon xanthan gum
½ teaspoon baking powder
½ teaspoon baking soda
¼ teaspoon salt
20 ounces semi-sweet chocolate, chopped

1. Beat butter and sugar at medium speed in large bowl of electric mixer until light and creamy. Add egg, peppermint extract, and vanilla extract, and beat well.

2. Add flour, cocoa powder, xanthan gum, baking powder, baking soda, and salt; mix until a soft, smooth dough is formed.

3. Divide dough into two equal halves. Drop first half in small mounds across a large sheet of plastic wrap. Fold the plastic over the dough and shape into a long, 1 ½-inch-diameter log, leaving plastic open at the ends. Twist ends and flatten dough at each end. Try to smooth log by rolling back and forth on counter. Repeat with second half of dough. Refrigerate both rolls until well chilled.

4. Preheat oven to 350°F. Position rack in center of oven. Lightly grease cookie sheet with cooking spray.

5. Using a thin, sharp knife, slice chilled dough into ¼-inch slices and place ½ inch apart on cookie sheet. Bake in center of oven for about 8-10 minutes until cooked through (do not over-bake). Allow cookies to sit on the cookie sheet for 2-3 minutes, then transfer to a wire rack and cool completely. *If you chill the cookies at this point until they are very cold, they will firm up and be less fragile for dipping in the chocolate.*

6. Melt chocolate in a double boiler and keep warm. Dip cookies in warm chocolate face down, then turn with an offset spatula (or butter knife) to completely coat. Lift cookie out of pan with the spatula, and then hold it between two fingers while you smooth the chocolate coating and skim off any extra-thick spots with the offset spatula (or butter knife). Place cookie on parchment paper to cool (put the piece of parchment on a baking sheet near the melted chocolate; start by placing cookies at the far end so you don't drip over finished cookies). Allow cookies to cool completely; it is easiest to chill them on the baking sheet in the refrigerator. Store cookies in refrigerator (or a very cool room) in an airtight container.

SNICKERDOODLES

Makes about 50 cookies

After three days, store in refrigerator. Can be kept in refrigerator for two weeks or frozen for up to one month.

* To make cinnamon sugar, combine 3 tablespoons granulated sugar and 1 teaspoon ground cinnamon (or more, to taste) in a small bowl.

What is more classic than a Snickerdoodle? Every family recipe box seems to have a version of this holiday and snack time favorite. The foundation for this one is a simple sugar cookie recipe (from *Gluten-Free Baking Classics*). It only takes a short time to make up the dough, roll it into balls, mash them slightly with a fork, and then sprinkle the tops with cinnamon sugar. You can bake the cookies right away or make the dough and store it in the refrigerator or freezer; you'll be able to make fresh cookies whenever you want them. The sweet smell of cinnamon coming from the oven will have everyone in your home running to the kitchen.

¾ cup unsalted butter
1 cup granulated sugar
1 large egg
1 tablespoon pure vanilla extract
1 ¾ cups Brown Rice Flour Mix (220 grams)
¼ cup sweet rice flour
1 teaspoon baking powder
1 teaspoon xanthan gum
¼ teaspoon salt
Cinnamon sugar*

1. Beat butter and sugar in large bowl of electric mixer until light and creamy. Add egg and vanilla and mix until smooth.

2. Add flours, baking powder, xanthan gum, and salt; beat until a thick, smooth dough is formed.

3. Chill dough in refrigerator for 30 minutes, or until firm enough to handle. You can also shape dough into a round, wrap in plastic wrap and chill for later use. Unbaked dough can be stored in refrigerator for up to one week or frozen for up to two months. To freeze, wrap in plastic wrap and then wrap in foil.

4. Preheat oven to 350°F. Position rack in center of oven. Lightly grease cookie sheet with cooking spray.

5. Use your hands to shape dough into 1-inch balls and place 1 inch apart on cookie sheet. Use a fork to press ball of dough to desired thickness: thinner for crisper cookies, and thicker for softer cookies. Sprinkle with cinnamon sugar.

6. Bake in center of oven for about 12-15 minutes (this depends on thick-

ness) until a very light golden color. Allow cookies to sit on the cookie sheet for 2-3 minutes, then transfer to a wire rack and cool completely. Store in an airtight container.

THUMBPRINT COOKIES

Makes 24 cookies

Filled cookies can be kept in refrigerator for three days or frozen for up to one month. Unbaked dough can be stored in refrigerator for up to one week or frozen for up to two months. To freeze, wrap dough in plastic wrap and then wrap in foil.

Thumbprints are one of those classic American cookies that people always seem to make at the holidays. You'll see them everywhere for about a month, and then you won't see them again until the following year. In reality, they were never one of my favorite cookies. I always thought they were either too big, too doughy, too dry, too flavorless, or too soggy (when they were filled and left at room temperature). But I kept getting requests for thumbprints from readers, and so I was determined to find a recipe that I could look forward to making and eating. After a lot of research into old and new versions (the new recipes were all tweaks of the originals), I found the common thread and started testing. The result is this delicious, firm-yet-crumbly cookie. I like to fill them with jam, but my sons really liked the Nutella version better. In my house, I make a plate of each.

½ cup unsalted butter
½ cup granulated sugar (see Cook's Note below)
1 large egg
1 ½ teaspoons pure vanilla extract
1 ⅓ cups Brown Rice Flour Mix (167 grams)
¼ cup finely ground almonds
½ teaspoon baking powder
½ teaspoon xanthan gum
¼ teaspoon salt
¼ – ½ cup jam or Nutella

1. Beat butter and sugar together in large bowl of electric mixer until light and creamy. Add egg and vanilla and mix until smooth.

2. Add flour, ground almonds, baking powder, xanthan gum, and salt; beat at medium-high speed until a soft, smooth dough is formed. Chill dough in refrigerator for 30 minutes, or until firm enough to handle.

3. Preheat oven to 350°F. Position rack in center of oven. Lightly grease cookie sheet with cooking spray.

4. Use your hands to shape dough into 24 balls and place 1 inch apart on cookie sheet. Very slightly flatten the tops of each ball and using your thumb, or the underside of a rounded (measuring) teaspoon, make a deep indentation into the center of each cookie (but try not to push down to the bottom of the cookie).

5. Bake cookies for about 8 minutes; remove pan and gently press down the centers of the cookies again. Return to oven and bake another 12–14 minutes, or until tops are light golden (the color of wheat) and bottoms are light golden brown (the color of Amstel Light Beer).

If planning to serve the cookies within one day:

6. While cookies are baking, warm jam in a small saucepan over low heat until it softens and becomes slightly pourable (if using Nutella, do not warm in a pan; it should be at room temperature). After the cookies have finished baking, immediately fill the indentation in each cookie with enough warm jam (or Nutella) to bulge over the top of the cookie. Allow cookies to sit on the cookie sheet for 2 minutes, then transfer to a wire rack and cool completely. Store filled cookies in an airtight container in refrigerator (first chill filled cookies before stacking them in container to firm up the jam; separate layers of filled cookies with parchment paper). After three days, store any leftovers in freezer (this will help to keep the cookies from absorbing moisture from the jam).

If not serving the cookies within one day:

7. Do not fill with jam (or Nutella). Store unfilled cookies in refrigerator for up to one week and then fill with jam (or Nutella) only when ready to serve. For longer storage, freeze unfilled cookies for up to one month and then fill with jam when ready to serve. Follow instructions for filling and storing filled cookies in Step 6 above.

Cook's Note: The cookie itself is not overly sweet and relies more on the filling to up the sweet factor; you can add another 2-3 tablespoons of sugar if desired.

PEANUT BUTTER COOKIES

Makes about 36 cookies. Recipe can be doubled.

After three days, store in refrigerator. Can be kept in refrigerator for two weeks or frozen for up to one month.

These old-fashioned peanut butter cookies will vanish out of your cookie jar. Their crisp-on-the-outside, chewy-on-the-inside texture and rich, nutty flavor make them the perfect treat to serve with a glass of milk. Put some out on a plate for the hungry mouths around your table in the afternoon after school or sports practices, or pack them to go for Saturday afternoon hikes and fishing trips.

½ cup unsalted butter or shortening
¾ cup chunky peanut butter (not "natural-style")
½ cup packed dark brown sugar
⅓ cup granulated sugar
1 large egg
1 teaspoon pure vanilla extract
1 cup Brown Rice Flour Mix (125 grams)
2 tablespoons sweet rice flour
¾ teaspoon baking soda
½ teaspoon baking powder
½ teaspoon xanthan gum
⅛ teaspoon salt
Granulated sugar, optional

1. Beat butter in large bowl of electric mixer until smooth and creamy. Add the peanut butter and sugars and beat 2-3 minutes until fluffy. Add egg and vanilla and mix until smooth.

2. Add flours, baking soda, baking powder, xanthan gum, and salt; beat until a thick, smooth dough is formed. If needed, chill dough in refrigerator for 15-30 minutes, or until firm enough to handle. You can also shape dough into a round, wrap in plastic wrap, and chill for later use. Unbaked dough can be stored in refrigerator for up to one week or frozen for up to two months. To freeze, wrap in plastic wrap and then wrap in foil.

3. Preheat oven to 350°F. Position rack in center of oven. Lightly grease cookie sheet with cooking spray.

4. Use your hands to shape dough into 1-inch balls, and place 1 inch apart on cookie sheet. Use a fork to press ball of dough to desired thickness and to make a crosshatch pattern: thinner for crisper cookies and thicker for softer cookies (if needed, dip fork in warm water to keep it from sticking to dough). Sprinkle tops with additional granulated sugar, if desired.

5. Bake in center of oven for about 12 minutes until a very light golden color (check after 10 minutes; bake time depends on thickness and how soft or firm you want the cookies). Allow cookies to sit on the cookie sheet for 2-3 minutes, then transfer to a wire rack and cool completely. Store in an airtight container.

LEMON TEA COOKIES

*Makes about 60 cookies.
Recipe can be cut in half.*

*After three days, store
cookies in refrigerator.
Can be kept in
refrigerator for two
weeks or frozen for up to
one month. Unbaked
dough can be stored in
refrigerator for up to one
week or frozen for up to
two months. To freeze,
wrap plastic-wrapped log
of dough in foil.*

These light, melt-in-your-mouth cookies have a bright lemon flavor. Dust them with powdered sugar after they cool, and you'll have a lemon "melt-away" cookie that your friends and family will love. Perfect for a teatime treat, a holiday cookie tray, or a picnic lunch, this is a cookie you'll find yourself making all year long.

¾ cup unsalted butter
½ cup confectioners' sugar
1 tablespoon packed grated lemon rind
2 teaspoons pure vanilla extract
¾ teaspoon pure lemon extract
1 ⅔ cups Brown Rice Flour Mix (208 grams)
⅓ cup sweet rice flour
½ teaspoon xanthan gum
¼ teaspoon salt
½ – ¾ cup confectioners' sugar, for coating cookies

1. Beat butter and confectioners' sugar in large bowl of electric mixer until light and fluffy. Add lemon rind, vanilla extract, and lemon extract, and mix until smooth.

2. Add flours, xanthan gum, and salt; beat until a smooth dough is formed.

3. Drop half of dough in small mounds across a large sheet of plastic wrap. Fold the plastic over the dough and shape into a long, 1-inch-diameter log, leaving plastic open at the ends. Twist ends and flatten dough at each end. Try to smooth log by rolling back and forth on counter. Repeat with second half of dough. Refrigerate both rolls until well chilled.

4. Preheat oven to 350°F. Position rack in center of oven. Lightly grease cookie sheet with cooking spray.

5. Using a thin, sharp knife, slice chilled dough into ¼-inch slices and place 1 inch apart on cookie sheet. Bake in center of oven for about 12 minutes, or until a very light golden color. Allow cookies to sit on the cookie sheet for 2–3 minutes, then cool slightly on a rack. Put confectioners' sugar in a small bowl, then coat cookies several at a time until they are completely covered. Store in an airtight container.

MORAVIAN SPICE COOKIES

Wheat flour-based Moravian cookies have graced holiday cookie plates for generations, but you'll be amazed at how good they are in their new gluten-free form. Spicy, crisp, and just a little bit exotic, these cookies are delicious. My classic recipe pairs the rich, sweet flavors of molasses and brown sugar to the warm embrace of cinnamon, ginger, and cloves. Even if you've never made them before, the steps below will carefully guide you to ensure that you get perfectly formed, crisp cookies with just the right bite.

1 ¼ cups Brown Rice Flour Mix (155 grams)
1 teaspoon baking soda
1 teaspoon ground cinnamon
1 teaspoon ground ginger
¾ teaspoon xanthan gum
½ – ¾ teaspoon ground cloves
¼ teaspoon salt
3 tablespoons vegetable shortening
¼ cup packed dark brown sugar
⅓ cup molasses

1. Combine flour, baking soda, cinnamon, ginger, xanthan gum, cloves, and salt in a small bowl. Set aside.

2. Beat shortening, brown sugar, and molasses in large bowl of electric mixer until smooth and creamy. Add flour mixture; mix until very well combined. Be sure to scrape bottom of bowl. Shape dough into two 1-inch high disks. Roll each disk between two large sheets of wax paper until very thin (less than ⅛-inch, if possible). Then put each rolled-out piece of cookie dough in the refrigerator or freezer to chill until very cold (if not baking within four hours, wrap the rolled dough in plastic wrap so that it doesn't dry out).

3. Preheat oven to 325°F. Position rack in center of oven. Line large cookie sheet with parchment paper.

4. Cut rolled out cookie dough with a 2-inch fluted cookie cutter. Lift cookies onto prepared cookie sheet with a spatula and place about ½ inch apart. If you have trouble lifting the cookies off the wax paper, cover the dough with the other sheet of wax paper and return it to the freezer until the cookies are hard enough to lift onto the cookie sheet.

Makes about 60 cookies

After two weeks, store baked cookies in refrigerator. Can be kept in refrigerator for two weeks or frozen for up to six weeks. Unbaked dough can be kept in refrigerator for up to five days or frozen for up to six weeks. To freeze, wrap in plastic wrap and then foil.

5. Bake in center of oven for 8-10 minutes until cooked through *(cookies will crisp as they cool, but if not fully baked, they will not get crisp)*. Allow cookies to sit on the cookie sheet for 1 minute. Lift cookies on parchment paper onto a rack to cool. Store in an airtight container.

Cook's Note: For slightly less spice use ¾ teaspoon ground cinnamon, ¾ teaspoon ground ginger, and ½ teaspoon ground cloves.

ANISE SESAME COOKIES

Aromatic and enticing, my anise sesame cookies have a slightly soft, crumbly texture, and just enough sweetness to pair well with an after-dinner dessert wine or a late morning cup of coffee. The subtle anise flavor and slight nutty crunch of the sesame seeds are a winning combination. The cookies are easy to make and just addictive enough that you may want to make an extra batch to hide away in your freezer.

½ cup shortening
6 tablespoons granulated sugar
1 large egg
1 teaspoon pure anise extract
1 cup Brown Rice Flour Mix (125 grams)
¼ cup sweet rice flour
¼ teaspoon very finely ground anise seeds
½ teaspoon baking powder
¾ teaspoon xanthan gum
⅛ teaspoon salt
1 tablespoon sesame seeds
1 large egg, beaten

1. Beat shortening and sugar together in large bowl of electric mixer until light and creamy. Add egg and anise extract and mix until smooth.

2. Add flours, anise seed, baking powder, xanthan gum, and salt; beat at medium-high speed until a soft, smooth dough is formed. Mix in sesame seeds. Chill dough in refrigerator for 30 minutes, or until firm enough to handle.

3. Preheat oven to 350°F. Position rack in center of oven. Lightly grease cookie sheet with cooking spray.

4. Spoon the dough into 24 equal-sized portions on a sheet of wax paper. Use your hands to shape dough into 24 2-inch-long log-shaped ovals (about ⅝-inch high), and place 1 inch apart on cookie sheet. Press very slightly on the tops to flatten the logs (the logs should now be about ½ inch high, with rounded ends and a slightly flattened top). Brush tops and sides with beaten egg. Bake in center of oven 16–18 minutes; cookie tops will be a pale golden color, and bottoms should be light golden brown. Allow cookies to sit on cookie sheet for 2 minutes, then transfer cookies to a wire rack and cool completely. Store in an airtight container.

Makes 24 cookies. Recipe can be doubled.

After three days, store cookies in refrigerator. Can be kept in refrigerator for two weeks or frozen for up to one month. Unbaked dough can be stored in refrigerator for up to one week or frozen for up to two months. To freeze, wrap dough in plastic wrap and then wrap in foil.

LEMON SANDWICH COOKIES

Makes about 30 filled cookies. Recipe can be doubled.

Filled cookies can be kept in refrigerator for five days or frozen for two to three weeks (they absorb moisture from the filling over time; the rate depends on how often you open the container). Unfilled cookies can be kept in refrigerator for up to two weeks or frozen for one month. Unbaked dough can be stored in refrigerator for up to one week or frozen for one month. To freeze, wrap logs in plastic wrap and then in foil.

Pass around a big plate of these old-fashioned lemon sandwich cookies and watch them disappear. The delicate, crunchy cookie has a great-tasting, bright lemon flavor. And the cool, rich cream cheese filling is tangy with just the right amount of sweetness. These cookies are the perfect indulgence to have on hand for afternoon snacks or an after-dinner treat.

½ cup unsalted butter
½ cup granulated sugar
1 large egg
1 teaspoon packed grated lemon rind
¾ teaspoon pure lemon extract
½ teaspoon pure vanilla extract
1 ½ cups Brown Rice Flour Mix (188 grams)
½ teaspoon baking powder
½ teaspoon xanthan gum
¼ teaspoon salt

Filling

4 ounces cream cheese, at room temperature
4 tablespoons unsalted butter, softened
1 teaspoon pure lemon extract
¼ teaspoon pure vanilla extract
1 ¼ cups confectioners' sugar

1. Beat butter and sugar together in large bowl of electric mixer until light and creamy. Add egg, lemon rind, lemon extract, and vanilla extract; mix until smooth.

2. Add flour, baking powder, xanthan gum, and salt; beat at medium-high speed until a soft, smooth dough is formed.

3. Shape dough into a flat square and wrap in wax paper; refrigerate for 30 minutes. Divide dough in half. Take the first half and shape it into a 1 ½-inch-round by 6 ½-inch-long log by rolling it in the plastic wrap (break the dough into small mounds, place in a row on a large sheet of plastic wrap, then roll); leave plastic open at the ends. Twist ends, and flatten dough at each end. Try to smooth log by rolling back and forth on counter. Repeat with second half of dough. Refrigerate both rolls until very well chilled.

4. Preheat oven to 350°F. Position rack in center of oven. Lightly grease cookie sheet with cooking spray.

5. Take the first log, and using a thin, sharp knife, slice the chilled dough into 30 slices (about $\frac{1}{8}$-inch thin) and place about 1 inch apart on cookie sheet. Bake in center of oven for about 12–14 minutes, or until tops are a light golden color; bottoms should be very dark golden. Allow cookies to sit on the cookie sheet for 2 minutes, then transfer to a wire rack and cool completely. Repeat with second log of dough. Put cookies on a large plate, cover with foil, and freeze until hard (this will make it easier to handle them when you are spreading on the filling).

6. *To make Filling:* Beat cream cheese and butter in large bowl of electric mixer until smooth. Add lemon extract and vanilla extract, then gradually add confectioners' sugar and beat until very light and creamy.

7. *To fill cookies:* Spoon about 1 heaping teaspoon of filling onto the flat side of one cookie. Top with another cookie, flat side down. Repeat with remaining cookies. Store in a tightly sealed container in refrigerator.

CHOCOLATE BROWNIE COOKIES

Makes 40 cookies

Best when eaten within three days of baking. After three days, store in refrigerator. Can be kept in refrigerator for two weeks or frozen for up to three weeks.

* I recommend Nielsen-Massey Pure Chocolate Extract.

These delectable cookies have the rich, chocolate flavor of brownies. You can mix the dough in minutes and have a plate of warm cookies to serve in no time. Originally created with grownups in mind (that plan failed miserably when plates of freshly baked cookies became a kid magnet), they are not overly sweet. But the cookies are rich and "chocolatey" enough to satisfy a dessert craving by just eating one or two.

½ cup unsalted butter, softened
¾ cup packed dark brown sugar
2 large eggs
2 tablespoons Kahlua Liqueur (or strong coffee)
1 teaspoon pure vanilla extract
½ teaspoon pure chocolate extract*
1 cup Brown Rice Flour Mix (125 grams)
2 tablespoons sweet rice flour
⅓ cup unsweetened cocoa powder (not Dutch processed)
½ teaspoon baking soda
½ teaspoon xanthan gum
½ teaspoon salt
¼ teaspoon baking powder
⅔ cup mini chocolate chips

1. Preheat oven to 350°F. Position rack in center of oven. Lightly spray cookie sheet with cooking spray.

2. Beat butter and sugar at medium speed in large bowl of electric mixer until well blended. Add eggs, Kahlua, vanilla extract, and chocolate extract; beat until smooth. Reduce speed to low and add flours, cocoa powder, baking soda, xanthan gum, salt, and baking powder ; mix until smooth. Mix in chocolate chips.

3. Drop by rounded teaspoon onto prepared baking sheets. Bake for about 8 minutes until cooked through; do not over-bake. Allow cookies to sit on the cookie sheet for 2 minutes, then transfer to a wire rack and cool completely. Store in airtight container.

OLD-FASHIONED PUMPKIN COOKIES

Makes 60 small cookies

Best when eaten within three days of baking. After three days, store in refrigerator. Can be kept in refrigerator for two weeks or frozen for up to three weeks.

When it's time for dessert, bring out a plate of these Old- Fashioned Pumpkin Cookies. This traditional cookie is filled with nutrient- and fiber-rich pumpkin and the home-spun flavors of cinnamon and nutmeg. They're easy to make and can be baked earlier in the day, or even the day before you plan to serve them. Keep them stored in an airtight container until it's time to eat.

½ cup unsalted butter, softened
1 cup granulated sugar
1 cup Libby's® 100% Pure Pumpkin
1 large egg
1 teaspoon pure vanilla extract
1 ¾ cups Brown Rice Flour Mix (220 grams)
¼ cup sweet rice flour
1 ¼ teaspoons ground cinnamon
1 teaspoon baking soda
1 teaspoon baking powder
¾ teaspoon xanthan gum
½ teaspoon ground nutmeg
½ teaspoon salt
Vanilla Icing or White Chocolate Glaze (recipes follow)

1. Preheat oven to 350°F. Position rack in center of oven. Lightly spray cookie sheet with cooking spray.

2. Beat butter and sugar at medium speed in large bowl of electric mixer until well blended. Add pumpkin, egg, and vanilla; beat until smooth. Reduce speed to low and add flours, cinnamon, baking soda, baking power, xanthan gum, nutmeg, and salt; mix until smooth.

3. Drop by rounded teaspoon onto prepared baking sheets. Bake for about 12–15 minutes, until cooked through and edges are slightly browned and firm. Allow cookies to sit on the cookie sheet for 2 minutes, then transfer to a wire rack and cool completely.

4. Drizzle Vanilla Icing or White Chocolate Glaze (recipes below) over cookies. Store in airtight container.

Vanilla Icing

1 ¼ cups confectioners' sugar
2 tablespoons milk

1 teaspoon light corn syrup
½ teaspoon pure vanilla extract

1. Combine confectioners' sugar, milk, light corn syrup, and vanilla in a small bowl, and stir until smooth and creamy. Add more milk if necessary.

White Chocolate Glaze

4 ounces white chocolate
2 ½ tablespoons unsalted butter

1. Melt white chocolate and butter in a small heavy saucepan over medium-low heat; stir constantly until smooth. Immediately remove from heat and cool slightly. *Glaze can be made ahead and rewarmed in microwave. Store tightly covered in refrigerator for up to three weeks.*

CHOCOLATE WHOOPIE PIES

Makes 22 small whoopie pies. Recipe can be cut in half.

Best when eaten within three days of baking. Store in the refrigerator in a tightly sealed container up to five days, or at room temperature for up to two days (after two days at room temperature, the cookies start to absorb too much moisture from the filling). Can be frozen and then stored in a tightly sealed container for up to three weeks (freeze until solid in a single layer before stacking between parchment paper).

Who doesn't love a little whoopie now and then? When I started seeing whoopie pies in stores, bakeries, and farm markets in every conceivable size, color, and flavor, I knew it was time to make them myself. I stayed as close to "classic" as possible; my gluten-free version has a tender, flavorful chocolate cake-like cookie and a semi-classic vanilla filling. I say "semi" because there seems to be a lot of debate in the whoopie pie world about exactly what was in the original filling. Modern-day recipes feature everything from straight shortening to a mixture of butter and shortening, or butter and marshmallow cream, to a more time-consuming cooked version with milk and flour. I opted for easy and delicious, and went with the butter-marshmallow cream combination. You'll find these cookies are great for snacking, lunches, parties, and picnics. They're even better on the second day, so you might have to hide them. (And they freeze really well.)

½ cup unsalted butter
1 cup granulated sugar
1 large egg
1 ½ teaspoons pure chocolate extract
1 teaspoon pure vanilla extract
1 ½ cups Brown Rice Flour Mix (188 grams)
⅔ cup unsweetened cocoa powder (not Dutch processed)
1 teaspoon baking soda
1 teaspoon baking powder
¾ teaspoon xanthan gum
½ teaspoon salt
¾ cup plus 3 tablespoons milk

Filling

¾ cup unsalted butter, softened
2 tablespoons milk
2 teaspoons pure vanilla extract
1 ½ cups confectioners' sugar
1 cup marshmallow cream

1. Preheat oven to 350°F. Position rack in center of oven. Line cookie sheet with parchment paper.

2. Beat butter and sugar in large bowl of electric mixer until pale and fluffy. Add egg and beat until smooth and creamy. Mix in chocolate

extract and vanilla extract. Add flour, cocoa powder, baking soda, baking power, xanthan gum, salt, and milk; mix about 2-3 minutes until creamy.

3. Drop by tablespoon onto prepared baking sheets about 2 inches apart (make 44 cookies). Smooth tops of cookies with fingertip, if needed. Bake about 10 minutes until cooked through and springy to the touch; do not over-bake or they dry out (if undercooked, they will deflate). Cool on baking sheets for 2 minutes; remove to wire racks to cool completely.

4. *To make Filling:* Beat butter in large bowl of electric mixer until smooth. Add milk and vanilla, then gradually add confectioners' sugar and beat until light and creamy. Add marshmallow cream and beat until light and fluffy.

5. *To fill cookies:* Spoon about 1 heaping tablespoon of filling onto the flat side of one cookie. Top with another cookie, flat side down. Repeat with remaining cookies.

PUMPKIN WHOOPIE PIES

Makes 30 mini whoopie pies. Recipe can be cut in half.

Best when eaten within three days of baking. Store in refrigerator in a tightly sealed container for up to five days, or at room temperature for up to two days (after two days at room temperature, the cookies start to absorb too much moisture from the filling). Can be frozen and then stored in a tightly sealed container for up to three weeks (freeze until solid in a single layer before stacking between parchment paper).

Whoopie pie fans all seem to have their favorites flavors, but chocolate and pumpkin are the only ones I ever get requests for. These pumpkin whoopie pies have all the warm flavors of a big Thanksgiving pumpkin pie blended into a small, hand-held treat. My recipe makes honey colored, cake-like cookies that are tender and moist. The vanilla filling is really soft and light because I combined a classic, cream cheese filling with quintessential marshmallow cream. Once you bake up a batch and serve them on a plate to your family and friends, this recipe is sure to become a much-requested part of your own whoopie pie-baking repertoire.

2 large eggs
1 cup granulated sugar
1 cup Libby's® 100% Pure Pumpkin
2 tablespoons molasses
1 teaspoon pure vanilla extract
1 ⅔ cups Brown Rice Flour Mix (208 grams)
1 ¼ teaspoons ground cinnamon
1 teaspoon baking soda
1 teaspoon baking powder
¾ teaspoon xanthan gum
½ teaspoon ground nutmeg
½ teaspoon ground ginger
½ teaspoon salt
½ cup canola oil

Filling

4 ounces cream cheese, at room temperature
6 tablespoons unsalted butter, softened
2 teaspoons pure vanilla extract
1 ½ cups confectioner's sugar
1 cup marshmallow cream

1. Preheat oven to 350°F. Position rack in center of oven. Line cookie sheet with parchment paper.

2. Beat eggs in large bowl of electric mixer until lemon colored. Slowly add sugar a little at a time; beat until mixture turns pale yellow and thick. Mix in the pumpkin, molasses, and vanilla; beat until very

smooth. Add flour, cinnamon, baking soda, baking power, xanthan gum, nutmeg, ginger, salt and oil; mix about 1 minute until smooth and well blended.

3. Drop by rounded teaspoon onto prepared baking sheets about 1 inch apart (make 60 cookies*). Smooth tops of cookies with finger tip, if needed. Bake 10-12 minutes, until cooked through and springy to the touch. Cool on baking sheets for 2 minutes; remove to wire racks to cool completely.

4. **To make Filling:** Beat cream cheese and butter in large bowl of electric mixer until smooth. Add vanilla, then gradually add confectioners' sugar and beat until light and creamy. Add marshmallow cream and beat until light.

5. **To fill cookies:** Spoon about 1 heaping tablespoon of filling onto the flat side of one cookie. Top with another cookie, flat side down. Repeat with remaining cookies.

Cook's Notes: Cookies are very moist the first few days and are best stored in a single layer. Use a small spatula to lift them from solid surfaces (i.e., cookie sheets and containers) so the bottoms remain intact.

To make 22 slightly larger whoopie pies, make 44 cookies and bake 12 to 14 minutes.

LADYFINGERS

Makes 40 cookies

Can be made a day ahead. Store in tightly sealed container for two days at room temperature or up to two weeks in the freezer. Best when eaten within two days of baking.

When I was young, my mother would serve ladyfingers with whipped cream and fresh strawberries when they were in season. I really loved this simple dessert combination and started to miss it after several years on a gluten-free diet. I tried some of the gluten-free ladyfingers sold in stores, but they lacked the soft texture and fresh flavor of the wheat versions, so I decided to make them myself. My gluten-free ladyfingers are light and spongy, with just the right touch of vanilla. You can use them to make tiramisu and trifle, or you can serve them alongside berries and whipped cream as my mother did. They're so delicious you might even be tempted to eat one by itself with a cup of tea.

¾ cup Brown Rice Flour Mix (95 grams)
½ teaspoon baking powder
¼ teaspoon xanthan gum
⅛ teaspoon salt
3 large eggs, separated, at room temperature
¾ cup granulated sugar, divided
1 large egg
2 teaspoons pure vanilla extract
¼ teaspoon pure almond extract
Confectioners' sugar for dusting over top, optional

1. Preheat oven to 350°F. Position two racks in upper and lower middle of oven. Line two large cookie sheets with parchment paper and spray very lightly with cooking spray.

2. Whisk flour, baking powder, xanthan gum, and salt together in a small bowl. Set aside.

3. Beat the 3 egg whites in large bowl of electric mixer. Start mixer at medium speed and beat until whites are foamy. Gradually increase speed to high. Add ¼ cup of the sugar, 1 tablespoon at a time, beating until sugar dissolves and whites form medium soft peaks (make sure it is not too soft). Do not scrape bowl while beating. Set aside.

4. Beat the 3 egg yolks and 1 large egg in large bowl of electric mixer until thick and lemon colored. Add remaining ½ cup sugar gradually, 1 tablespoon at a time, and continue to beat until light. Add flour mixture, vanilla extract, and almond extract; mix until smooth. Batter will be thick.

5. Fold $\frac{1}{3}$ of the beaten egg whites into the batter to lighten it; gently fold in remaining egg whites. Use a pastry bag with a $\frac{1}{2}$-inch smooth round opening at the tip. Fill the pastry bag with the batter and squeeze it onto the prepared baking sheet in 4-inch long finger-shaped strips that are 1 inch apart. Put 20 ladyfingers on each cookie sheet in two rows of 10.

6. Bake for 7 minutes and then quickly switch the baking sheets around in the oven; bake another 5 to 7 minutes until the cookies are lightly browned. Remove the cookie sheets from the oven and slide the parchment paper (with the cookies still on it) onto a counter. When the cookies are completely cool, remove them with a spatula. If desired, sprinkle with additional confectioners' sugar before serving.

MADELEINES

Madeleines are tiny sponge-cake like cookies that are baked in a shell-shaped mold. Fragrant, tender, and sporting a wonderful crisp outer crust, they are truly delectable fresh from the oven. Although classic French versions sometimes include honey and nuts, my two gluten-free favorites are vanilla and lemon (both are below). They're simple to make and almost indistinguishable from wheat versions. Enjoy them both with a cup of tea, or for dessert after a special meal.

¾ cup Brown Rice Flour Mix (95 grams)
½ teaspoon baking powder
¼ teaspoon xanthan gum
⅛ teaspoon salt
2 large eggs, at room temperature
⅔ cup granulated sugar
2 teaspoons pure vanilla extract
6 tablespoons unsalted butter, melted and cooled
Confectioners' sugar for dusting over top

1. Preheat oven to 375°F (if you have dark pans,* preheat oven to 350°F). Position rack in center of oven. Spray two 12-mold (3-inch each) madeleine pans with cooking spray and dust with plain rice flour. I strongly recommend using a non-stick pan (light or dark non-stick).**

2. Whisk flour, baking powder, xanthan gum, and salt together in a small bowl. Set aside.

3. Beat eggs in large bowl of electric mixer until lemon- colored. Slowly add sugar a little at a time, then beat until mixture turns pale yellow and thick. Mix in the vanilla. Sprinkle a small amount of the flour mixture over the top of the egg mixture and fold it in to lighten it, then gently fold the rest of the flour mixture into the egg mixture.

4. Spoon a couple tablespoons of the batter into the melted butter to lighten it, then gradually fold the melted butter mixture into the lightened batter in three additions. Spoon about 1 tablespoon of the batter into the center of each prepared mold (don't worry if it isn't perfectly smooth).

5. Place one of the pans in the center of the rack and bake about 10 minutes (darker non-stick pans may take a little less time) until puffed and lightly browned around the edges (the tops should spring back when

Makes 24 3-inch cookies

Can be made a day ahead. Store in tightly sealed container for two days at room temperature or up to two weeks in the freezer (rewarm very briefly in the microwave to freshen). Best when eaten immediately, or at least within several hours (keep tightly sealed so they don't dry out).

*Dark pans work well in this recipe.

**If not using a non-stick pan, grease really well.

touched). Do not over-bake or they will dry out. You want to pull them out as soon as they spring back when touched. Repeat with second pan.

6. Unmold the cookies onto a rack (you may need to gently pry some of them out of the pan with a knife or your fingers). Turn each cookie shell side up so it doesn't get indents from the rack. Cool slightly and dust with confectioners' sugar. Serve as soon as possible.

LEMON MADELEINES

In step 3, add 1 teaspoon pure lemon extract, 1 packed teaspoon grated lemon rind, and only 1 teaspoon pure vanilla extract (not 2 teaspoons as in the ingredient list above).

ORANGE WALNUT BISCOTTI

When you're looking for something a little different, these delectable orange walnut biscotti will hit the spot. Crunchy and fragrant with fresh orange, they're perfect alongside your morning coffee or as an afternoon treat with a cup of tea. I also like to serve them after dinner with a chilled dessert wine. So grab a zester and grate yourself some fresh orange rind to make this special recipe. You'll be glad you did.

2 cups Brown Rice Flour Mix (250 grams)
¾ cup granulated sugar
1 packed tablespoon grated orange rind
1 teaspoon baking powder
¾ teaspoon xanthan gum
2 large eggs
⅓ cup canola oil
1 ½ teaspoons pure orange extract
½ teaspoon pure vanilla extract
1 cup coarsely chopped walnuts

1. Preheat oven to 325°F. Lightly grease a large cookie sheet with cooking spray and dust with rice flour.

2. Combine flour, sugar, orange rind, baking powder, and xanthan gum in large bowl of electric mixer. Add eggs, oil, orange extract, and vanilla extract; beat at medium speed until well combined. Mix in walnuts. Dough will be very sticky.

3. Use a spatula and floured hands to shape dough into three logs, each measuring 8 inches long, 2 inches wide, and 1 inch high. Place logs 2 ½ inches apart on prepared cookie sheet.

4. Place in center of oven and bake 30 minutes until light golden. Logs will spread and flatten slightly. Remove to a cutting board and cool 8 minutes.

5. Using a serrated knife, cut logs on the diagonal into ½- to ¾-inch-wide slices. Place biscotti back on the cookie sheet, standing up, and return to oven. Bake about 25 minutes more, until light golden brown. Remove from oven and cool completely on a rack. Store in an airtight container.

Makes about 36 cookies

After three days, store in refrigerator. Can be kept in refrigerator for three weeks or frozen for up to six weeks.

Other Sweet Treats

Chocolate Soufflé

Oatmeal Fig Bars

Pecan Pie Bars

Coconut Custard Bars

Coconut Custard Bars with Chocolate Chips

Lemon Cheesecake Bars

Pumpkin Cheesecake Bars

Chocolate Icebox Cake

Rugelach, Kifli, and Kolacki

Hamanstaschen

Apple Turnovers

Strawberry Buttermilk Shortcakes

Yeast Doughnuts

Fried and Baked

Churros

THIS CHAPTER HAS SOME VERY SPECIAL HEIRLOOM RECIPES THAT YOU AND YOUR FAMILY or friends might have been missing. I revisited some of the many requests I've received over the years to convert cherished family recipes, added a few of my own favorites, and set to work. The result is a mouthwatering collection of recipes that are surprisingly simple to make—even the apple turnovers and the rugelach, which involve some of the more complicated techniques. But as always, I give very specific, detailed instructions for every step to ease your way.

Some of the recipes will become favorites that you'll find yourself making often, like the pecan pie bars, coconut custard bars, or cheesecake bars. Others, like the hamanstaschen, you might save for holidays. But no matter when you decide to fry up a batch of crisp-on-the-outside, tender-on-the-inside yeast doughnuts, or bake up a batch of delicate rugelach, you'll be happy to have these carefully converted gluten-free versions to share with those around your table.

Dairy substitutes: My butter substitute of choice for most of the baked goods in this chapter is Earth Balance® Buttery Spread or Buttery Sticks (not the Shortening Sticks). I did *not* test dairy free versions of the Lemon Cheesecake Bars, Pumpkin Cheesecake Bars, Rugelach, or the Apple Turnover recipes.

This chapter uses the following pans:
- 6-cup (1 ½ quart) soufflé dish
- 9-inch square baking pan
- 8-inch square baking pan
- Large, shiny cookie sheets (or baking sheets) of medium to heavy weight. For best results, I do not recommend super-thick, insulated, or dark metal cookie sheets for my recipes.
- Heavy 3-quart saucepan to fry yeast doughnuts and churros
- Non-stick 6-doughnut baking pan, optional, to make baked yeast doughnuts

The Last Word on Sweet Treats

- Set up before starting the recipe: Assemble all the ingredients.
- Measure carefully.
- Preheat the oven to the proper temperature (make sure the oven is calibrated correctly).
- Do not open the oven door more than necessary.
- Use a timer in case you get distracted.
- Use a candy thermometer to maintain oil temperature for doughnuts and churros.

CHOCOLATE SOUFFLÉ

This no-fail chocolate soufflé is not only wheat-free, it's completely flour free. No more excuses when you're out of flour mix—you'll be able to make a fabulous chocolate dessert whenever the mood strikes. This very dependable and delicious recipe makes a light, airy soufflé that will impress those around your table. Be sure to use a top-quality chocolate for the best results.

Serves 4

½ cup heavy cream
4 ounces good quality semi-sweet chocolate, finely chopped
2 tablespoons Kahlua Liqueur (or brandy)
3 eggs yolks from large eggs, at room temperature*
½ teaspoon pure vanilla extract
5 egg whites from large eggs, at room temperature*
¼ cup granulated sugar
1 tablespoon granulated sugar for dusting soufflé dish

* Separate eggs when they are cold, and then let them warm to room temperature.

1. Preheat oven to 400°F. Position rack in center of oven. Butter a 6-cup (1 ½- quart) soufflé dish and dust with granulated sugar. You can also use an 8-cup (2 quart) soufflé dish; the soufflé will rise well, but it won't rise over the top of the dish to the same extent.

2. Combine heavy cream, chocolate, and Kahlua in a heavy medium saucepan over low heat; stir constantly until chocolate is melted. Remove from heat.

3. Beat egg yolks in a small bowl with a whisk. Add a little bit of the hot chocolate sauce and beat well to temper the eggs. Add egg yolk mixture to chocolate sauce and mix until well blended. Add vanilla and stir to combine. Set aside.

4. Put egg whites in large clean bowl of electric mixer. Use clean whisk attachment on medium speed to beat egg whites until foamy. Turn mixer to medium-high and add sugar a little at a time. Turn mixer to high and beat egg whites until stiff peaks form (or hand-whisk egg whites in a large copper mixing bowl).

5. Stir about a cup of the whites into the chocolate mixture to lighten it. Then quickly pour this mixture onto one side of the electric mixer bowl containing the stiff egg whites. Gently fold the egg whites into the chocolate mixture using a large rubber spatula (this should not take longer than about 45–50 seconds. Don't worry if a few streaks of egg white remain). Pour into prepared soufflé dish. Place in oven and turn down oven temperature to 375°F.

6. Bake for about 30 minutes, until soufflé has risen and set. Do not open oven while soufflé is baking (or until at least 30 minutes have passed). Serve immediately.

OATMEAL FIG BARS

Chewy oatmeal, sweet, tender figs, and crunchy walnuts all wrapped into one mouth-watering treat. These oatmeal fig bars will really hit the spot when you're looking for a little comfort baked up in the shape of a bar. They taste best at room temperature, when all the flavor nuances of the figs, oatmeal, and walnuts are more pronounced. But they freeze really well, so you just might want to keep some tucked away in the freezer; that way you can pull out a couple whenever the mood strikes (just be sure to let them come to room temperature). If you're not a fig lover, you can play around with the fruit in the filling and substitute dried apricots or cherries.

Makes 16 bars

Best when eaten within four days of baking. Store in a tightly sealed container in the refrigerator. Bars can be wrapped with plastic wrap and then with foil and stored in freezer for up to three weeks.

Crust

- 1 cup Brown Rice Flour Mix (125 grams)
- 1 cup gluten-free rolled oats
- ½ cup packed dark brown sugar
- 1 teaspoon xanthan gum
- 10 tablespoons cold unsalted butter (cut into small pieces)
- ½ cup coarsely chopped walnuts, for topping
- ⅓ cup more dark brown sugar, for topping

1. Preheat oven to 350°F. Position rack in center of oven. Grease bottom of 8-inch square baking pan with cooking spray and generously dust with rice flour.

2. Combine flour, oats, ½ cup dark brown sugar, and xanthan gum in large bowl of electric mixer; make sure brown sugar is well incorporated. Add butter and mix on low speed until crumbly. Gently press ⅔ of crust mixture into bottom of baking pan (if you pack the dough too densely, the crust will be hard to get out of the pan. If you pack it too loosely, the crust will be a bit crumbly). Bake in center of oven for 20–22 minutes until very light golden.

3. ***To make topping:*** Mix walnuts and ⅓ cup of the dark brown sugar into remaining ⅓ of crust mixture; set aside.

Fig Filling

- 8 ounces dried Calimyrna figs, trimmed and chopped (about 1 ½ cups)
- ¼ cup granulated sugar
- ½ teaspoon ground cinnamon

1 cup water
1 teaspoon pure vanilla extract

1. Combine figs, sugar, cinnamon, and water in heavy saucepan. Bring to a boil, reduce heat to medium-low, and simmer, uncovered, until figs are very tender and water has evaporated (about 10-15 minutes). Stir occasionally until sugar is dissolved. Remove from heat and transfer to a food processor (you should have a little less than 1 ½ cups before you puree it); add vanilla and puree until smooth.

2. Spread filling onto partially baked crust. Crumble topping over filling and pat it gently into place. Bake in center of oven for about 25 minutes, until topping is set and golden brown. Cool on a wire rack and then chill until cold before cutting into bars. Cut into 16 squares (or triangles) and remove from baking pan. Serve at room temperature (the bars are best at room temperature because the flavors are more pronounced).

PECAN PIE BARS

These addictive pecan pie bars will become a much-requested part of your baking repertoire. More substantial and flavorful than ordinary pecan bars, they're faster and easier to make than pecan pie, and perfect for dessert buffet tables, picnics, barbecues, and afternoon snacks.

Crust

    1 cup Brown Rice Flour Mix (125 grams)
    2 tablespoons granulated sugar
    2 tablespoons packed dark brown sugar
    1 teaspoon xanthan gum
    5 tablespoons cold unsalted butter

1. Preheat oven to 350°F. Position rack in center of oven. Grease bottom of 9-inch square baking pan with cooking spray and generously dust with rice flour.

2. Put flour, sugar, dark brown sugar, and xanthan gum in large bowl of electric mixer; mix to blend. Add butter and mix on low speed until crumbly. Gently press into bottom of baking pan (if you pack the dough too densely, the crust will be hard to get out of the pan. If you pack it too loosely, the crust will be a bit crumbly).

3. Bake in center of oven for 10 minutes or until very light golden.

Pecan Filling

    ⅔ cup granulated sugar
    ⅔ cup light corn syrup
    ⅓ cup unsalted butter
    ¼ teaspoon salt
    2 large eggs
    2 teaspoons pure vanilla extract
    1 ½ cups pecans, chopped

1. Combine sugar, corn syrup, butter, and salt in heavy saucepan over medium heat; stir frequently until sugar is dissolved. Remove from heat.

Makes 16 bars

Best when eaten within four days of baking. Bars can be wrapped with plastic wrap and then with foil and stored in freezer for up to three weeks. Pecan Pie Bars freeze well.

2. Beat the eggs in a small bowl and quickly whisk into saucepan. Add vanilla and pecans; mix well. Pour onto partially baked crust.

3. Bake in center of oven for about 25 minutes until center is set. Cool on a wire rack, then chill until cold before cutting into bars. Cut into 16 squares (or triangles) and remove from baking pan. Serve at room temperature or slightly chilled.

COCONUT CUSTARD BARS

Makes 16 bars

I created these flavorful custard bars one spring day when I was hungry for something "coconuty." I didn't feel like a coconut cream pie or a cake with icing. I wanted something simple, like a lemon square. I searched for a recipe but found none along the lines of what I was craving, so I tinkered a bit and came up with this delectable treat. They're thicker than a lemon square, more along the lines of a coconut custard pie bar, and they have a lovely, unique texture because the recipe uses coconut milk instead of whole milk or cream. Bake up a batch soon, to soothe any coconut longings you're harboring of your own.

Store any leftover bars in a tightly sealed container in refrigerator. Best when eaten within four days of baking. Bars can be wrapped with plastic wrap and then with foil and stored in freezer for up to three weeks. Coconut Custard Bars freeze well.

Crust

1 cup Brown Rice Flour Mix (125 grams)
¼ cup granulated sugar
1 teaspoon xanthan gum
5 tablespoons cold unsalted butter, cut into 5 pieces

1. Preheat oven to 350°F. Position rack in center of oven. Grease bottom of an 8-inch square baking pan with cooking spray and generously dust with rice flour.

2. Put flour, sugar, and xanthan gum in large bowl of electric mixer; mix to blend. Add butter, and mix on low speed until crumbly. Gently press into bottom of baking pan (if you pack the dough too densely, the crust will be hard to get out of the pan. If you pack it too loosely, the crust will be a bit crumbly).

3. Bake in center of oven for 15 minutes or until very light golden.

Coconut Filling

3 large eggs
⅔ cup granulated sugar
2 tablespoons Brown Rice Flour Mix
½ teaspoon baking powder
⅛ teaspoon salt
¾ cup well shaken canned coconut milk
¼ - ½ teaspoon coconut extract (to taste)
½ teaspoon pure vanilla extract
⅔ cup sweetened flaked coconut

1. Beat eggs in large bowl of electric mixer at high speed until foamy. Add sugar, flour, baking powder, salt, coconut milk, coconut extract, vanilla extract, and flaked coconut. Beat until well blended. Pour into partially baked crust.

2. Bake in center of oven for about 35 minutes or until set (knife will come out clean). Cool on wire rack, then chill until cold before cutting into bars. Cut into 16 squares (or triangles) and remove from baking pan. Serve at room temperature or slightly chilled. Can be made a day ahead.

COCONUT CUSTARD BARS
with Chocolate Chips

Follow Step 1 to make the Coconut Filling, then stir ½ cup chocolate chips into the filling or sprinkle them over the top. Proceed with Step 2.

LEMON CHEESECAKE BARS

Makes 9 to 16 bars

Store in refrigerator for up to three days. Bars can be wrapped with plastic wrap and then with foil and stored in freezer for up to two weeks.

When you have the hankering for a little cheesecake, but you don't feel like making a whole one, these bars will come in very handy. The recipe makes a classic lemon-laced cream cheese filling on a delicious shortbread crust. In less than an hour, you'll have a great dessert for a quiet dinner with friends or a summer barbecue. These cheesecake bars are also ideal for serve-yourself holiday dessert tables.

Crust

> 1 cup Brown Rice Flour Mix (125 grams)
> ¼ cup granulated sugar
> 1 teaspoon xanthan gum
> 5 tablespoons cold unsalted butter

1. Preheat oven to 350°F. Position rack in center of oven. Grease bottom of 9-inch-square baking pan with cooking spray and generously dust with rice flour.

2. Put flour, sugar, and xanthan gum in large bowl of electric mixer; mix to blend. Add butter and mix on low speed until crumbly. Gently press into bottom of baking pan (if you pack the dough too densely, the crust will be hard to get out of the pan. If you pack it too loosely, the crust will be a bit crumbly).

3. Bake in center of oven for 10 minutes or until very light golden.

Cream Cheese Filling

> 2 8-oz. packages cream cheese (not low fat)
> ⅔ cup granulated sugar
> 2 large eggs
> 8 ounces sour cream (low-fat can be used)
> 3 tablespoons lemon juice and grated rind of 1 medium lemon
> 1 teaspoon pure vanilla extract

1. Beat cream cheese until smooth in large bowl of electric mixer at medium speed. Reduce speed and slowly add sugar. Beat in eggs one at a time. Scrape bowl and beaters. Add sour cream, lemon juice, grated lemon rind, and vanilla, and mix until well blended. Pour onto partially baked crust.

2. Bake in center of oven for 35–40 minutes until puffed and set. Cool pan on wire rack and then chill until cold. Cut into 9 or 16 squares and remove from baking pan. Serve chilled or at room temperature.

PUMPKIN CHEESECAKE BARS

Makes 9 bars

Store in refrigerator for up to three days. Bars can be wrapped with plastic wrap and then with foil, and stored in freezer for up to two weeks.

I always make a pumpkin cheesecake for Thanksgiving, and it has become one of several desserts that people seem to expect on my holiday dessert table. But sometimes it would be nice to have a little pumpkin cheesecake even when I don't have an extra twelve or more people in the house to help eat it. That's where these bars work their magic. Perfectly sized for autumn dinners with friends, evenings sipping hot mulled cider in front of a bonfire, Sunday brunches, and potlucks—you'll find lots of happy excuses to make them all season long.

Crust

> 1 cup Brown Rice Flour Mix (125 grams)
> 2 tablespoons granulated sugar
> 2 tablespoons packed dark brown sugar
> 1 teaspoon xanthan gum
> 5 tablespoons cold unsalted butter

1. Preheat oven to 350°F. Position rack in center of oven. Grease bottom of 9-inch square baking pan with cooking spray and generously dust with rice flour.

2. Put flour, sugars, and xanthan gum in large bowl of electric mixer; mix to blend. Add butter and mix on low speed until crumbly. Gently press into bottom of baking pan (if you pack the dough too densely, the crust will be hard to get out of the pan. If you pack it too loosely, the crust will be a bit crumbly).

3. Bake in center of oven for 10 minutes or until very light golden.

Cream Cheese Filling

> 2 8-oz. packages cream cheese (not low fat)
> ⅓ cup granulated sugar
> ½ cup packed dark brown sugar
> 2 large eggs
> 1 ¼ cups pumpkin puree
> 1 tablespoon bourbon whisky
> 1 teaspoon pure vanilla extract

2 ½ teaspoons ground cinnamon
½ teaspoon ground nutmeg
½ teaspoon ground ginger
⅛ teaspoon salt

1. Beat cream cheese until smooth in large bowl of electric mixer at medium speed. Reduce speed and slowly add the sugars. Beat in eggs one at a time. Scrape bowl and beaters. Add pumpkin, bourbon, vanilla, cinnamon, nutmeg, ginger and salt and mix until well blended. Pour onto partially baked crust.

2. Bake in center of oven for 35-40 minutes until puffed and set. Cool pan on wire rack and then chill until cold. Cut into 9 squares and remove from baking pan. Serve chilled or at room temperature.

CHOCOLATE ICEBOX CAKE

Makes one long log cake

Best when eaten within two days of putting the whipped cream on the cookies to make the cake.

*You may need more whipped cream than the recipe calls for, depending on how generous you are spreading it between the cookies; I am generous and use more. It is important to have a thick layer on the outside, because the cake absorbs a lot of the whipped cream while resting in the refrigerator.

It all started when my friend Betsy told me she was making a chocolate icebox cake using Nabisco Famous Chocolate Wafers over the Thanksgiving holiday. After years of eating gluten-free, I realized I hadn't made (or eaten) this iconic dessert from my childhood in more than a decade. It was time. Time for a little gluten-free nostalgia. I decided to make the cake the way I remembered it—a long log shape that is sliced on the diagonal; when you place each cut slice on a plate, it looks a little zebra-like. The cookies are stacked side by side, with sweetened whipped cream slathered in between each of them. Then, the whole cookie log is covered with more whipped cream and chocolate shavings. It's fun and delicious, and kids, both young and old, will gobble it up.

1 batch of Chocolate Wafers (recipe follows)
Whipped Cream Topping (recipe follows)*
Grated chocolate or chocolate shavings

1. Spread about 1 tablespoon of whipped cream on one side of each cookie, then stack them in either a long log shape laid across a long serving plate (or to make "cupcakes," stack 4 cookies vertically).

2. Cover the entire outside of the log with the remaining whipped cream and sprinkle grated chocolate or (chocolate shavings) over the top.

3. Refrigerate at least 10 to 12 hours, or up to one day. The cookies should become soft as they absorb some of the moisture from the whipped cream topping. Slice pieces of cake on a diagonal. Serve chilled.

CHOCOLATE WAFERS

Makes about 36 cookies

My gluten-free chocolate wafer is crisp and full of chocolate flavor. Try to cut it as thin as possible, about ⅛ inch, which is easiest to do when the dough is very cold. Try not to over-bake the cookies, but if you under-bake them, they won't be as crisp.

½ cup unsalted butter
½ cup granulated sugar
½ cup packed dark brown sugar
1 large egg white
1 teaspoon pure vanilla extract

½ teaspoon pure chocolate extract*
1 cup Brown Rice Flour Mix (125 grams)
½ cup unsweetened cocoa powder (not Dutch processed)
½ teaspoon xanthan gum
¼ teaspoon baking soda
¼ teaspoon salt

1. Beat butter, granulated sugar, and dark brown sugar in large bowl of electric mixer at medium speed until very well blended. Add egg white, vanilla extract, and chocolate extract, and beat well.

2. Add flour, cocoa powder, xanthan gum, baking soda, and salt; mix until a soft, smooth dough is formed.

3. Drop the dough in small mounds across a large sheet of plastic wrap. Fold the plastic over the dough, and then shape into a 9-inch-long log, leaving plastic open at the ends. Twist ends and flatten dough at each end. Try to smooth log by rolling back and forth on counter. Refrigerate until well chilled.

4. Preheat oven to 350°F. Position rack in center of oven. Line cookie sheet with parchment paper.

5. Using a thin, sharp knife, slice chilled dough into ⅛-inch slices and place 1 inch apart on cookie sheet (be sure the surface of the dough is very smooth before cutting). Bake in center of oven for about 10 minutes until cooked through (do not over-bake). Allow cookies to sit on the cookie sheet for 2 minutes, then transfer to a wire rack and cool completely.

Whipped Cream

2 cups heavy cream
¼ cup confectioners' sugar
1 ½ teaspoons pure vanilla extract

1. Combine heavy cream, confectioners' sugar, and vanilla in large bowl of electric mixer, and beat until stiff peaks form.

Cookies can be kept in refrigerator for two weeks or frozen for up to one month. Unbaked dough can be stored in refrigerator for up to three days or frozen for up to two months. To freeze, wrap plastic-wrapped log of dough in foil.

*I recommend Nielsen-Massey Pure Chocolate Extract.

RUGELACH, KIFLE, AND KOLAKI

Recipe can be doubled

Best when eaten within three days of baking. Refrigerate after one day.

Kifle is a delicate pastry that my family first tasted when friend Natalie Fizer brought us a huge plate as a gift from her Ukrainian-born mother. We devoured them and quickly learned how to make them ourselves. After many years of eating gluten-free, I started to miss baking and eating kifle, so I took out my yellowed recipe and started trying to convert it. While at work, I noticed that it looked exactly like the rugelach and kolacki recipes I'd been sent by readers who wanted help converting their own treasured recipes. After a lot of testing, I came up with a dough that tastes delicious and handles well. The trick is to recognize that there is a "sweet spot" in the chilling process: If the dough is too cold, it will crack when you try to roll it; if it's too warm, it will stick to the parchment paper. The beauty of gluten-free baking is that you never have to let the dough rest to relax the gluten. But here, you have to chill it enough to be able to work with it. I like to fill my pastry with just jam alone, but I've included a nut-sugar-cinnamon option that I sometimes use for a change of pace. Of course, you can use your own family fillings to recreate food memories.

Dough

- 1 cup Brown Rice Flour Mix (125 grams)
- 2 tablespoons granulated sugar
- ½ teaspoon xanthan gum
- ½ teaspoon baking powder
- ¼ teaspoon salt
- 6 tablespoons unsalted butter, at room temperature (but not soft)
- 4 ounces cream cheese (not low fat), at room temperature
- 1 teaspoon rice flour, divided (or more if needed), for rolling dough

Nut Filling

- ½ cup finely chopped walnuts (or nut of choice)
- ½ cup golden raisins, chopped
- 3-4 tablespoons granulated sugar, or to taste
- ¾ teaspoon ground cinnamon

Glaze, optional

- 1 well beaten egg or 3 tablespoons heavy cream
- 1-2 tablespoons granulated sugar or cinnamon sugar**, optional

½ cup apricot, raspberry, or fig jam, or other filling of choice*
Confectioners' sugar, optional (for sifting over cooled, baked Rugelach/ Kifli/Kolacki)

*Jams that contained high fructose corn syrup seemed to melt out of the dough and burn more quickly than those containing regular granulated sugar in my tests.

**Combine 1-2 tablespoons sugar and ¼ – ½ teaspoon ground cinnamon.

RUGELACH

1. Mix flour, sugar, xanthan gum, baking powder, and salt in a small bowl. Set aside.

2. Combine butter and cream cheese in large bowl of electric mixer and beat until well blended and light. Add the flour mixture and mix at very low speed until dough holds together.

3. Move dough onto a piece of plastic wrap and form it into two smooth, equal-sized disks. Wrap each disk in plastic wrap and then chill for 30 minutes to 1 hour in the refrigerator until firm enough to roll. Dough can be frozen at this point for up to one month; wrap in plastic wrap, and then use foil as an outer wrap.

4. *To make Nut Filling (if using):* combine nuts, raisins, sugar, and cinnamon in a small bowl. Set aside.

5. Preheat oven to 350°F. Position rack in center of oven. Line cookie sheet with parchment paper.

6. Take one disk of dough from the refrigerator and roll it between two sheets of wax paper to form a 9-inch round. Take off the top sheet of wax paper and make sure the outer edges are evenly smooth (you can cut and move pieces of dough around the disk, if necessary). Sprinkle ½ teaspoon of the rice flour over the dough and very lightly spread it with your hand. Put the wax paper back over dough and turn the whole rolled disk upside down so that the floured side is on the bottom. Remove the top sheet of wax paper. Repeat with second disk. If dough becomes difficult to work with at any time, return it to the refrigerator until it is no longer sticky.

7. Spread each round with half the jam and half the Nut Filling (if using). Lightly push the nut filling into the dough using the back of a spoon or the extra sheet of wax paper. Use a very thin, sharp knife, or pizza cutter, to cut each round into quarters, then cut each quarter into three pieces. Starting at the large edge, loosely roll up each wedge and place it on the cookie sheet. If the dough is too cold, it will crack when you try to roll it; let it sit for a few minutes. If it's too warm, it will stick to the parchment paper; put it back in the refrigerator for a few minutes. Make sure the points (of dough) are tucked under each rugelach.

8. *To use optional Glaze:* Brush each rugelach with beaten egg or heavy cream (make sure the egg doesn't drip down underneath; it will burn). Sprinkle tops with plain granulated sugar or cinnamon sugar; the sugar will give it a nice crisp outer shell.

Makes 24

9. Bake for 25–30 minutes, until rugelach are puffed, lightly browned (the tops should be firm and will be crisp if you sprinkled them with sugar), and bottoms are browned. Depending on the temperature of your dough and the color and thickness of your pan, your rugelach might be done in less time. Transfer to a rack and cool to room temperature. Lightly dust with confectioners' sugar just before serving, if desired. Store in an airtight container at room temperature.

KIFLI and KOLACKI

Follow Steps 1 through 5 above.

Makes 32

6. Take one disk of dough from the refrigerator and roll it between two sheets of wax paper to form an 8-inch square. Take off the top sheet of wax paper; make sure the outer edges are smooth and even (you can fold them in). Sprinkle ½ teaspoon of the rice flour over the dough, and very lightly spread it with your hand. Put the wax paper back over dough, and turn the whole rolled square upside down so that the floured side is on the bottom. Remove the top sheet of wax paper. Repeat with second disk. If dough becomes difficult to work with at any time, return it to the refrigerator until it is no longer sticky

7. Use a very thin, sharp knife, or pizza cutter, to cut each square into 16 2-inch squares. Spoon 1 scant teaspoon of jam and/or nut filling onto each square, then bring two of the opposite corners together into the center and pinch tightly to close; or roll up corner to corner on the diagonal. If the dough is too cold, it will crack when you try to pinch or roll it; let it sit for a few minutes. If it's too warm, it will stick to the parchment paper; put it back in the refrigerator for a few minutes.

8. ***To use optional Glaze:*** Brush each Kifli/Kolacki with egg wash or heavy cream (make sure the egg doesn't drip down underneath; it will burn), and sprinkle tops with granulated sugar.

9. Bake about 15-20 minutes, until Kifli or Kolacki are puffed, tops are golden, and bottoms are very lightly browned. (The dough here is rolled slightly thinner than in the rugelach recipe above and will take less time to bake; it will be slightly lighter in color.) Transfer to a rack and cool to room temperature. Lightly dust with powdered sugar just before serving, if desired. Store in an airtight container at room temperature.

HAMANTASCHEN

Makes 26–28 cookies

Hamantaschen can be kept in refrigerator for five days or frozen for up to three weeks. Best when eaten within three days of baking.

*Jams that contained high-fructose corn syrup seemed to melt and burn more quickly than those containing regular granulated sugar in my tests.

Every year in the late winter, the siren call goes out for gluten-free hamantaschen recipes. I'd helped many a new-to-gluten-free-baker convert a treasured family recipe, but I didn't have one of my own to offer. Now, however, after a lot of research and a bit of trial and error, I'm a newly converted hamantaschen fan. Boy, are they good! So even if you, like me, never had the chance to taste one of these little beauties before, here's your chance. Follow the recipe carefully, especially the steps for chilling and pinching the dough, and you'll be arranging a plate of perfectly formed hamantaschen in no time at all.

2 cups Brown Rice Flour Mix (250 grams)
½ cup granulated sugar
¾ teaspoon xanthan gum
½ teaspoon baking powder
⅛ teaspoon salt
½ cup unsalted butter cut into small pieces
1 large egg
1 tablespoon orange juice
1 teaspoon pure vanilla extract
1 cup very cold jam, preserves, or filling of choice*
Confectioners' sugar for garnish, optional

1. Mix flour, sugar, xanthan gum, baking powder, and salt in large bowl of electric mixer. Add butter and mix until crumbly and resembling coarse meal.

2. Add egg, orange juice, and vanilla. Mix on medium-low speed until dough completely holds together and is soft and pliable; this might take a couple of minutes. The dough should be damp but not sticky.

3. Turn dough out onto a piece of plastic wrap and form it into two smooth, equal-sized disks. Wrap each disk in plastic wrap and then chill for 30 minutes. Dough can be frozen at this point for up to one month; wrap in plastic wrap and then use foil as an outer wrap.

4. Line a large cookie sheet with parchment paper. Take one disk of dough from the refrigerator and roll it between two sheets of wax paper to ⅛-inch thickness. If dough seems tacky, refrigerate for 15 minutes before proceeding. Take off the top sheet of wax paper and cut dough into 3-inch circles using a cookie cutter. Use a wide spatula (like one you would use to flip pancakes) to move the dough circles to the prepared

cookie sheet. Re-roll remaining scraps of dough between wax paper and chill it until firm enough to cut. You should get about 13-14 circles in total from the first disk of dough.

5. Spoon 1 heaping teaspoon of chilled preserves or filling of choice onto the middle of each cookie. To create the customary triangular-shaped cookie (which looks like a tri-cornered hat): Fold up two sides of the dough, and pinch them together where they meet. Fold up the third side of the dough and pinch the two other corners together. Make sure no seams are visible and that the sides are pulled tightly; the filling should remain exposed in the middle. Make sure the filling comes at least to the top of the top edges of the dough and then very gently press the edges of the top of the dough over filling so that it isn't standing up straight. If the dough gets too warm to work with, put the cookie sheet (with the dough on it) in the refrigerator or freezer until it becomes firm enough to handle. Repeat the whole process with the other disk of dough.

6. Chill cookies on baking sheet in refrigerator until very cold. Preheat oven to 375°F. Position rack in center of oven.

7. Bake about 18–20 minutes, until the cookies are golden and the edges are starting to brown. Move hamantaschen to a rack and cool completely. Lightly dust with confectioners' sugar just before serving, if desired. Store in an airtight container at room temperature for same-day use. The cookies can actually be kept at room temperature for two days, but they will soften.

APPLE TURNOVERS

Makes 4 turnovers.
Recipe can be doubled.

Best when eaten within three days of baking. Refrigerate in a tightly sealed container after one day.

Most apple turnover recipes use store-bought puff pastry or pie crust pastry to make the outer dough. But as I started researching pastry doughs to create my own gluten-free version, I discovered the existence of "sour cream kipel pastry" in an old cookbook from the beginning of the 1900s. It's a flaky European pastry similar to puff pastry, but without as many layers. I searched for it in modern-day cookbooks and found variations of it made into cookies, but it wasn't until I read through Dori Greenspan's cookbook *Baking: From My Home to Yours* and looked up her recipe for apple turnovers that I felt I had hit gold. She used a sour cream pastry to make *her* turnovers that looked incredibly like the pastries in my old cookbook. And the dough was made almost exactly the same way. Greenspan said she had gotten the recipe from someone years before but couldn't even remember when. No matter. She had given me the confidence to give it a try. And you know what? It works perfectly in its new gluten-free form. This dough is a revelation: It's light and flaky, especially if you fold and chill it according to the directions. So if you've been searching for a delicious, flaky dough in order to recreate an old family favorite, you might want to try this one. And be assured that once you've folded and chilled it, you can shape it any way you want. In fact, I used this dough, with less sugar and a bit of baking powder, to make my Pigs In Blankets (see page 220).

Testing Notes: This isn't really a difficult recipe to make, but it does require a careful reading of the directions and a practice run to get it perfect.

1 cup Brown Rice Flour Mix (125 grams)
2 tablespoons granulated sugar
½ teaspoon xanthan gum
⅛ teaspoon salt
5 tablespoons unsalted butter, cut into small pieces
3 tablespoons sour cream (not low fat)
1–2 Granny Smith apples (or tart cooking apples)
1 tablespoon unsalted butter
3 tablespoons granulated sugar
½ teaspoon cinnamon (or to taste)
⅛ teaspoon nutmeg (or to taste)
2 teaspoons corn starch
1 large well-beaten egg, to brush on pastry
Granulated sugar, for garnish

1. Combine flour, sugar, xanthan gum, and salt in large bowl of electric mixer. Add butter and mix until crumbly and resembling coarse meal. Add sour cream and mix on medium-low speed until dough is just starting to hold together but is still all in quarter-sized pieces.

2. Move dough (still in pieces) to a large sheet of plastic wrap and press it together to form a smooth, rectangular shaped disk; wrap it tightly and chill for 1 hour in the refrigerator until firm enough to roll.

3. Roll pastry dough into an 8 x 15-inch rectangle between two sheets of wax paper, and then fold it into thirds along the 15-inch side, as though you were folding a letter (it should end up being 8 x 5 inches, but the dimensions do not have to be exact). Wrap tightly in plastic wrap and refrigerate at least 3 hours and up to two days. If not using within 6 hours, cover with foil so the dough doesn't dry out. Dough can be frozen at this point for up to one month; wrap in plastic wrap and then use foil as an outer wrap. Defrost in refrigerator.

4. Peel, core, and cut apples into 8 slices; cut each slice into ¼-inch thick pieces (across the short way, not into long ¼-inch slices). You will need 1 ½ cups of cut-up apple pieces. Melt butter in a small sauté pan over medium high heat. Add apples, sugar, cinnamon, and nutmeg, and cook until apples have softened, about 4 minutes. Add corn starch and boil for another minute or two until liquid has thickened and reduced (if apples start getting too soft, remove them and just boil the drained liquid). Use a spatula to scrape the apples and thickened sauce into a small bowl. Cover with plastic wrap and store in refrigerator until ready to use. Bring to room temperature before proceeding.

5. Preheat oven to 375°F. Position rack in center of oven. Line cookie sheet with parchment paper.

6. Take the dough out of the refrigerator and allow it to warm up enough to roll without getting sticky. Roll dough into a 10 ¾ –to 11-inch square between two sheets of wax paper (it will be a little less than ⅛ inch thick) and cut into four equal-sized squares. The dough should be pliable enough to bend (if it's still too cold, let it rest a bit). Divide apple filling between the four squares and gently mound it towards one side of each square. Very slightly moisten the edges of the squares with water using your finger. Fold pastry over the filling to create a triangle, then seal the edges by pressing down with the tines of a fork (if dough is too soft to work with, return it to the refrigerator or freezer for a few minutes). Carefully move turnovers to prepared cookie sheet (if turnovers are too soft to move, return them to the refrigerator or

freezer for a few minutes).

7. Brush turnovers with beaten egg and sprinkle with granulated sugar. Bake 25 to 30 minutes until dark golden and firm to the touch. Cool on a rack for at least 15 minutes before serving. Store in an airtight container at room temperature.

STRAWBERRY BUTTERMILK SHORTCAKES

When fresh strawberries are in season, grab this recipe and your container of flour mix and bake up a batch of these delicate buttermilk shortcakes. You won't even need a biscuit cutter: just spoon small mounds of dough onto the prepared baking sheet and gently pat them into shape. My family and friends like the fruit piled high, so my recipe calls for two pounds of berries, but you could easily get by with just one. I also like to serve the shortcakes with fresh peaches, when they are in season later in the summer. But even if you only make these delicious cakes in the dead of winter, and serve them with defrosted frozen raspberries and lemon curd, you'll have people asking for more.

Strawberry Filling

2 pounds fresh strawberries
¼ – ⅓ cup granulated sugar (or more to taste)

Shortcakes

2 cups Brown Rice Flour Mix (250 grams)
¼ cup granulated sugar
4 teaspoons baking powder (see Cook's Note below)
¾ teaspoon xanthan gum
½ teaspoon salt
¼ teaspoon baking soda
½ cup cold unsalted butter, cut into small pieces*
1 large egg
¾ cup lowfat buttermilk (dairy free instructions below)
2 teaspoons pure vanilla extract
1 large egg to brush on top
Rice flour, for shaping dough
Granulated sugar to sprinkle on top

Whipped Cream Topping

1 cup heavy cream
2–3 tablespoons confectioners' sugar
1 ½ teaspoons pure vanilla extract

1. **Make Strawberry Filling:** Remove the stems and lightly wash berries; pat dry with a paper towel. Slice berries and place in a large bowl. Stir

Makes 8 shortcakes

Store leftover shortcakes in an airtight container in refrigerator, or cover with plastic wrap and then with foil and store in freezer for up to three weeks. Best when eaten within three days of baking. Rewarm in a preheated 350°F oven for about ten minutes, or several seconds in a microwave.

*If you plan to use a butter substitute, measure it first, and then chill it until it is very cold.

in sugar and allow to sit at room temperature for at least 30 minutes to macerate.

2. ***Make Shortcakes:*** Preheat oven to 400°F. Position rack in center of oven. Line heavy baking sheet with parchment paper.

3. Combine flour, sugar, baking powder, xanthan gum, salt, and baking soda in large bowl of electric mixer. With mixer on low, cut butter into flour mixture until it resembles a coarse meal. Put mixture into a small bowl and set aside.

4. Beat egg in the same large bowl of electric mixer until very light and foamy. Add flour mixture and start the mixer on low speed, then pour the buttermilk and vanilla on top of the flour mixture; mix at medium-low speed for about 30 seconds until dough comes together.

5. Use a large spoon to drop 8 mounds of batter onto prepared baking sheet 1 inch apart. Use rice flour to lightly flour hands and then very gently pat each mound into a 2 ½-inch round (they don't have to be perfectly shaped). Brush tops with well-beaten egg and sprinkle with granulated sugar.

6. Place shortcakes in center of oven. Bake 20-25 minutes, until very dark golden and cooked through. Cool 15 minutes on a rack.

7. ***Make Whipped Cream Topping:*** Combine heavy cream, confectioners' sugar, and vanilla in large bowl of electric mixer; beat until stiff peaks form.

8. ***To serve:*** Cut shortcakes in half and place bottom half (cut side up) on dessert plate. Top with some of the strawberry filling, a little of the juice, and then some whipped cream; place top half of the shortcake over the whipped cream. Top with more whipped cream, strawberries and juice. Serve immediately.

Dairy-free Buttermilk: Combine ¾ cup rice or soy milk with 2 teaspoons lemon juice or distilled vinegar. Use only ¾ cup of the combined liquid in this recipe.

Cook's Notes: These are best made right before you are going to use them, but can be made four hours ahead. Place baked and cooled shortcakes in a tightly sealed container, or wrap in plastic wrap and then leave at room temperature. For longer storage, place in refrigerator or freezer. Use a double-acting, slow-acting baking powder like Davis or Clabber Girl. This gives you time to pat out the dough before the carbon dioxide gas is released.

YEAST DOUGHNUTS
Fried and Baked

A classic glazed yeast doughnut is crisp on the outside and light and tender on the inside. It should make you smile, and it should also make you want to reach for another. My gluten-free version will make you do just that. In fact, truth be told, some members of my household didn't stop reaching until the plate was empty. The fried version takes longer to make than the baked version, but it's worth the wait (the dough rises while it's being chilled in the refrigerator, which makes it easier to roll and cut); these beauties are perfect when they come out of the oil hot. The baked doughnuts are light and tender, and they taste delicious. However, you'll find they're very pale, and they don't have the same crisp outer layer as their fried siblings.

FRIED YEAST DOUGHNUTS

I used a 3-inch doughnut cutter with a 1-inch center hole, but you can make whatever size you want, including jelly doughnuts; you'll just have to adjust the frying time. Depending on when you're planning to fry the doughnuts, you can prep the dough the day before and let it rise overnight in the refrigerator.

Serve doughnuts warm or at room temperature. Best when eaten the day they are made. Wrap any leftover doughnuts (is that possible?) in plastic wrap, then foil, to store in freezer for up to two weeks. Rewarm briefly in microwave.

Makes 7 doughnuts. Recipe can be doubled.

1 ¼ cups Brown Rice Flour Mix (155 grams)
2 tablespoons granulated sugar
¾ teaspoon ground nutmeg
½ teaspoon xanthan gum
¼ teaspoon salt
1 ¼ teaspoons active dry yeast granules (not quick-rise)*
½ cup skim or lowfat milk, heated to 110°F
1 large egg, at room temperature
2 tablespoons unsalted butter, slightly melted
1 teaspoon pure vanilla extract
Rice flour, for shaping dough

*1 ¼ teaspoons is one half of a ¼-oz. packet of dried yeast. Use the whole packet if you are doubling the recipe.

1. Mix flour, sugar, nutmeg, xanthan gum, salt, and yeast in a large bowl of electric mixer.

2. Add milk, egg, butter, and vanilla to bowl, and mix until just blended. Scrape bowl and beaters; beat at medium speed for 2 minutes. Scrape dough down into a mound at the bottom of the bowl. Loosely cover bowl with a piece of plastic wrap and let dough rise in refrigerator until doubled in size and thoroughly chilled, about 4 to 12 hours (this will also make it easier to roll and cut the dough).

3. Lightly sprinkle rice flour over a large sheet of parchment paper. Use a rubber spatula to stir the dough to deflate it and move it onto the parchment paper in a ball; sprinkle more flour over the top and sides. With floured hands, lightly roll dough around in the flour and then pat it out into a ³⁄₈-inch thick round. Cut 5 doughnuts with 3-inch doughnut cutter. Gather up scrapes and holes and repeat; cut 2 more doughnuts. Slide the parchment paper onto a cookie sheet or tray; cover with a light cloth and let doughnuts rise in a warm place (about 80° F) for 30 minutes to an hour, until doubled in size (or a little more than double).

4. In large 3-quart saucepan, heat 2 inches of canola oil to 350°F (use a candy thermometer to maintain temperature). While oil is heating up, cut up the big sheet of parchment paper under the doughnuts so that each doughnut is sitting on its own little square of parchment paper.

5. Fry only two doughnuts at a time (unless you use a bigger pot and more oil). Cook doughnuts about 1 minute until medium golden brown; turn with a slotted spoon. Cook other side for about one minute; remove with slotted spoon to a paper towel-lined plate. Blot off any residual oil. Repeat with remaining doughnuts, making sure oil is heated to 350°F before proceeding.

6. Cool doughnuts on a rack for 10 to 15 minutes, then dip tops into Vanilla Glaze (recipe below); allow glaze to firm up before serving. Or, while doughnuts are still warm, brush tops with melted butter and dip in granulated sugar or cinnamon sugar.

BAKED YEAST DOUGHUTS

This baked version uses slightly less flour than the fried version because you don't have to worry about rolling and cutting the dough. With less flour, the doughnut is very light and airy, even if it doesn't have the golden brown, crisp crust of the fried version.

Makes 6 doughnuts. Recipe can be doubled.

1 cup Brown Rice Flour Mix (125 grams)
2 tablespoons granulated sugar
³⁄₄ teaspoon ground nutmeg
½ teaspoon xanthan gum
¼ teaspoon salt
1 ¼ teaspoons active dry yeast granules (not quick-rise)*
½ cup skim or lowfat milk, heated to 110°F
1 large egg (room temperature)
2 tablespoons unsalted butter, slightly melted
1 teaspoon pure vanilla extract

*1 ¼ teaspoons is one half of a ¼-oz. packet of dried yeast. Use the whole packet if you are doubling the recipe.

1. Mix flour, sugar, nutmeg, xanthan gum, salt, and yeast in a large bowl of electric mixer.

2. Add milk, egg, butter, and vanilla extract to bowl and mix until just blended. Scrape bowl and beaters; beat at medium speed for 2 minutes. Scrape dough down into a mound at the bottom of the bowl. Cover bowl with a light dish towel and let dough rise in a warm place (about 80°F) until dough has doubled in size (about an 1 hour).

3. Grease a non-stick 6-doughnut baking pan with cooking spray. Stir the dough to deflate it, and then spoon it into the doughnut pan (you could pipe it from a bag, but you will lose a lot of dough; I tried it, and I don't recommend it). Carefully smooth tops with a table knife or offset spatula. Cover with a light cloth and let doughnuts rise in a warm place for about an hour, until doubled in size.

4. Place rack in center of oven and preheat to 375°F while doughnuts are rising. Put pan in center of oven and bake at 375°F for 8 to 9 minutes, until cooked through and bottoms are lightly browned. Remove each doughnut by using a thin silicone spatula to loosen it, then place them on a rack to cool for 10-15 minutes.

5. Dip top of each doughnut into Vanilla Glaze (recipe below); allow glaze to firm up before serving. Or, while doughnuts are still warm, brush tops with melted butter and dip in granulated sugar or cinnamon sugar.

Vanilla Glaze

¾ cup confectioners' sugar
1 teaspoon pure vanilla extract
2 tablespoons half-and-half or milk

1. Combine confectioners' sugar, vanilla, and half-and-half in a small bowl and stir until smooth and creamy.

CHURROS

Makes about 16
4-inch churros. Recipe
can be doubled

Serve churros warm.
Best when eaten within
several hours of when
they are made. Even
though I strongly think
you should just eat them
all, you can wrap any
leftover churros in plastic
wrap, then foil, to store
in freezer for up to two
weeks. Rewarm briefly in
350° F oven.

*To make cinnamon
sugar, combine ⅓ cup
granulated sugar and 1
teaspoon cinnamon (or
to taste) in a small bowl.

After watching wheat-eating diners devour churros for the last several years here in the New York metro area, I got curious. What's the big deal? Well, now I know. This classic light and puffy Mexican treat is really good! Even better, churros are actually pretty easy to make, and they don't take a lot of time (there's no waiting for the dough to rise as with yeast doughnuts). In a matter of minutes you'll be able to give into the craving for these crispy-on-the-outside, moist-and-tender-on-the-inside, cinnamon sugar-dusted morsels. A quick puff paste, a pastry bag, a pair of kitchen shears, and a small pot of hot oil, and you'll be cinnamon sugar-dusting up your own churros in no time at all!

½ cup plus 1 tablespoon Brown Rice Flour Mix (70 grams)
2 teaspoons granulated sugar
⅛ teaspoon xanthan gum
⅛ teaspoon salt
¼ cup unsalted butter, cut into 4 pieces
½ cup fat-free milk
½ teaspoon pure vanilla extract
2 large eggs
Cinnamon Sugar*

1. Combine flour, sugar, xanthan gum, and salt in small bowl and set aside.

2. Bring butter and milk to a boil in a 1-quart saucepan over medium heat. Try not to allow too much of the milk to evaporate. As soon as the milk mixture boils, remove pan from heat and add flour mixture all at once. Use a soup spoon and stir vigorously to combine. The dough should come together in a tight ball.

3. Return the pan to medium heat and cook about 1 to 1 ½ minutes, stirring constantly, until dough has a smooth appearance and oil from the butter begins to glisten on the surface. The bottom of the pan will be coated with a thin film of dough.

4. Transfer the dough to the large bowl of an electric mixer. Begin to mix dough at medium speed and add the vanilla and then the eggs one at a time. Allow the first egg to be fully absorbed and the dough to become smooth and shiny, before adding the second. After each addition, the dough will separate into slippery little lumps before coming back together. Beat until dough is very smooth in consistency and is a very pale color (2–3 minutes).

5. In a 3-quart saucepan, heat 2 inches of canola oil to 350°F (use a candy thermometer to maintain temperature).

6. Use a pastry bag with a ½-inch star tip. Fill the pastry bag with warm batter. Hold the bag several inches above the hot oil, and squeeze out the batter; use a kitchen shears or a sharp knife to cut 4-inch lengths of batter and let them drop into the hot oil. Fry about four churros at a time (unless you use a bigger pot and more oil). Cook about 1 minute until medium golden brown; turn with a slotted spoon. Cook other side for about one minute; remove with slotted spoon to a paper towel-lined plate. Blot off any residual oil. Repeat with remaining batter, making sure oil is heated to 350°F before proceeding.

7. Cool churros on a rack for about 3 minutes, then roll in cinnamon sugar.

10

Breads and Other Savories

Large Sandwich Bread

Large Multigrain Sandwich Bread

Large Oat Sandwich Bread

Large Rye Sandwich Bread

Walnut Sandwich Bread

Pecan Sandwich Bread

"No-Knead" Bread

Rustic Buttermilk Rye

Rustic Multigrain Bread

Rustic Oat Bread

Brioche Loaf

Brioche Hamburger Buns

Panettone

Sesame Breadsticks

Multigrain Breadsticks

Cheese Soufflé

Pig in Blankets

Dumplings for Soup and Stew

Asian Dumpling Dough

Pierogi and Vareniki Dough

THIS CHAPTER FEATURES DELICIOUS RECIPES FOR BREAD AND SEVERAL OTHER SAVORY ITEMS that you may have been hungry for. I know that after more than a decade of gluten-free eating, I really wanted *good* Asian dumplings again. I also started to miss the pierogies that were given as a gift to my family every Christmas from a friend with Ukrainian roots. And even though I thought I could live without pigs in blankets, I really like being able to make up a batch when the folks in my home are watching a ball game.

The bottom line on the breads in this chapter is that, after literally hundreds of hours of research and testing (described below), my bread recipes are still very much based on the same flour mix and techniques. I still feel that one of the nice things about gluten-free bread baking is how quickly you can bake up a good-tasting bread with a tender texture. But just in case you want to prep ahead and bake later, I've added a description (below) of what happens to my bread recipes with delayed or chilled double rises.

I still don't add modified starches or other non-bread ingredients to my recipes, so it isn't possible to leave them out on the counter for days at a time like many store bought breads (or those made with ingredients that don't typically show up in a "real" bread). My breads are still at their best in terms of flavor and texture on the first day of baking. But they can all be frozen and be refreshed by warming, and happily, it works well.

The Search for a New Bread Paradigm

I went back out into the gluten-free bread-baking wilderness when I began to develop recipes for this book. Because I had created my bread flour mix and my first collection of bread recipes back in 2004, I wanted to find out what, if anything I could add or change to make my breads taste better, or last longer, or rise better—or just be better in any way whatsoever. I revisited my flour and starch selections, choice of gums, oven temperature, pan choice, rising techniques and baking times. Full of self-doubt that there could be a better way, I used up a lot of flour and kitchen time. I also explored the world of industrial gluten-free baking to see if I could swap in commercial baker techniques and ingredients to home baking.

An interesting and somewhat troubling trend (at least, to me) is that some home bakers are starting to incorporate more highly processed food ingredients, other than xanthan gum, into their breads in the quest to make their dough "kneadable."

I expected to find this in industrial baking, because I knew commercial bakers would want to make use of currently available bread dough handling equipment whenever possible. But in the last several years, there seems to be a growing tendency for some home bakers to want to fix gluten-free dough, rather than accept its essential nature as looser and almost batter-like. But it's that essential nature that leads to a higher quality, less processed food-like gluten-free bread. And yes, I know xanthan gum is processed, and that I use it in my recipes (and that it's also added to a lot of shelf-stable processed food), but I try to use as little as possible—a lot less than what you'd find in other gluten-free recipes or store-bought goods. It is for this very reason, because I already use a small amount of xanthan gum in my baking, that I'm even more hesitant to "pile on" by adding other industrially processed ingredients to the food I make and eat.

Flours: I revisited using brown rice flour in addition to, or in place of, millet and sorghum, and decided against it even though most gluten-free commercial bakeries and many gluten-free cookbook writers use it in their breads. To my palate, brown rice flour still doesn't have as much sweet, nutty grain flavor as either millet or sorghum. Adding it to my blend along with the millet and sorghum didn't add any appreciable benefit. In fact, it gave my breads a bit of that glossy look the frozen rice-based breads have at the store. I also decided that, even though I personally don't eat a lot of baked goods on a weekly basis (except when I'm in the middle of a testing frenzy), I think it's important to have as much grain diversity in our diets as possible. I do not want all my baked goods to be rice based.

In addition to taking another look at rice flour, I reconsidered almond flour, seed flours, and even coconut flour because they have all been embraced by some gluten-free bread bakers. I gave them another look, but they do not produce a close facsimile of a classic wheat bread.

Flour to starch ratio: I retested my breads to see what would happen if I changed the ratio of whole grain flour to starch, because I was curious about whether I would think differently now than I did years ago when I first developed my flour mix. I conducted the tests with two recipes: My basic sandwich bread (which contains egg, milk, and more fat), and an artisan bread (which contains very little fat and no eggs or milk). What would happen if I used the same 2-to-1 ratio of whole grain to starch that I used in my all-purpose brown rice flour mix? My breads became very dense and brick-like.

I tried again. What if, instead of my adding the normal extra ¼ cup of whole grain to a 2-cup multigrain bread (and reducing the bread flour mix down to 1 ¾ cups), I added ½ cup whole grain to 1 ½ cups of my mix? It produced dense breads that tasted good and had nice, even crumb. But the breads didn't have the larger air holes or the very soft-on-the-first-day texture I looked for in my breads.

I tried *again* with less extra-added whole grain—⅓ cup added to 1 ⅔ cups bread flour mix—and found that, although it still made a too-dense sandwich bread, it actually created a very hearty kind of heavier country bread that people might enjoy.

I know I did. Ultimately, I developed three recipes for this book using ⅓-cup extra whole grain in a 2-cup loaf instead of ¼ cup (which was my old way). My new "rustic" breads have a chewy texture and are full of flavor. If you like heavier breads, it's hard to stop eating them. Except for the new rustic bread recipes, I ended up leaving my flour-to-starch ratio the way it was.

Starches: First, I retested various combinations of potato starch, tapioca starch, and corn starch to be able to see if I could make my breads better, and to revisit what happened when any one was left out (see Chapter 2 in this book, *"Frequently Asked Questions,"* about starch replacements for more information). I know that many gluten-free bakers/writers say starches are interchangeable, *but they are not.* Each starch has an essential nature and can contribute certain qualities to the finished baked good depending on the recipe and on how it's calibrated. Although it is easy enough to switch out one starch for another to accommodate allergies or other concerns, the three of them together, when used with millet and sorghum flour, create a really nice bread.

Second, I decided to revisit possibly using one of the modified starches available to home bakers in my bread recipes. I had tried Expandex many years ago, but couldn't get any information from the company that sold it about what chemicals were used to manufacture it or whether any tests had been done to determine its long-term effect on the body. I decided not to include it in my recipes at the time. Now though, as I re-explored the somewhat magical and scary world of modified starches to see what was new, I found that most of them are still only available to commercial bakers and food companies (except for Expandex, Instant Clear Jel, and Ultratex 3). But more importantly, I spoke with food scientists from several companies to get a better understanding about how and why the many different kinds of modified starches are made, and, I looked for published research into their effect on the body.

Modified tapioca, potato, and corn starches are created through a series of industrial-processing techniques that involve physical, chemical, or enzymatic modifications of native starches. Starch manufacturers do this to give the native starches certain characteristics that they wouldn't normally have—like not breaking down when heated, or jelling at a lower temperature, or retaining liquid for a longer time, or being a replacement for fats.

At some level, I have to admit it's a marvel of modern-day industrial engineering: Scientists can chemically change the molecular structure of a starch so that it won't break down in our gluten-free baked goods. The baked good will then rise higher and stay fresh longer. In fact, many of the processed foods we see on the shelves of grocery stores—including gluten-free items—are loaded with modified starches. Look closely at the label of many gluten-free breads, crackers, and other snack and cereal products, including some baking mixes, and you'll see just how prevalent they are.

But when I looked for research about their effect on the body, I found very little done on humans, and no long-term studies over ninety days. Think about this: It took years before we understood the effect of trans fats, another seemingly innocent, but highly processed ingredient on our bodies, and modified starches are a very, very highly processed ingredient. Knowing what I now know, I've come to consider modified starches a bit of *Frankenfood*. Although I've always tried to limit my intake of processed foods in general, I'm now even more careful about purposely eating foods that contain modified starches to an infrequent few. And because I'm not looking to make processed food at home, there are no modified starches in my recipes.

Protein isolates as extra added "protein" to replace gluten: Commercial food manufacturers add all kinds of protein isolates to a wide assortment of processed foods, including meat and cheese products, pet foods, snack foods, and baked goods. In addition to vegetarians and body builders who use them for extra protein, you'll also find protein isolates listed as an ingredient in low-carb cookbooks going back more than a decade, because they were touted as an excellent option for making low-carb, protein-rich breads and other baked goods.

I found the first sightings of a home baker specifically using whey protein isolate to develop gluten-free baked goods on a blog written by Mike Eberhart in December 2007 (he has since written a cookbook). He considered it a "miracle GF baking ingredient" because it gave the dough a more pliable texture. Since then, its use has become more prevalent. The trouble is that, just like the modified starches discussed above, whey, pea, hemp, and soy protein isolates are very highly processed food ingredients (e.g., whey protein isn't just dried-out curds and whey). And even though I understand that body builders and vegetarians use them to supplement their protein intake, and that people who require a low-carb diet for health reasons might want to make baked goods with them, I really believe that most people are better off getting their protein from real (recognizable) food. Since my goal is to develop, to the best of my abilities, simple, classic breads that don't resemble processed food, I do not include it in my recipes.

Psyllium husk to replace xanthan gum and/or add fiber: Psyllium is a bulk laxative, fiber supplement, and colon cleanser produced from the seed of the Plantago plant, a plant that has a long history of medicinal use here on Earth.

I decided to test it as a replacement for xanthan gum in my simple submarine sandwich bread (from *Gluten-Free Baking Classics*) to see if the essential nature of my bread would improve in such an appreciable better way that I might want to consider reworking the dozens of bread recipes I've already published. I choose my artisan sub bread because the recipe reads like a wheat submarine sandwich bread recipe, except for the gluten-free flour mix and the xanthan gum, and it makes a good-tasting, golden brown loaf with a nice, soft, airy crumb structure. I purposely did not choose a bread recipe with a lot of ingredients, because then it would be harder to see the effect of changing one ingredient.

The result? Xanthan gum made a prettier, better textured, better tasting, lighter, and more airy bread than psyllium husk in my simple submarine bread recipe (to read more about the test and view actual pictures posted on my blog in April 2014, see *"Chapter Notes"* at the end of this introduction).

What happened? The final loaf volume of gluten-free loaves depends on the stability of the gel formed by the hydrocolloids added to the dough. Xanthan gum is a thickener, stabilizer, emulsifier, and foaming agent. It provides structure and is stable over a broad range of temperatures. Pysllium husk, however, forms a gel that is stable only up to temperatures of about 176°F (80°C)[1], depending on the amount used in the recipe. So while psyllium husk is very useful for holding in the carbon dioxide-based gas bubbles during proofing, once you put the bread into a hot oven and it starts to bake and the internal temperature rises, the loaf will ultimately collapse—if you are depending only on psyllium husk to give structure to the bread.

It turns out that many of the cookbook writers or bloggers who feel they are successfully creating baked goods using psyllium husk to replace xanthan gum create recipes that contain eggs and, very often, baking soda. What is happening in their recipes is this: At the point where the psyllium husk starts to fail as a gel, if the bread contains tapioca starch or even potato starch (which many do), the tapioca starch can act like a bridge until the egg proteins take over to help hold the bread up. The tapioca is able to act like a bridge because it gelatinizes at a higher temperature than psyllium husk (or potato starch, for that matter). Then, the proteins in the egg provide some of the structure necessary to hold the bread up. But if you've ever made a bread that uses just eggs, and no xantham gum for extra added support, you already know that the xantham gum does a better job. The baking soda is added to help the bread rise, because the dough is being tightly held together by the psyllium husk.

Writers whose recipes don't contain eggs often use seed gels, sometimes in large quantities. But the recipes that depend on seed gels instead of eggs to help the psyllium husk powder provide structure have a problem similar to those with the eggs, in that the breads will still turn out denser and more tightly textured. And as I noted in Chapter 3, although I might use flax seed gel as an egg replacer when I bake for people who have egg allergies, it really is better suited to helping hold things together (as an emulsifier). Flax gels are weak structure builders because they don't have the relatively strong protein network of eggs to reinforce dough and batter. They won't hold the rise as well as xanthan gum, and more importantly, they can give baked goods a slightly gummy texture.

The significance of having to add eggs and baking soda to make a bread recipe work when using psyllium husk powder is important. Perhaps if I *wanted* to add eggs or egg whites to my artisan breads in order to create a decent loaf, the test outcome would be different. But I don't. My thinking when I originally developed these recipes

---

[1]Haque, A., Richardson, R. K., Morris, E. R., & Dea, I. C. M. (1993). Xanthan-like weak gel rheology from dispersions of ispaghula seed husk. *Carbohydrate Polymers, 22*(4), 223-232.

was this: Wheat pizza crusts, baguettes, rustic flat breads, and country breads don't contain eggs (or the seed gels used to replace to eggs), and I wanted to maintain the integrity of original recipes to the best of my abilities. As a result, I didn't want my gluten-free versions to contain eggs, or the seed gels people use to replace eggs.

The bottom line on psyllium husk is this: It is possible to use psyllium husk to replace xanthan gum in gluten-free breads. You just have to understand that your end product will look and taste even more like a gluten-free bread.

And what about using psyllium husk to add extra added fiber to bread? If you look at the nutritional listing for psyllium husk and psyllium husk powder, you will see that it really is devoid of vitamins, minerals, and other phytonutrients, although it does have a lot of good fiber. I think it's important to get our fiber from plants and nuts and seeds, so that along with fiber, we get food for our bodies. That said, some people really need the extra added fiber they get from something like psyllium— in addition to the food they eat—so they may benefit from adding extra psyllium to their bread.

Double rises, chilled rises, and overnight rises: I tested both my enriched breads (eggs and milk) and my artisan breads (no eggs or milk) for the following—

- First rise in tea towel-covered bowl; second rise in tea towel-covered bread pan at 80°F
- First rise in plastic wrap-covered bowl for 4 hours in refrigerator; second rise in tea towel-covered bread pan at 80°F
- First rise in plastic wrap-covered bowl for 12 hours overnight in refrigerator; second rise in tea-towel covered bread pan at 80°F

The results? Double rises, chilled rises, and delayed rises all work fine for my recipes. But the final rise and final baked height will be slightly less high when there are two rises (chilled or not) instead of only one. In addition, the tops of the brioche and panettone become slightly mottled and won't look as smooth as when they only have one rise. That said, the brioche and panettone turn out better. Why? The second rise will be slower, and the breads won't rise quite as high in the oven, but as a result, they are also less likely to fall or sink in the middle. *This is a critical point if you are repeatedly having problems with cave-ins with any yeast dough, even after you have taken all the steps I offer below under "Double Checking"; i.e., you might want to consider a double rise to see if it helps.*

There are a couple of other benefits as well. Chilling the dough allows you to prep it the night before, or earlier in the day, and then do the final proofing just before you are ready to bake (or fry, in the case of yeast doughnuts).

Chilling the dough also makes it easier to handle and mold initially, but my breads still have a better shape when baked in a bread pan. Because my bread doughs don't contain extra ingredients like psyllium or protein isolates that make gluten-free doughs more malleable (and help to hold them in place on a baking sheet), and because they don't contain a lot of extra, unnecessary xanthan gum, they have a better shape when baked in a pan with some form of support. Also, it isn't necessary to knead gluten-free bread in order to make it come out well; bakers knead bread to develop the gluten, and there is no gluten to develop.

Sourdough breads: There's been a good deal of research conducted in food science labs on gluten-free sourdough fermentation as a means to produce functional ingredients in order to improve the flavor, aroma, nutrition, texture, and shelf life of gluten-free breads. But to date, there's been no road map or game-changing ingredient to emerge from it all for commercial bakers (much less home bakers; but this could change). In addition, commercial gluten-free sourdough bread production is miniscule and uneven across the country, and breads range from incredibly thick and dense to those with some small air pockets but little real sourdough flavor.

Moreover, on the home baking front, if you take more than a glance at all the gluten-free sourdough bread baking advice on gluten-free websites, blogs, and in cookbooks, you'll notice that each writer thinks that they have found "the" way, but all the ways are all totally different.

In the meantime, for someone like me, who doesn't eat bread more than once or twice a month (at least when I'm not testing bread recipes), it isn't worth the time and effort, or the expensive flour needed to keep the starter alive and in optimum health. And even if I did keep it alive, the chances that I would always want to make a sourdough bread each time I do bake bread are not good. My forays into sourdough baking in my own kitchen have not convinced me to spend a lot of time there, at least yet.

Dairy substitutes: My butter substitute of choice for most of the baked goods in this chapter is Earth Balance® Buttery Spread or Buttery Sticks (not the Shortening Sticks). My milk substitute of choice is rice milk. I did *not* test dairy free versions of the Brioche or the Pigs in Blankets.

For questions about making yeast free bread, substitutions for gelatin in the sandwich loaves, and baking at high altitudes, see Chapter 3, *Other Frequently Asked Questions*.

This chapter uses the following pans:
- 8 ½ x 4 ½-inch loaf pan (not nonstick, if possible)
- 9 x 5-inch loaf pan (not nonstick, if possible)
- 6-cup (1 ½ quart) soufflé dish
- Large, shiny cookie sheets (or baking sheets) of medium to heavy weight. For best results, I do not recommend super-thick, insulated, or dark metal cookie sheets for my recipes.

- Non-stick skillet with glass lid to cook Asian dumplings
- Large, heavy saucepan to boil periogies and vareniki

The Last Word on Breads

- Set up before starting the recipe: Assemble all ingredients.
- Measure carefully.
- Check the date on your yeast to make sure it is fresh. The recipes in this book use dependable ¼-ounce packets of active dry yeast granules readily available in grocery stores. I recommend Red Star Yeast (see Chapter 3, *Frequently Asked Questions* for more information about yeast).
- Most of the recipes in this chapter call for heating the liquid to 110°F; higher temperatures could kill the yeast.
- Are your eggs at room temperature? If not, you can warm them up in a bowl of warm water.
- Be sure to beat your bread dough the full amount of time called for in the recipe. It helps hydrate the dough and xanthan gum.
- If you only have a non-stick pan to use, be sure to flour it well after you grease it.
- To create a warm place for your breads to rise, you can preheat your oven to 80°F, turn the oven off, and then put the dough inside. If you can only preheat your oven to a temperature higher than 80°F, open it up and air it out before you put in the dough, or don't let it preheat all the way. If the oven is too warm, your bread will rise too quickly and then fall when you bake it.
- Preheat the oven to the proper temperature before baking; make sure the oven is calibrated correctly.
- Keep your bread out of the hot spots in your oven. The side of your bread that is baking in the hot spot of your oven will rise more and/or "open up" more than on the other side, and you can end up with an uneven bread. You can find out where your oven's hot spots are by baking a large sheet of bread slices and watching to see the area where slices brown first.
- Do not open the oven door more than necessary.
- Use an instant-read thermometer to check temperatures of liquids for breads and interiors of finished baked breads. You do not need a fancy, expensive one.
- Use a timer in case you get distracted.

Double Checking

Why doesn't my bread rise? Why doesn't my bread rise well? Why does my bread rise, and then fall?

Are you measuring the liquid correctly? Too much liquid can cause your bread to fall. If everything else on this list is correct, try reducing the liquid by 1 tablespoon. If you make bread when it's raining and the house is humid, your bread flour may absorb more moisture than it needs. The extra water in the dough will weigh it down. As in wheat baking, the amount of moisture in the air will affect the rise.

Or perhaps you were so careful about spooning the flour into the measuring cups that you ended up a little short of flour (either when you made the bread flour mix, or when you measured it for the recipe). If you think this might be the case, try adding a tablespoon or two of flour to the dough. If that works, try not to spoon the flour into the cup as lightly next time you're mixing and measuring flours.

Or perhaps you didn't wait until the bread had risen to the proper level because you figured enough time had elapsed, or you waited too long and let it over-proof.

Dark pans absorb more radiant heat than lighter-colored ones, so your breads may rise too quickly in the oven—and then fall. If you used a dark loaf pan, try lowering the temperature by 25°F the next time you bake.

Is your oven temperature correct? If your oven is running hotter than it should, it can contribute to a too-fast rise and then a fall.

Is your xanthan gum old or not working correctly?

If all else fails, try a double rise or a delayed rise. See "Double rises, chilled rises, and overnight rises" just above.

Chapter Notes: Read more about the test and see pictures at my blog: http://mygluten-freetable.com/2014/04/the-gluten-free-bread-baking-with-psyllium-husks-powder-test/

LARGE SANDWICH BREAD

Sometimes nothing but a big, thick sandwich will do. A large loaf of delicious bread is a great place to start. This tender loaf has the consistency of a homemade white bread and the rich taste of millet and sorghum, two ancient grains that will more than make up for the lack of wheat flavor. It will be softest on the first day, but after that it can be refreshed in the toaster or microwave.

In order to ensure a consistent rise for even the most inexperienced bakers, I've lowered my "normal" baking temperature (to slow the oven rise), omitted the foil cover, and reduced the baking time. I've also added a second set of instructions for a two-rise bread (first rise in the bowl, second rise in the bread pan). If you only do one rise, the bread will have larger air pockets. But if you find you are having problems with your loaves sinking a bit in the middle, you may want to try a two-rise bread.

Allow the bread to rise slowly. Don't put it in a place that is too warm- the ideal temperature is about 80°F. A fast rise will contribute to an unstable bread that is likely to fall, and the xanthan gum also needs time to "set" in gluten-free breads.

Makes one 1 lb. 14 oz. loaf

Use a heavy serrated knife to pre-slice the bread into 16 slices, not including ends (or 18 thinner slices). Wrap bread well in plastic wrap and then foil. Store on the counter for up to two days, in refrigerator for up to three days, or freezer for up to three weeks.

* If you don't want to use the gelatin, add an extra egg yolk or leave it out entirely.

2 large eggs (room temperature)
¼ cup canola oil
3 cups Bread Flour Mix (384 grams)
2 to 3 tablespoons sugar (to taste)
2 ½ teaspoons xanthan gum
1 ½ teaspoons unflavored gelatin*
¾ teaspoon salt
1 packet (¼ oz.) active dry yeast granules (not quick rise)
1 cup plus 3 tablespoons skim or 1% or 2% milk (110°F)

1. Lightly grease a 9 x 5-inch loaf pan with cooking spray and dust with rice flour. (Your bread will rise more dependably when baked in a lighter colored metal pan that isn't non-stick.)

2. Mix eggs and canola oil together in a small bowl and set aside.

3. Mix all dry ingredients in large bowl of electric mixer. Quickly add warm milk and egg and oil mixture to the bowl; mix until just blended. Scrape bowl and beaters, and then beat at high speed for 3 minutes.

For one rise: Spoon dough into prepared pan and smooth top with a table knife or offset spatula; cover with a light cloth and let rise in a warm place for about 35 to 60 minutes, or until dough is just below the top of the pan.

For two rise: Scrape dough down into a mound at the bottom of the bowl; cover bowl with a light cloth and let it rise in a warm place (about 80°F), or at room temperature, until dough has doubled in size, about 30 minutes to 1 hour. Use a rubber spatula to very gently, but completely, deflate the dough and then spoon it into prepared pan. Carefully smooth top with a table knife or offset spatula. Cover pan with a light cloth and let rise in a warm place for about 30–60 minutes, or until dough is just below the top of the pan. If your home is 70°–80°F, you can leave the bread on the counter. Or, you can use a warm oven (no more than 80°F) to help the bread rise. If you have only one oven, you will have to pull the bread out before it is finished rising in order to preheat the oven.

4. Position rack in center of oven. Preheat oven to 375°F while bread is rising (do not use a convection oven; bread will brown too quickly).

5. Place bread on center rack in oven (but keep out of hotspots) and bake for about 35 to 40 minutes, until instant read thermometer registers about 205°F. Bread should have a hollow sound when tapped on the sides and bottom. Remove bread from oven and turn onto a rack to cool.

Cook's Note: Dry ingredients can be mixed ahead and stored in plastic containers for future use. But do not add yeast until just ready to bake bread.

LARGE MULTIGRAIN SANDWICH BREAD

Gluten-free bakers are fortunate in some respects: There's a tempting variety of whole grain flours we can use to make multigrain breads. Everyone has their favorite, but mine remains teff. It makes a flavorful, hearty loaf that reminds me of whole wheat. And it makes a delicious sandwich, especially when fresh, although the slices take well to being rewarmed after the first day.

In order to ensure a consistent rise for even the most inexperienced bakers, I've lowered my "normal" baking temperature (to slow the oven rise), omitted the foil cover, and reduced the baking time. I've also added a second set of instructions for a two-rise bread below (first rise in the bowl, second rise in the bread pan). If you only do one rise, the bread will have larger air pockets. But if you find you are having problems with your loaves sinking a bit in the middle, you may want to try a two-rise bread.

Allow the bread to rise slowly. Don't put it in a place that is too warm- the ideal temperature is about 80°F. A fast rise will contribute to an unstable bread that is likely to fall, and the xanthan gum also needs time to "set" in gluten-free breads.

Makes one 1 lb. 14 oz. loaf

Use a heavy serrated knife to pre-slice the bread into 16 slices, not including ends (or 18 thinner slices). Wrap bread well in plastic wrap and then foil. Store on the counter for up to two days, in refrigerator for up to three days, or freezer for up to three weeks.

* If you don't want to use the gelatin, add an extra egg yolk or leave it out entirely.

    2 large eggs (room temperature)
    ¼ cup canola oil
    2 ⅔ cups Bread Flour Mix (340 grams)
    ⅓ cup teff flour
    2–3 tablespoons sugar, to taste
    2 ½ teaspoons xanthan gum
    1 ½ teaspoons unflavored gelatin*
    ¾ teaspoon salt
    1 packet (¼ oz.) active dry yeast granules (not quick rise)
    1 cup plus 3 tablespoons skim or 1% or 2% milk (110°F)
    2 tablespoons sesame seeds
    2 tablespoons flax seed
    2 tablespoons sunflower seeds

1. Lightly grease a 9 x 5-inch loaf pan with cooking spray and dust with rice flour. (Your bread will rise more dependably when baked in a lighter colored metal pan that isn't non-stick.)

2. Mix eggs and canola oil together in a small bowl and set aside.

3. Mix all dry ingredients in large bowl of electric mixer. Quickly add warm milk and egg and oil mixture to the bowl; mix until just blended. Scrape bowl and beaters, and then beat at high speed for 3 minutes. Add seeds and mix well.

For one rise: Spoon dough into prepared pan and smooth top with a table knife or offset spatula; cover with a light cloth and let rise in a warm place for about 35 to 60 minutes, or until dough is just below the top of the pan.

For two rise: Scrape dough down into a mound at the bottom of the bowl; cover bowl with a light cloth and let it rise in a warm place (about 80°F), or at room temperature, until dough has doubled in size, about 30 minutes to 1 hour. Use a rubber spatula to very gently, but completely, deflate the dough and then spoon it into prepared pan. Carefully smooth top with a table knife or offset spatula. Cover pan with a light cloth and let rise in a warm place for about 30-60 minutes, or until dough is just below the top of the pan. If your home is 70°– 80°F, you can leave the bread on the counter. Or, you can use a warm oven (no more than 80°F) to help the bread rise. If you have only one oven, you will have to pull the bread out before it is finished rising in order to preheat the oven.

4. Position rack in center of oven. Preheat oven to 375°F while bread is rising (do not use a convection oven; bread will brown too quickly).

5. Place bread on center rack in oven (but keep out of hotspots) and bake for about 35 to 40 minutes, until instant read thermometer registers about 205°F. Bread should have a hollow sound when tapped on the sides and bottom. Remove bread from oven and turn onto a rack to cool.

Cook's Note: Dry ingredients can be mixed ahead and stored in plastic containers for future use. But do not add yeast until just ready to bake bread.

LARGE OAT SANDWICH BREAD

Substitute ⅓ cup gluten-free oat flour for ⅓ cup teff flour.

Use 1 cup plus 2 tablespoons skim or 1 or 2% milk (110°F) instead of 1 cup plus 3 tablespoons.

Optional: In Step 5, make a slash down the center of the bread with a sharp, pointy knife, and sprinkle whole gluten-free rolled oats across the top, if desired, before placing in the oven.

LARGE RYE SANDWICH BREAD

How do you make rye bread without rye flour, which has gluten? The trick is to use teff flour to provide the hearty richness and color this bread is known for. A touch of rye flavoring, available in a gluten-free form from Authentic Foods (see page 19), provides the necessary finishing touch.

1 ½ teaspoons gluten-free rye flavor*
2–3 tablespoons caraway seeds (or to taste)

In Step 3 above: Add rye flavor to dry ingredients. Substitute caraway seeds for sesame, flax and sunflower seeds.

*This bread has a classic New York deli-style rye taste. After you make it the first time, you can adjust the amount of rye flavor. If you prefer it milder, decrease it in ½-teaspoon increments. For a stronger rye flavor, increase it in ¼-teaspoon increments.

WALNUT SANDWICH BREAD

Makes one 1 lb. 14 oz. loaf

Use a heavy serrated knife to pre-slice the bread into 16 slices, not including ends (or 18 thinner slices). Wrap bread well in plastic wrap and then foil. Store on the counter for up to two days, in refrigerator for up to three days, or freezer for up to three weeks.

*If you don't want to use the gelatin, add extra egg yolk or leave it out entirely.

This walnut sandwich bread has a rich flavor and a complex, hearty texture that comes from the finely ground nuts in the dough. It's perfect toasted for breakfast and topped with fruit preserves and nut butters, or served alongside cheese or soup. It also makes a great sandwich with leftover roast chicken.

2 large eggs (room temperature)
¼ cup Canola oil
2 ⅔ cups Bread Flour Mix (340 grams)
⅓ cup finely ground walnuts
2–3 tablespoons sugar, to taste
2 ¼ teaspoons xanthan gum
1 ½ teaspoons unflavored gelatin*
¾ teaspoon salt
1 packet (¼ oz.) active dry yeast granules (not quick rise)
1 cup plus 3 tablespoons skim, 1% or 2% milk (110° F)
¾ cup chopped walnuts

1. Lightly grease a 9 x 5-inch loaf pan with cooking spray and dust with rice flour. (Your bread will rise more dependably when baked in a shiny metal pan that isn't non-stick.)

2. Mix eggs and canola oil together in a small bowl and set aside.

3. Mix all dry ingredients (except chopped walnuts) in large bowl of electric mixer. Quickly add warm milk and egg and oil mixture to the bowl; mix until just blended. Scrape bowl and beaters, and then beat at high speed for 3 minutes. Mix in chopped walnuts. Spoon dough into prepared pan and smooth top with a table knife or offset spatula; cover with a light cloth and let rise in a warm place for about 35 to 60 minutes, or until dough is just below the top of the pan. If your home is 70° to 80°F, you can leave the bread on the counter. Or, you can use a warm oven (no more than 80°F) to help the bread rise. If you have only one oven, you will have to pull the bread out before it is finished rising in order to preheat the oven.

4. Position rack in center of oven. Preheat oven to 375°F while bread is rising (do not use a convection oven; bread will brown too quickly).

5. Place bread on center rack in oven (but keep out of hotspots) and bake for about 35 to 40 minutes, until instant read thermometer registers about 205°F. Bread should have a hollow sound when tapped on the sides and bottom. Remove bread from oven and turn onto a rack to cool.

Cook's Note: Dry ingredients can be mixed ahead and stored in plastic containers for future use. Do not add yeast until just ready to bake bread.

PECAN SANDWICH BREAD

Substitute ⅓ cup finely ground pecans for the ⅓ cup finely ground walnuts.

Substitute ¾ cup chopped pecans for the ¾ cup chopped walnuts.

NO-KNEAD BREAD

Makes one small boule-shaped loaf

Use a heavy, serrated knife to slice the bread. Wrap leftover bread well in plastic wrap and then foil. Store in freezer for up to three weeks.

Several years ago I developed a strong desire to try to make a gluten-free version of Jim Lahey's No-Knead Bread. Mark Bittman popularized the original recipe in an article in the New York Times in November 2006, and it spread like wildfire across the baking community. But I didn't want to make a gluten-free version filled with eggs, sugar, and oil like the ones I had noticed online. I wanted to see if I could make a true converted version of the original: flour, yeast, salt, and water. The bread had been a revelation to wheat bakers at the time because Laheys' very wet dough self-kneaded over a period of 12 to 18 hours as it sat on the counter. Given enough time, the enzymes in the dough broke down the gluten and allowed it to realign, thereby allowing the baker to sidestep the whole kneading process. The resulting bread was also crisp on the outside and tender and moist on the inside, a direct result of Lahey's ingenious baking method: He baked the dough in a very hot oven in a preheated, heavy, covered pot that acted like a steam- injection oven. The recipe didn't require any real "work" on the part of the baker except for figuring out how to get the dough into the preheated Dutch oven without burning your hands and arms.

But would Lahey's technique work for my bread flour mix? As a gluten-free baker, I was already accustomed to not kneading my very wet bread dough. The big allure for me was the possibility of making more crusty bread than I was already making. I tried it with one of my wettest doughs, a dough that also had fewest ingredients and the same proportion of flour to water as Lahey's recipe (my Submarine Sandwich Bread dough from *Gluten-Free Baking Classics*, the same bread I used in the psyllium husk powder test discussed in the introduction to this chapter on page 191). I left out the teaspoon of olive oil and the sugar, lowered the quantity of yeast to 1/2 teaspoon, but kept in the xanthan gum. I let it sit for 14, 18, and 24 hours in three consecutive tests. I used my 5-quart cast iron Dutch oven.

The results? The recipe made a beautiful boule with a crackly crust, a soft, chewy interior, and a tangy, very slight sour dough-like taste. The 14-hour version baked up the best—it had a gorgeous, rounded dome top. The 18-hour version was a fraction less high but tasted the same. The 24-hour version was less high overall, and as it was baking, one of my son's friends said my home smelled like the Jack Daniels Distillery. Hmmm. My advice is to try this bread, but stick with 14- to 18-hour rise time.

Testing Note: I did not double my recipe (Lahey's recipe used 3 cups of flour) because for me, this bread is all about the crust, and I wanted as much of it as possible (and you will, too, after you try it). A double recipe gives a lot more interior. But this recipe makes a perfectly sized boule to serve with a salad or cheese course. That said, you can double it, but you might have to adjust the final baking time when you remove the lid.

1 ½ cups Bread Flour Mix (190 grams)
1 teaspoon xanthan gum
¾ teaspoon salt
½ teaspoon active dry yeast granules (not quick-rise)
¾ cup plus 1 tablespoon water, room temperature

1. Mix all dry ingredients in large bowl of electric mixer. Pour water into mixing bowl and mix until just blended. Scrape bowl and beaters, and then beat at high speed for 2 minutes.

2. Spoon dough into a large bowl that has been liberally greased with olive oil. Cover tightly with plastic wrap and allow to sit at room temperature (70°–75°F is ideal) for 14 to 18 hours. Dough will have doubled and appear cracked.

3. Line another medium bowl with a large piece of parchment paper. Gently fold the dough over itself several times with a rubber spatula until it looks smoother, and then scoop it onto the paper in the bowl; smooth out the paper underneath the dough to the best of your abilities. Cover with a tea towel and allow to rise at room temperature (70°-75°F is ideal) for 2 hours. It will not double and may not look like it has risen much at all.

4. After the first hour and fifteen minutes, place a large Dutch oven (5-quart cast iron or enamel) in the center of the oven, and set the oven temperature to 400°F (i.e., you are preheating the Dutch oven for the last 45 minutes of the total 2-hour rise time).

5. After the two-hour rise, remove the hot pot from the oven, carefully lift the parchment paper with dough on it and place it in the center of the pot. Close the lid and place it back in the oven for 30 minutes. Remove the lid and bake another 35 minutes, until crust is dark golden brown. Remove bread from oven and turn onto a rack to cool.

Cook's Note: Dry ingredients can be mixed ahead and stored in plastic containers for future use. But do not add yeast until just ready to bake bread.

RUSTIC BREADS

Makes one small round loaf

Loaves can be stored in refrigerator for up to two days or freezer for up to three weeks (sliced or left whole); wrap well in plastic wrap and then foil. Defrost in plastic wrap. Rewarm in preheated 350°F oven for 10–15 minutes; sprinkle bread with a bit of water and wrap in foil. Or if bread is already sliced, microwave slices for a few seconds until defrosted, and then toast under the broiler.

The three rustic bread recipes below came out of my experiments using a cast iron Dutch oven to make the no-knead bread. I loved the very crisp crust and firm bottom my no-knead bread had when I baked it in a cast iron pot, and I became intrigued to see what would happen if I used a cast iron skillet for a different bread recipe. So instead of baking my newly developed rustic bread recipes in a layer cake pan, as I had been doing, I tried them in one of my small cast iron skillets. Although the loaves didn't have exactly the same crackly crust as the ones baked in the covered Dutch oven, the bottoms were, indeed, crustier. Moreover, because my rustic breads contained a slightly higher proportion of whole grain flour than my regular artisan breads, the dough was thicker and didn't spread out as much in the pan. I found I was still able to get a round shape when I scooped the dough into the center of the skillet, but without the formal sides that a layer cake pan provides. My breads looked more "rustic"; it was just what I wanted. However, the breads did not rise into a boule shape like the no-knead bread; they were a bit flatter overall.

I normally warn against using a dark pan to bake my breads because it can negatively affect the rise (the bread develops a crust and browns before it can fully rise). But these particular breads were already rising less than my others because of the amount of extra whole grain flour I had added (see the section titled "Flour to starch ratio" in the introduction to this chapter on page 189). But just in case, I also tested baking them in a heavy but lighter-colored skillet. The result? I found that using the darker cast iron skillet didn't affect the rise for this bread recipe.

Thus my rustic breads were born. The buttermilk in the rye version gives it a delicious tang, even without a sourdough starter. The multigrain version is rich and flavorful, and the oat bread is tender and slightly nutty. Enjoy them all alongside soups and salad, or as the base for hors d'oeuvres and tapas. The buttermilk rye is great topped with melted Gruyere cheese or smoked salmon. I love the oat brushed with a little olive oil and topped with goat cheese and fresh summer tomatoes. And the multigrain is a great base for thin slices of smoked ham or roast chicken. Enjoy them all!

RUSTIC BUTTERMILK RYE BREAD

1 ⅔ cups Bread Flour Mix (213 grams)
⅓ cup teff flour
¼ cup buttermilk powder
4 teaspoons granulated sugar

1 ¼ teaspoons xanthan gum
¾ teaspoon salt
¾ teaspoon rye flavor*
1 packet (¼ oz.) of active dry yeast granules (not quick-rise)
1 cup plus 1 tablespoon water heated to 110° F
1 tablespoon olive oil
1 tablespoon caraway seeds
1 large egg, beaten (to glaze top of bread)

*An excellent gluten-free rye flavor is available from Authentic Foods (see page 19 for details).

RUSTIC MULTIGRAIN BREAD

1 ⅔ cups Bread Flour Mix (213 grams)
⅓ cup teff flour
4 teaspoons granulated sugar
1 ¼ teaspoons xanthan gum
¾ teaspoon salt
1 packet (¼ oz.) of active dry yeast granules (not quick-rise)
1 cup plus 1 tablespoon water heated to 110° F
1 tablespoon olive oil
1 tablespoon sesame seeds
1 tablespoon sunflower seeds
1 tablespoon golden flax seeds
1 large egg, beaten (to glaze top of bread)

RUSTIC OAT BREAD

1 ⅔ cups Bread Flour Mix (213 grams)
¼ cup gluten-free oat flour
3 tablespoons gluten-free rolled oats
4 teaspoons granulated sugar
1 ¼ teaspoons xanthan gum
¾ teaspoon salt
1 packet (¼ oz.) of active dry yeast granules (not quick-rise)
1 cup plus 2 tablespoons water heated to 110° F
1 tablespoon olive oil
1 large egg, beaten (to glaze top of bread)

1. Line the bottom of a cast iron skillet 6 inches wide across the bottom (8 inches across the top) with a piece of parchment paper (cut to fit). Do not grease pan.

2. Mix all dry ingredients in large bowl of electric mixer. Add water and

olive oil, and mix until just blended. Scrape bowl and beaters, and then beat at high speed for 3 minutes. Add seeds, if using. Spoon dough into center of prepared pan, but do not flatten the dough or spread it out to touch the edges. Use a table knife or offset spatula to smooth the surface of the dough; dampen it with water to get a nice smooth surface. Cover with a light cloth and let rise in a warm place until double in size, about 1 hour (the dough should rise and spread to touch the sides of the pan).

3. Place rack in center of oven. Preheat oven to 400°F while bread is rising (do not use a convection oven, because it will brown the bread too quickly).

4. Brush bread with beaten egg; try not to get it on the side of the pan (or spray very lightly with canola oil baking spray if you are egg intolerant. It will help darken the crust). Bake in center of preheated oven for 35-40 minutes. When done, bread should have a hollow sound when tapped on the top and bottom and be very dark golden brown. Your instant-read thermometer should register 205°–210°F. You can bake it longer to make a thicker crust; the color will deepen, and the internal temperature will continue to rise. Remove bread from pan and cool on a rack at least 30 minutes before slicing. The loaf should be 2 inches high in the middle.

Cook's Note: Dry ingredients can be mixed ahead and stored in plastic containers for future use. Do not add yeast until just ready to bake bread. You can adjust the amount of bread flour mix and teff (or oat) flour to 1 ½ cups bread flour mix and ½ cup teff (or oat) flour to create a denser but still delicious bread.

BRIOCHE

Brioche is a rich French yeast bread made with copious amounts of butter and eggs. It has a golden brown crust and a fine textured crumb with a beautiful golden hue. Many American recipes call for relatively large amounts of sugar, but classic French versions typically use a bit less. I choose to use less, but you can add another tablespoon to the amount listed below. My gluten-free version is really very easy to make, and it's practically foolproof if you follow the directions (be sure to lower the heat from 375°F to 350°F when you put the brioche loaf in the oven).

After the brioche has cooled, slice it thick and serve it with fresh butter and preserves for breakfast or tea, or use it to make tea sandwiches, French toast, bread pudding, or strata. You also can use the base recipe to make hamburger buns (directions below), or bake it in small brioche molds (set aside and chill a small amount of dough to make the top knots, and then put them on at the last minute). When inspiration strikes, you can adjust the base recipe below to make Baba au Rhum and Savarin.

Testing notes: Somewhere during the last 20 years, many well-known cookbook writers started to consider it essential to chill brioche dough overnight in order to "develop the flavor." Moreover, many took what was a relatively simple recipe and complicated it in order to differentiate their own version. But before that, many cookbooks, including an early English translation of the *Escoffier Cook Book*, *Mastering the Art of French Cooking* by Julia Child, and *The Lutece Cookbook* by Andre Soltner, baked the brioche after two rises in a temperate room. The recipes indicated that bakers could chill the dough for the second rise if they wanted to bake the bread at a later time, or in order to make the dough easier to shape (especially when making a *tete á brioche*), but it wasn't an essential step in the recipe. In any case, I found my own loaves to be so enriched with butter and eggs that the flavor was not marginally improved when left overnight (and brioche is not supposed to be so "yeasty" that it tastes like sourdough). That said, if you want to prep the dough the night before and bake it in the morning, yes you can. After about an hour in the refrigerator, the brioche stops rising because the butter gets cold and congeals. But more importantly, if your home is very warm, you may want to consider letting the dough rise the refrigerator so that it doesn't over-ferment and take on a stale beer-like smell.

When the brioche only has one rise, the top is smoother. If you want the perfectly smooth tops of the hamburger buns in the picture, only let the dough rise once in the pan. I usually make my brioche hamburger buns with only one rise. The loaf bread, however, has a tendency to over-rise and then fall without the second rise.

Makes one 1-lb. loaf

Wrap brioche well in plastic wrap and then foil. Store on the counter for up to one day, in refrigerator for up to two days, or in freezer for up to three weeks. Rewarm very briefly in microwave until soft (wrapped in dampened paper towels if brioche seem dry), or defrost slightly in microwave and then toast. For best toast results, use a toaster that is already heated up so the slice of brioche doesn't dry out before it browns (I start my toaster and let it run through one cycle before I put in the brioche).

Another interesting note: Wheat bakers typically brush the sides of the pan they bake their brioche in with butter, but butter made the sides of my brioche loaves more tender, so they tended to "keyhole" (cave in at the sides) a little bit. The sides stayed firmer with canola oil baking spray.

½ cup skim or 1% or 2% milk, heated to 110°F
1 packet (¼ oz.) active dry yeast granules (not quick-rise)
2 cups Bread Flour Mix, divided (256 grams)
2 tablespoons granulated sugar, divided
2 teaspoons xanthan gum
¾ teaspoon salt
3 large eggs (room temperature is best)
8 tablespoons unsalted butter, slightly softened (not warm),
    cut into 8 pieces
1 large egg, beaten (to glaze top of bread)

1. Combine warm milk (110°F), yeast, 1 tablespoon of the flour, and 1 tablespoon of the sugar in measuring cup; stir until well blended. Cover with a towel and set aside for 10 minutes until mixture becomes foamy.

2. Mix all dry ingredients in large bowl of electric mixer. Add milk/yeast mixture and eggs and mix until just blended. Add butter one piece at a time until you've added it all. Scrape bowl and beaters, and then beat at high speed for 4 minutes. Dough will be smooth and glossy. Scape dough down into a mound at the bottom of the bowl. Cover bowl with a light cloth and let it rise at room temperature (but not above 80°F, or the butter will start to melt), until dough has doubled in size, about 1 to 2 hours. You can also let the dough rise in the refrigerator for 4 to 12 hours covered with plastic wrap.

3. Lightly grease a 9 x 4 x 4-inch loaf pan with cooking spray and dust very lightly with rice flour (See Cook's Notes below) or a 9 x 5-inch loaf pan with cooking spray (your brioche will rise more dependably when baked in a lighter- colored metal pan that isn't non-stick). Use a rubber spatula to very gently, but completely, deflate the dough and then spoon it into prepared pan. Carefully smooth top with a table knife or offset spatula (slightly dampen knife with water if it is sticking to the dough). Cover with a light cloth and let rise at room temperature (up to 80°F) for about 1 hour, until dough has doubled.

4. Place rack in center of oven and preheat to 375°F while brioche is rising (do not use a convection oven, because it will brown the surface too quickly).

5. Brush brioche very generously with beaten egg; place in center of oven and lower temperature to 350°F. Bake about 35 minutes for 9 x 4 x 4-inch pan (about 30 minutes for 9 x 5-inch pan). Your instant-read thermometer should register 190-195°F when inserted in center of loaf (try not to let it get over 200°F, or loaf will be drier than it should be). Remove bread from oven and cool in the pan on a rack for 2 minutes, then remove from pan and cool on rack before slicing.

Cook's Notes: Dry ingredients can be mixed ahead and stored in plastic containers for future use. Do not add yeast until just ready to bake brioche.

USA Pans makes a 9x4x4 inch loaf pan sold on the King Arthur Flour Company website (about $18.00); the same pan is sold as a "Pullman loaf pan" with an accompanying top (which you don't need for this recipe) on Sur La Table, Amazon, and other kitchen supply stores or websites. This pan will make a more traditional sandwich shape loaf.

The 9 x 5-inch pan will make a slightly less high loaf that is perfect for French toast and smaller tea sandwiches.

BRIOCHE HAMBURGER BUNS

When the dough for these brioche hamburger buns has only one rise, the tops of the buns are smoother and prettier. If you want the perfectly smooth tops of the hamburger buns in the picture, only let the dough rise once in the pan: mix the ingredients and then put them in the pan right away to rise. I usually make my brioche hamburger buns with only one rise.

Makes 6 hamburger buns

Follow Steps 1 and 2 above.

3. Generously grease a six-bun hamburger bun pan with cooking spray and dust very lightly with rice flour (each bun form is about 4 ½ inches in diameter) or six 4 ½ to 5-inch pie pans.

4. Use a rubber spatula to very gently, but completely, deflate the dough and then spoon it into each of the prepared bun forms (or pie pans). Carefully smooth and flatten tops of buns with a table knife or offset spatula (slightly dampen knife with water if it is sticking to the dough). Cover with a light cloth and let rise at room temperature (but not more than 80°F) for about an hour until doubled in size (if dough was chilled, it will rise nicely at 80°F).

Wrap buns well in plastic wrap and then foil. Store on the counter for up to one day, in refrigerator for up to two days, or freezer for up to three weeks. To reheat, warm very briefly in the microwave until soft (wrap in dampened paper towels if buns seem dry).

5. Place rack in center of oven and preheat to 375°F while buns are rising (do not use a convection oven because it will brown the surface too quickly).

6. Brush buns generously with beaten egg; place in center of oven and lower temperature to 350°F. Bake 15-20 minutes. Buns should have a heavy but somewhat hollow-ish sound when tapped on top. Do not over-bake or the buns will be dry. Tops should be golden brown. Remove buns from oven and turn onto a rack to cool before slicing.

Cook's Note: To serve, slice buns with a serrated knife and top with burger, or slice, brush with butter, and then briefly brown in a fry pan before topping with burger.

PANETTONE

*Makes one 7-inch
Panettone*

*Wrap panettone well in
plastic wrap and then
foil. Store on the counter
for up to one day, in
refrigerator for one day
or freezer for up to three
weeks. Rewarm briefly in
microwave until soft
wrapped in dampened
paper towels.*

The panettone we see in bakeries and specialty markets supposedly had its beginnings in Milan, Italy, where bakers created this sweetened, rich yeast bread for the Christmas holidays. When I first started researching what I hoped were "classic" recipes, I was surprised to find so many different variations. Although the base recipes were all remarkably similar to brioche, unlike brioche, there seemed to be a wide assortment of add-ins: grated lemon rind and/or orange rind, vanilla and/or Marsala wine, raisins, slivered almonds, candied fruit and/or citron. I choose to leave out the almonds, but you can add-in whichever combination you like, or the ones that best reflect your family traditions.

½ cup golden raisins (do not use hard, dried out raisins)
1 tablespoon Marsala wine
½ cup skim or 1% or 2% milk, heated to 110°F
1 packet (¼ oz.) active dry yeast granules (not quick-rise)
2 cups Bread Flour Mix, divided (256 grams)
¼ cup granulated sugar, divided
2 teaspoons xanthan gum
¾ teaspoon salt
2 teaspoons grated orange rind
1 teaspoon grated lemon rind
3 large eggs (room temperature is best)
8 tablespoons unsalted butter, slightly softened and cut into
    8 pieces
1 teaspoon pure vanilla extract
⅓ cup good quality diced candied fruit and/or citron
1 large egg, beaten (to glaze top of bread)
Confectioners' sugar, optional

1. Mix raisins and Marsala wine in a small bowl and set aside for 30 minutes.

2. Combine warm milk (110°F), yeast, 1 tablespoon of the flour and 1 tablespoon of the sugar in measuring cup; stir until well blended. Cover with a towel and set aside for 10 minutes until mixture becomes foamy.

3. Drain raisins and discard wine. Mix all dry ingredients in large bowl of electric mixer. Mix in grated orange and lemon rind. Add milk/yeast mixture, eggs, and vanilla and mix until just blended. Add softened butter one piece at a time until you've added it all. Scrape bowl and beaters,

and then beat at high speed for 4 minutes. Dough will be smooth and glossy. Mix in drained raisins and candied fruit. Scape dough down into a mound at the bottom of the bowl. Cover bowl with a light cloth and let dough rise at room temperature (but not above 80°F or the butter will start to melt), until dough has doubled in size, about 1 to 2 hours, You can also let the dough rise in the refrigerator for 4 to 12 hours covered with plastic wrap.

4. Spray a 1 ½ quart soufflé pan (7 ½ inches diameter) with baking spray and dust very lightly with rice flour. Use a rubber spatula to very gently, but completely, deflate the dough and then spoon it into prepared pan; carefully smooth top with a table knife or offset spatula. Cover with a light cloth and let rise at room temperature (up to 80°F) for about 1 hour, until dough has about doubled and is just below the top of the soufflé dish.

5. Place rack in center of oven and preheat to 375°F while panettone is rising (do not use a convection oven because it will brown the surface too quickly).

6. Brush panettone generously with beaten egg and place in center of oven. Turn oven down to 350°F. Bake for 40 minutes, then check for doneness. Your instant-read thermometer should register 190°F to 195°F when inserted into center of loaf (try not to let it get over 200°F or loaf will be drier than it should be). If not done, loosely cover top with aluminum foil to prevent over-browning and bake about 10 minutes more, then check for doneness again. Remove panettone from oven and cool in the soufflé pan on a rack for 5 minutes, then remove from soufflé pan and cool on rack before slicing. To serve, dust top with confectioners' sugar, if desired.

Cook's Note: Dry ingredients can be mixed ahead and stored in plastic containers for future use. Do not add yeast until just ready to bake panettone.

SESAME BREADSTICKS

Makes 14 breadsticks

Store any leftovers tightly wrapped in plastic wrap and then foil. Store in freezer for up to three weeks. To reheat, freshen breadsticks by sprinkling with a bit of water, wrap in foil, and warm in preheated 350ºF oven for about 10 minutes; open foil for last 3 minutes.

These chewy, crusty breadsticks are quick and easy to make and sure to please those around your table. Make them to serve along side soups and salads for a hearty meal or as a lightning fast gluten-free bread for holiday tables. My own family likes the breadsticks sprinkled with coarse salt, but you can top them with any combination of seeds or spices.

1 ½ cups Bread Flour Mix (190 grams)
2 tablespoons granulated sugar
2 tablespoons sesame seeds
1 teaspoon xanthan gum
½ teaspoon salt
1 packet (¼-oz.) dry quick rise yeast granules
1 teaspoon olive oil
¾ cup plus 1 tablespoon water (110ºF)
1 large egg, beaten, optional
Sesame seeds (or coarse salt), optional

1. Spray large baking sheet with baking spray.

2. Mix all dry ingredients in large bowl of electric mixer. Pour olive oil and warm water (110ºF) into mixing bowl; mix until just blended. Scrape bowl and beaters and then beat at high speed for 2 minutes.

3. Scoop dough into medium sized pastry bag (or large plastic bag with tip cut off). Pipe dough onto baking sheet to make 14 8-inch long by ½-inch wide breadsticks that are 1-inch apart from each other. Cover with light cloth and let rise in warm place (about 80ºF) for about 30 minutes, until dough has about doubled in size. You can use a warm oven (no more than 80ºF) to help the breadsticks rise. If you have only one oven, you will have to pull them out before they are finished rising in order to preheat the oven.

4. Place shelf in center of oven. Preheat oven to 400ºF while breadsticks are rising. Brush with egg white and then sprinkle with seeds (or coarse salt). For an egg-free version, spray evenly with baking spray and then sprinkle with seeds or salt. To make light colored but crisper breadsticks, do not spray with cooking spray (the fat in the spray makes the crust darker, but a bit more tender).

5. Bake breadsticks in center of preheated oven for about 20 minutes until golden brown all over and crisp on bottom. Remove from pan and serve immediately (breadsticks are best when fresh).

Cook's Note: Dry ingredients can be mixed ahead and stored in plastic containers for future use. But do not add yeast until just ready to bake bread.

MULTIGRAIN BREADSTICKS

Substitute 1 ¼ cups bread flour (160 grams) and ¼ cup teff flour for 1 ½ cups bread flour mix.

CHEESE SOUFFLÉ

Soufflés always remind me of special occasions and little French restaurants. They have a reputation for being complicated to make, but like a dance, once you know the steps, you'll be able to whip up a soufflé in no time at all. Try this simple cheese soufflé for Sunday brunch or supper at the end of a busy day. If you have a well-stocked pantry and refrigerator, you'll be able to have it on the table in no time. I like to fold in leftover broccoli or spinach from dinner the night before (make sure it isn't wet). But if you don't have leftover vegetables, you can quickly cook some up in time to allow them to cool a bit before you add them to the egg and cheese mixture. Many soufflé aficionados like to dust the insides of the soufflé dish with a couple of table-spoons of finely shredded Parmesan cheese, but it isn't necessary. If the mood strikes, you can also add a pinch of nutmeg, a touch of paprika, or a little Dijon mustard (or dry mustard) to the egg yolks.

> ¼ cup unsalted butter
> 3 tablespoons potato starch
> 1 cup milk, warmed
> ¼ – ½ teaspoon salt
> Freshly ground pepper to taste
> 4 large eggs, separated*
> 4 ounces, Gruyere or Parmesan, coarsely shredded
> 1 cup cooked chopped broccoli, warm or at room
>   temperature, optional

It's easier to separate eggs when they are cold. But it's easier to whip egg whites when they are at room temperature; give yourself enough time to allow the eggs to sit out until they're no longer cold after you separate them.

1. Preheat oven to 400°F. Position rack in center of oven. Butter a 6-cup (1 ½ quart) soufflé dish or spray with cooking spray. You can use an 8-cup (2 quart) soufflé dish and the soufflé will rise well, but it just won't rise over the top of the dish to the same extent.

2. Melt butter in heavy medium saucepan over low heat. Mix potato starch into melted butter and cook slowly, stirring constantly for 1 minute (roux will look foamy, not paste-like). Gradually stir in warm milk. Increase heat to medium and cook, stirring constantly, until white sauce is smooth, thick and at the boiling point. Remove from heat. Add salt and pepper.

3. Beat egg yolks in a small bowl with a whisk. Add a little bit of the hot sauce and beat well to temper the eggs. Add egg yolk mixture to sauce and mix until well blended. Stir in shredded cheese and broccoli and

mix well. Set aside. The soufflé base can be prepped up to an hour ahead and left to rest until you are ready to whip up the egg whites and fold them into it. Cover with a plate or plastic wrap.

4. Put egg whites in large clean bowl of electric mixer. Use clean whisk attachment to beat egg whites until foamy on medium speed. Turn mixer to high and beat egg whites until stiff peaks form (or hand whisk the egg whites in a large copper mixing bowl).

5. Stir about a cup of the whites into the egg/cheese mixture to lighten it. Then quickly pour this mixture onto one side of the electric mixer bowl containing the stiff egg whites. Gently fold the egg whites into the egg/cheese mixture using a large rubber spatula (this should not take longer than about 45–50 seconds. Don't worry if a few streaks of egg white remain). Pour into prepared soufflé dish. Place in oven and lower temperature to 375°F.

6. Bake for 30-35 minutes until soufflé has risen and set. Do not open oven while soufflé is baking (until at least 25 minutes have passed). Serve immediately.

PIGS in BLANKETS

Makes 30 pigs in blankets.
Recipe can be doubled.

I don't think I've ever seen leftover pigs in blankets on a serving tray. No matter how many I make, they seem to disappear quickly. You might have been missing out on these favorites as you passed them by at parties, but no more. This is a delicious recipe made with a dough that's light and flaky, especially if you fold and chill it according to the directions. (I use a sweeter variation of this versatile dough, without the baking powder, to make apple turnovers; see recipe on page 176). Read the directions carefully and completely before you start. And then make up a batch of pigs in blankets today and have a party!

> 1 cup Brown Rice Flour Mix (125 grams)
> 2 teaspoons granulated sugar
> ½ teaspoon baking powder
> ½ teaspoon xanthan gum
> ⅛ teaspoon salt
> 5 tablespoons cold unsalted butter, cut into small pieces
> 3 tablespoons cold sour cream (not low fat)
> 6 5-inch frankfurters or 30 mini frankfurters
> 1 large, well-beaten egg, for glaze

1. Combine flour, sugar, baking powder, xanthan gum and salt in large bowl of electric mixer. Add butter and mix until crumbly and resembling coarse meal. Add sour cream and mix on medium-low speed until dough is just starting to hold together, but is still all in quarter-sized pieces.

2. Move dough (still in pieces) to a large sheet of plastic wrap and press it together to form a smooth, rectangular shaped disk; wrap it tightly and chill for 1 hour in the refrigerator until firm enough to roll.

3. Roll pastry dough into an 8 x 15-inch rectangle between two sheets of wax paper and then fold it into thirds along the 15-inch side, as though you were folding a letter (it should end up being 8 x 5 inches, but the dimensions do not have to be exact). Wrap tightly in plastic wrap and refrigerate at least 3 hours and up to two days. If not using within 6 hours, cover with foil so the dough doesn't dry out. Dough can be frozen at this point for up to one month; wrap in plastic wrap and then use foil as an outer wrap.

4. Preheat oven to 400°F. Position rack in center of oven. Lightly grease baking sheet with cooking spray.

5. Take the dough out of the refrigerator and allow it to warm up enough to roll without getting sticky. Roll dough into a 10 x 9-inch rectangle between two sheets of wax paper (it should be about $\frac{1}{8}$ inch thick). Then, cut into two 5 x 9-inch rectangles. Then, cut each rectangle into three 5 x 3-inch rectangles, for a total of six rectangles.

6. *To use 5-inch frankfurters:* Dry off frankfurters with a paper towel. Roll one 5 x 3-inch piece of dough around each frank and seal edges of dough by pressing them together. Cut into five equal sized pieces (if dough is too soft to work with, return it to the refrigerator or freezer for a few minutes).

   To use cocktail-sized frankfurters: Dry off frankfurters with a paper towel. Cut each 5 x 3-inch rectangle into five 1 x 3-inch strips. Roll a strip of dough around each cocktail frank and seal edges of dough by pressing them together (if dough is too soft to work with, return it to the refrigerator or freezer for a few minutes).

7. *To bake immediately:* Arrange pigs in blankets on prepared baking sheet seam side down. Brush top and sides with beaten egg. Bake 20 minutes until pastry is slightly puffed and golden brown, and frankfurters are cooked through. Immediately move to a platter, cool about 5 minutes and serve warm with mustard.

8. *To bake within two days:* Arrange pigs in blankets seam side down, side-by-side in a tightly sealing container (press a piece of plastic wrap over the pigs in the container to keep them from being exposed to any air). Pigs in blankets may be prepared up to this point 2 days ahead and kept in refrigerator. When ready to bake, proceed as in Step 7.

9. *To freeze for future use:* Freeze pigs in blankets on a parchment lined baking sheet until firm. Remove pigs from baking sheet and place them on a large piece of plastic wrap; make sure they are all touching with no space in between. Wrap tightly in plastic wrap and then foil; freeze for up to one month. When ready to bake: Place frozen pigs on prepared baking sheet and brush with beaten egg. Add a few minutes to the baking time above.

DUMPLINGS
For Soup and Stews

Makes 12 round dumplings. Recipe can be doubled.

Store leftover dumplings in a separate tightly sealed container from sauce. Reheat dumplings in microwave or in a saucepan with a bit of sauce over very low heat.

Dumplings come in all shapes and sizes and can be found in many cultures across the globe, but this particular recipe was based on the dumplings found in traditional chicken and dumpling recipes made by home cooks here in the United States. Although these delicate morsels are typically made with wheat, fat, and liquid, my gluten-free version cooks up as light and tender as the original. You just mix up the dough, carefully shape it into little balls, and then lower them into a big pot of simmering broth or stew. So if you've been missing the down-home comfort of chicken and dumplings, this easy-to-make recipe is so good you won't miss the original wheat versions for a minute.

1 cup Brown Rice Flour Mix (125 grams)
1 tablespoon baking powder
1 teaspoon sugar
½ teaspoon xanthan gum
½ teaspoon salt
2 tablespoons fresh chopped herbs (parsley, chives, etc.), optional
2 tablespoons very cold butter or butter substitute
½ cup skim or low-fat milk (or rice milk)

1. Combine flour, baking powder, sugar, xanthan gum, salt, and herbs (if using) in large bowl of electric mixer. Add butter and mix until crumbly and resembling coarse meal. With mixer on low speed, add milk and mix until well combined, about 30 seconds. Do not overbeat.

2. Scrape the dough onto a large plate or sheet of wax paper and divide it into 12 small, equal pieces with a knife or spoon. Without applying too much pressure, quickly shape each piece into a ball; edges do not need to be perfectly smooth. Use a very light touch so you don't end up making 12 small cannon balls (don't press on the dough; just lightly smooth it into shape).

3. Bring broth, soup, or stew to a gentle simmer in a heavy, tightly sealed saucepan or Dutch oven (SIMMER—DO NOT BOIL, or dumplings will toughen). Quickly place the dumplings on the surface of the liquid and cover the pot tightly. Gently simmer over a low heat for 12-15 minutes until the dumplings are cooked and dry in the center (test by piercing gently with a fork—dumpling should be tender). Do not open the pot

for first 10-12 minutes to help hold in the steam (which helps to cook the dumplings). Allow the dumplings to sit for two to three minutes in covered pot before serving.

Cooks Note: These dumplings are tender when formed gently and cooked for enough time. If chewy or doughy, they were pressed too hard or are underdone.

ASIAN DUMPLING DOUGH
Pot Stickers and Gyoza

Makes 14–16 dumplings. Recipe can be doubled.

Store leftover dumplings in a tightly sealed container in refrigerator.

Really good gluten-free Asian food is still hard to find in most areas of the country. And for pot-sticker and gyoza lovers like me, it's particularly hard. But take heart. You can make perfectly crisp on the bottom, slightly chewy Asian dumplings with this simple gluten-free dough. It's simple to make and it doesn't require a lot of ingredients: flour mix, hot water and a little salt and xanthan gum. You can fill the dough with whichever fillings you miss the most, or use the quick and easy one I created for my dumpling tests at the end of the recipe. I tested both rolling out and then cutting the dough with a biscuit cutter, and simply pressing little balls of dough out into circles between parchment paper. I found the later to work perfectly. I also tried frying dumplings in both non-stick and regular skillets, and I'm here to report that you should save yourself the heartbreak of torn dumplings—buy a good non-stick pan with a glass cover.

> 1 cup Brown Rice Flour Mix (125 grams)
> $\frac{1}{2}$ teaspoon xanthan gum
> $\frac{1}{8}$ teaspoon salt
> 7 tablespoons boiling water
> 1 generous cup prepared filling of your choice (suggestion below)
> Dipping sauce of you choice (suggestion below)
> Canola oil for frying

1. *To make dough:* Combine flour, xanthan gum and salt in large bowl of electric mixer. Add water and mix at medium high speed for 2-3 minutes, until dough is soft and pliable and sticking to the sides of the bowl (it will feel a lot like your earlobe). If you find the dough isn't getting soft after 2 full minutes, or that it looks very dry, add some more of the boiling water 1 teaspoon at a time (and you may need the extra water anyway if you aren't using finely ground rice flour). Wrap dough tightly in plastic wrap and let stand at room temperature for 20 minutes (or wrap in plastic wrap and then foil and refrigerate for later use, but bring to room temperature before proceeding).

2. *To form dumplings:* Roll dough into a cylinder, then break or cut it into 14 or 16 pieces and roll each piece into a perfectly shaped ball. Keep balls covered in plastic wrap so they don't dry out. Place one ball between two pieces of parchment paper and press into a 3 or 3 ½- inch

circle with your fingers or the palm of your hand (you can also use a small rolling pin). If possible, try to make the middle, where the filling will be sitting, thicker than the edges. Repeat with other dough balls.

3. If filling dumplings right away, lay circles of dough on a large sheet of parchment paper and keep covered with plastic wrap so they don't dry out. If keeping prepared dough to use another day, I found it useful to place each finished dough circle on a small, square of parchment paper (cut from a larger sheet) and then stack them on top of each other; wrap the stack of dough circles tightly in plastic wrap and then in foil so they don't dry out. Dough can then be kept in refrigerator for three days. Bring to room temperature before proceeding.

4. **To fill dumplings:** Spoon about a tablespoon of filling onto each dough circle. Place one dough circle in the palm of your hand and fold it in half over the filling to form a crescent shape. Pinch or pleat the edges together to completely seal the dumpling (use your finger to very lightly dampen the edges of one side of the circle with a little water if it doesn't stick well).

5. **To cook dumplings:** Heat 1-2 tablespoons of canola oil in a non-stick skillet* over medium high heat (the amount of oil depends on the size of the skillet and how many dumplings you fry at a time). Arrange the dumplings in the pan so they are very slightly touching and fry until the bottoms are dark golden brown, about 2-3 minutes.

6. Add ½ to ⅔ cup water, reduce heat to medium, cover pan (use a glass cover, if possible) and steam dumplings for 7-10 minutes until most of liquid evaporates (add a little more water if pan dries out before the filling is cooked through). Take off cover, shake pan to loosen dumplings, turn heat to medium-high and cook until all the liquid completely evaporates and the bottoms are dark brown and crisp. Remove cooked dumplings from pan and serve on a plate with dipping sauce.

*I recommend using a glass cover on your non-stick skillet to make it easier to check the liquid level while the dumplings cook. Calphalon makes a good, inexpensive one.

To make a quick and easy filling: Combine ½ pound ground pork or chicken, ¼ cup finely sliced scallions, ½ teaspoon minced garlic, ½ teaspoon minced ginger, 1 ½ teaspoons gluten-free soy sauce, 1 ½ teaspoons toasted sesame oil, and ⅛ teaspoon black pepper. Makes 1 very generous cup of filling.

To make a soy dipping sauce: Combine 2 tablespoons gluten-free soy sauce, 1 ½ tablespoons rice wine vinegar, 1 teaspoon roasted sesame oil, and 1 tablespoon finely sliced scallions. Add hot chili oil and/or a little sugar to taste.

PIEROGI and VARENIKI DOUGH

Makes 14–16 pierogies.
Recipe can be doubled.

Hungry for some old world comfort food? Think pierogies! This light, tender dough will have you effortlessly rolling and cutting and pinching and boiling up tender dumplings filled with your favorite fillings. When I started researching recipes, I found there were a lot of pierogi experts in the world —- and they all had their own way of doing things. I converted several different wheat recipes and learned a lot. Ultimately, I came up with an easy way to make a gluten-free dough that rolls and cuts easily and cooks up like a dream. Interestingly, I tried a highly acclaimed method of separating the dough into little balls and rolling the dumplings individually (as I do in my Asian dumping recipe), but it didn't work as well for this dough as the method I ultimately used in the recipe. And for those of you who didn't grow up serving periogies over the holidays filled with your family's favorite fillings, I offer up the very humble filling I used in my tests in the Cook's Notes at the end of the recipe.

> 1 cup Brown Rice Flour Mix (125 grams)
> ½ teaspoon xanthan gum
> ¼ teaspoon salt
> 1 large egg
> ¼ cup water
> 1 ¼ cups filling (see suggestion in Cook's Note)
> Rice flour, for shaping dough

1. ***To make dough:*** Combine flour, xanthan gum and salt in large bowl of electric mixer. Add egg and water and mix at medium-low speed for 2 minutes until dough is pliable (it will feel a lot like Play Doh). Wrap dough tightly in plastic wrap and let stand at room temperature for 30-45 minutes (or wrap in plastic wrap and then foil and refrigerate for later use; bring to room temperature before proceeding). If your home is warm, chill dough very slightly before forming pierogies.

2. ***To form pierogies:*** Sprinkle a little rice flour over the dough and roll it out between two sheets of parchment paper until it is about ⅛-inch thick (spread a little more rice flour over the dough if it is sticking). Use a 3-inch biscuit cutter to cut out as many circles as possible. Gather scrapes of dough, and reroll and cut out as many circles as you can (there is no gluten in the flour so you don't have to worry that the dough will become overworked and less tender).

3. ***To fill pierogies:*** Spoon about one tablespoon of filling onto each dough circle (form the filling into an oval shape). Pinch the edges together to form a crescent (use your finger to very lightly dampen the edges of one side of the circle with a little water if they don't stick well), then place it back on the parchment paper (see Cook's Notes below). Repeat with other dough circles. Keep finished pierogies covered with plastic wrap so they don't dry out. Uncooked pierogies can be kept in refrigerator for several hours before cooking in a tightly sealed container (layered between parchment paper), or on a parchment paper lined tray tightly covered with plastic wrap. They can also be frozen for up to one month: Freeze in a single layer on a parchment lined baking pan or tray and then transfer to a tightly sealed container or freezer bag. Bring to room temperature before cooking.

4. ***To cook pierogies:*** Bring a large pot of water to a gentle boil. Gently drop the pierogies into the water and stir them gently so they don't stick together. Do not overcrowd the pot (cook in batches, depending on the size of the pot). Gently boil for about 4-5 minutes total (they will float to the top after about 2-3 minutes, then cook for 1-2 minutes more depending on thickness of dough). You can check for doneness by tasting one to see if it is tender and cooked through. Remove from pot with a slotted spoon.

5. ***To serve:*** Serve immediately with melted butter or sour cream (and/or sautéed onions), or sauté in melted butter in a fry pan over medium high heat; cook until pierogies are golden brown and puffy. Boiled pierogies can also be kept in the refrigerator for three to four days in a tightly sealed container (layered between parchment paper) and then reheated in a fry pan with butter.

Cook's Note: You can patch the dough if necessary (dampen it). I am a shameless "patcher" and would fail class at Martha Stewart's Perfect-Pierogi School.

To make a quick and easy potato and cheese filling: Combine 1 cup mashed potatoes and ¼ cup shredded cheddar and/or farmers cheese. Season with salt and pepper to taste.

About the Author

Annalise Roberts is the author of three other gluten-free cookbooks that are sold in North America and overseas. Translated editions are available in South America and Eastern Europe. An expanded and revised edition of her best-selling book, *Gluten-Free Baking Classics* (April 2006), was released in September 2008. *Gluten-Free Baking Classics for the Bread Machine*, a collection of recipes developed for the large Zojirushi bread machine, was released in April 2009. *The Gluten-Free Good Health Cookbook* (January 2010), her third book written with her sister Claudia Pillow, provides food choice explanations and guidance, cooking advice, and more than 140 flavorful, culturally diverse, gluten-free recipes.

Annalise works with celiac support groups across North America and gives talks about gluten-free cooking and baking. After years of writing for her *foodphilosopher.com* website (one of the first gluten-free websites in the country, dating back to 2003), she now blogs sporadically at *www.mygluten-freetable.com*. She lives in the New York metropolitan area.

Measurement Equivalents and Metric Guidelines

U.S. Dry Volume Measurements

⅛ teaspoon	a pinch
3 teaspoons	1 tablespoon
⅛ cup	2 tablespoons
¼ cup	4 tablespoons
⅓ cup	5 tablespoon + 1 teaspoon
½ cup	8 tablespoons
¾ cup	12 tablespoons
1 cup	16 tablespoons
1 pound	16 ounces

Length

⅛ inch	3 mm
¼ inch	6 mm
½ inch	13 mm
1 inch	2.5 cm
4 inches	10 cm

Liquid Metric Equivalents

1 teaspoon	5 ml
1 tablespoon	15 ml
¼ cup	59 ml
⅓ cup	79 ml
½ cup	118 ml
⅔ cup	256 ml
¾ cup	177 ml
1 cup	237 ml
2 cups	473 ml

Oven Temperatures

80°F	26.7°C	
100°F	37.8°C	
300°F	150°C	Gas mark 2
325°F	165°F	Gas mark 3
350°F	180°F	Gas mark 4
375°F	190°F	Gas mark 5
400°F	200°F	Gas mark 6
425°F	220°F	Gas mark 7
450°F	230°C	Gas mark 8

Pan Size Equivalents

9 x 13-inch baking pan	22 x 33-cm baking pan
8 x 8-inch baking pan	20 x 20-cm baking pan
9 x 9-inch baking pan	22.5 x 22.5-cm baking pan
8 x 4-inch loaf pan	21.25 x 11.25-cm loaf pan
9 x 5-inch loaf pan	23 x 12-cm loaf pan
9-inch round cake pan	22-cm cake pan

Index

CPSIA information can be obtained
at www.ICGtesting.com
Printed in the USA
BVHW020403111019
560705BV00016B/85/P